An introduction to sociology

In recent years sociologists have had to give increased recognition to the contribution made to sociology by feminist perspectives and feminist research. However, this material has tended to remain marginal, to be seen as a separate topic, worthy of a chapter in textbooks and a few lectures.

This book aims to demonstrate the centrality of feminist perspectives and research to the sociological enterprise and to introduce students and the general reader to the wide range of feminist contributions to key areas of sociological concern. The authors argue that malesteam theories and research findings are at best incomplete, becuase they fail to take account of the perspective of women, and inadequate because the feminist challenge to malestream sociology requires that the discipline's theories and concepts be reconceptualised. The authors summarise the research findings of feminist sociology, demonstrating the need for sociology to be reformulated in order to incorporate the knowledge produced by feminists – that feminist scholarship challenges existing malestream theories and research findings.

This book will be essential reading for 'A' level and undergraduate (and other) students of sociology and related subjects. It will be of interest to the general reader concerned to understand the ways in which feminist scholarship enables us to make sense of the world we inhabit.

Pamela Abbott and Claire Wallace are both senior lecturers in sociology and social policy in Polytechnic South West at Plymouth. Claire Wallace has researched and published in the areas of work and youth, and Pamela Abbott in health, community care and women and social class. Together they teach courses on gender divisions and society and have written articles on the family.

Pamela Abbott taught sociology at 'A' level for ten years before moving into higher education and has examined 'A' level sociology for fifteen years. Claire Wallace was a research officer at the University of Kent at Canterbury before taking up her present post at Plymouth.

An introduction to sociology: feminist perspectives

**Pamela Abbott
and Claire Wallace**

Polytechnic South-West at Plymouth

London and New York

First published 1990 by Routledge
11 New Fetter Lane, London EC4P 4EE

Simultaneously published in the USA and Canada by Routledge
a division of Routledge, Chapman and Hall, Inc.
29 West 35th Street, New York, NY 10001

© 1990 Pamela Abbott and Claire Wallace

Typeset by LaserScript Limited, Mitcham, Surrey
Printed and bound in Great Britain by Mackays of Chatham PLC, Kent

British Library Cataloguing in Publication Data
Abbott, Pamela, *1947–*
  An introduction to sociology : feminist perspectives.
  I. Title II. Wallace, Claire, *1956–*
  301

Library of Congress Cataloging-in-Publication Data
Abbott, Pamela.
  An introduction to sociology : feminist perspectives / by Pamela Abbott and
Claire Wallace.
    p.   cm.
  Bibliography: p.
  Includes index.
  1. Sociology—Philosophy.   2. Sociology—Methodology.
3. Feminism—Philosophy.   4. Feminist criticism.   I. Wallace, Claire.
II. Title.
HM24.A215   1990   89–10313
301'.01—dc20   CIP

ISBN 0-415-01036-5   ISBN 0-415-01037-3 (pbk.)

Contents

301.01
A

Contents

Contents

Tables

Tables

Preface

This book, intended for students and the general reader interested in understanding the feminist contribution to sociology, provides an introduction to feminist perspectives in sociology that stands on its own or can be used in conjunction with more conventional introductory textbooks. As we see one of the major aims of sociology and feminism as being to enable us to understand our own society better we have used modern Britain as our focus. However, much of the argument applies equally to other societies. For those readers who want to incorporate feminist perspectives into their sociological understanding we suggest reading the appropriate chapter in this book after reading the corresponding chapter of a conventional textbook. The chapters in this book do not have to be read in the order in which they are written. We would suggest that you read Chapter one first. After that, you can follow your own interests or read the relevant chapters in line with the sequencing of the syllabus that you are following.

We are not presenting this as a 'true' account of social reality, nor do we see ourselves as neutral scientists merely recounting the work of sociologists and feminists. In recent years sociology textbooks have been criticized for being biased and leaving out key areas of sociological concern (see Marsland (1988) and correspondence in *Network*, the newsletter of the British Sociological Association – particularly issues dated October 1987 and June and July 1988). Indeed, we are ourselves critical of sociology textbooks because of the ways in which they have marginalized feminist knowledge. We write this book as two feminists, who argue that malestream research has ignored, distorted, and marginalized women and that feminists are concerned to reconceptualize the production of knowledge. All knowledge is partial and provisional, and this applies as much to feminist as to malestream knowledge. However, feminist knowledge takes account of the experiences of women as women. It starts from the position that in modern Britain women are subordinated and that it is necessary to explain this subordination in order that women can be liberated. We take this as a truth, as the starting point, not something that needs to be proved. Feminism is not one theoretical perspective within sociology, but a political movement concerned with furthering the cause of women's liberation. However, feminist knowledge has made an important contribution to sociology and has challenged the basic theoretical assumptions of malestream work, arguing that sociological theories, methods, and explanations need to be reconceptualized. It is with these arguments that we are concerned in this book.

Feminism is not a unified movement. While all feminists are agreed that women are subordinated and that it is necessary to develop strategies to liberate them, there are fundamental disagreements about the causes of that oppression and the strategies for achieving liberation. There are a large number of feminisms. In this book we have decided to order the material by reference to four major perspectives: liberal/reformist, Marxist, radical/revolutionary, and socialist feminism. We have chosen these because we feel that, to date, these are the major perspectives that have produced knowledge that is of relevance to sociology. However, any system of classification is fraught with problems, and trying to identify particular women with each of the different perspectives is a difficult and sometimes an arbitrary exercise. We may well have labelled some women in different ways to the way that they would label themselves, and some women have changed their position over time. The main problem comes with the division between Marxist and socialist feminisms. We have labelled Marxist feminists as those who see the class system as the main or most important determinant of women's subordination, and socialist feminists as those who hold a 'dual system' theory – that is, they give equal weight to the class and sex–gender systems in explaining women's subordination. This problem of distinguishing between different feminist perspectives is not just an academic one, but a personal one. We have to try to identify ourselves as well. One of us has been labelled as a 'new cultural Marxist feminist' and both of us in the past would have identified ourselves as Marxist. Now we tend to place ourselves as socialist feminists – giving equal priority to class and patriarchal relations.

It is important that you, the reader, are aware of our positions. We do not feel that it is possible for us to detach ourselves from our theoretical perspectives and become neutral reporters of other feminists' arguments and research findings. This is, of course, what we are trying to do – but it is important that you are aware that we are *not* neutral, nor is it possible for anyone to be neutral. This lack of neutrality is especially important for the reader to keep in mind when we are evaluating the adequacy of other women's work.

We hope you will enjoy reading this book and learn much from it. We have learned much from writing it and enjoyed the process of production. Feminism and sociology are not academic subjects that are just to be learned, but ways of coming to understand the society in which we live and our position in it. We hope that this book will stimulate you to look at the world afresh and come to new insights.

Acknowledgements

We should like to acknowledge the help that Roger Sapsford has given us at every stage of production; without his help the book would not have been typed on time. We should also like to thank our students at Plymouth Polytechnic, on whom we have tried out much of the material in this book. We alone, of course, remain responsible for the contents.

Chapter one

Introduction
The feminist critique of malestream sociology and the way forward

Sociology is a male-dominated discipline, and this has fundamental implications for its theories, methods, research and teaching. Despite at least twenty years' criticism of the discipline for its malestream orientation and bias, little has changed. While the majority of students taking the subject are women, the majority of lecturers are male. Women are excluded from the senior posts in the discipline, and women are taught 'malestream' sociology – that is, they are inducted into knowledge that plays a key role in justifying the inferior structural position of (the majority of) women in modern British society. Ann Oakley suggested in 1974 that:

> Male orientation may so colour the organisation of sociology as a discipline that the invisibility of women is a structured male view, rather than a superficial flaw. The male focus, incorporated into the definitions of subject areas, reduces women to a side issue from the start.
>
> (Oakley, 1974b: 4)

However, there has been some change. Sociologists can no longer afford to ignore women and gender divisions, and there is discussion about the changes needed for the malestream bias to be overcome. There has been a steady flow of books published by women writing from feminist perspectives in sociology. A publisher recently told us that when she started to publish feminist work in 1975 she was thought daft, but now the editorial committee 'love anything in that line'. However, much sociological research continues to focus on men and boys and to ignore women and girls. There is still a tendency to generalize from male samples to the whole population, and textbooks 'add women on' as an appendix – an extra topic or chapter – rather than incorporating research findings on women. While malestream sociology can no longer ignore feminist perspectives, it has tended to marginalize them – to see them as an addendum deserving at most one or two lectures or something that can safely be left for women to teach as an option course.

1

We write this introduction as two white feminist sociologists who have been teaching and researching for a number of years. For the past three years we have jointly taught courses in 'gender divisions and society' in a polytechnic. We are also fighting personal battles to incorporate feminist perspectives in our own teaching and to get colleagues to recognize that they need to rethink what they teach and the ways in which they teach it. The feminist challenge to malestream sociology is one that requires a radical rethinking of the content and methodology of the whole enterprise, one that recognizes the need to see society from the position of women as well as from the standpoint of men.

Many of the criticisms we have made above apply as much, if not more, to questions of ethnicity. Sociology is a discipline that has been and is dominated by white males who are middle class by destination if not by origin. Women have come into the discipline and challenged the blinkered view of malestream sociology, but they too have tended to be white. Black women have criticized many white feminist sociologists for their one-sided views. Blacks are even more under-represented in the discipline than white women. Acutely aware of this, we have attempted to incorporate material on black women and ethnic divisions where available.

In this book we try to explain the contribution that feminists have made and are making to sociology. We are concerned with helping the reader to understand the society in which we live, and for this reason we concentrate on modern Britain. We have not aimed to provide an exhaustive overview of the entire contribution of female sociologists to the theories and methodologies of sociology, nor a summary of all empirical research findings. Rather, we have selected material that enables us to demonstrate the contribution that feminism has made. As soon as we take the feminist criticisms of malestream sociology seriously we realize that we need to ask new, different questions and that in order to answer them we need to develop new tools, new concepts, and new theories. This is because malestream sociology has seen women's roles as natural and therefore not investigated them; sociology's tools, concepts and theories have been developed to investigate the public world of men and are inadequate for investigating the world that women inhabit and the relationships between men and women. Questions such as 'Why don't men look after children?' and 'Why do men have leisure?', become key issues to be researched and explained. Concepts such as social class are seen to be inadequate as theorized in malestream research (see Chapter two) and the methods used in malestream research are seen to be inadequate for investigating women's lives (see Chapter nine).

The sociological imagination

In the past, sociologists used to talk about sociology as the 'science of society'. By this they meant that sociology was concerned with carrying out research into the causes of social phenomena such as crime, unemployment, stratification, and so on. Once causes had been established then control and reform became possible. Sociology promised to provide a basis for both social control and reform.

However, the view that the social sciences and specifically sociology can be scientific in this sense has been seriously challenged. It has been argued that it is not possible for experimental research that can establish causation, such as is used in physics and chemistry for instance, to be carried out on human societies, and that it is impossible for sociologists to be value-free and objective about their subject-matter. Positivistic approaches to studying society based on the methodology of the natural sciences have been challenged by humanistic ones based on the premiss that human beings are different from inanimate objects and other species in that they act purposefully, and arguing that we should be concerned with understanding what is going on from the perspectives of human actors. Furthermore, the position from which the sociologist studies the world is always partial – it is always from a particular site. Theories – the ways in which we try to make sense of what is going on – whether our own everyday common-sense theories or sociological ones, do not arise out of the data, but on the contrary our theories determine what we select to examine in the first place and the range of possible explanations available to us. For example, theories that suggest that a woman's role is natural (biologically determined) limit the questions that we can ask about women and the range of possible answers to these questions. If we accept that it is women's biology that determines that they are the ones to look after children then we do not ask why men do not look after children. If women say that they are dissatisfied with their role as wives or mothers then our theory leads us to assume that there is something wrong with them – either they are not fully, biologically women or they are mentally ill, for example.

There are important differences between common-sense theories and sociological ones. The former are based on individual values, usually one-sided, and not based on strong evidence, and continue to be held in the face of contradictory evidence. We often refer to common-sense theories as 'prejudices'. We all have prejudices. The main point is that we are unreflexive about our common-sense theories – we often take them for granted and see them as natural and consequently true. Sociologists, on the other hand, try to be reflexive, to question taken-for-granted assumptions and to ask what evidence there is to support or challenge them. Furthermore, sociologists criticize the individualistic tendencies typical of common-sense explanations which tend to 'blame the victim' but to see the world around the victim as natural or inevitable. The American sociologist C. Wright Mills (1954) referred to this as 'the sociological imagination' – the ability to recognize that personal troubles are in fact public ills, that what we perceive as individual problems can be understood and explained only when we examine social, economic, and political factors. One example he used was the concept of unemployment. Often this is explained in individualistic terms such as an individual not wanting to work, individuals not being prepared to work for the wages offered, individuals not being prepared to travel to where work is available, and so on. Mills suggested that these individualistic explanations may explain why any given individual was unemployed, but they could not explain a high level of unemployment in a country as a whole. To do this it was necessary to look for other explanations, such as Government economic policy, the availability and cost of housing in areas where jobs are to be found, the types of job on offer compared with the skills of the unemployed, the level of income necessary to support a family, and so on.

Sociology, then, is about understanding the relationship between our own experiences and the social structures we inhabit. However, in the 1960s and 1970s women began to express the feeling that sociology did not relate to their experiences, because it examined the world only from the perspective of men. Indeed, existing theories and explanations could be challenged, they argued, if the perspective of women was also taken into account. The realization of this failure of sociology to speak to the experiences of women, and its consequent failure to theorize comprehensively, led feminists to examine more closely why this was the case – why sociology, despite its claims to neutrality, had a malestream bias. Dorothy Smith (1979) argued that this was because women's concerns and experiences were not seen as authentic, but subjective, while men's were seen as the basis for the production of true knowledge. Consequently, sociological knowledge portrayed women as men saw them, not as they saw themselves. Sociology also played a key role in maintaining women's subordinate and exploited position. While sociology claimed to put forward a detached and impartial view of reality, in fact it put forward a view from the perspective of men.

Feminist critiques of conventional sociology

Feminists have made a number of criticisms of sociology:

    1 that sociology has been mainly concerned with research on men and by implication with theories for men;

2 that research findings based on all-male samples are
  generalized to the whole of the population;
3 that areas and issues of concern to women are frequently
  overlooked and seen as unimportant;
4 that when women are included in research they are presented in
  a distorted and sexist way;
5 that sex and gender are seldom seen as important explanatory
  variables.

In summary, sociology is seen as, at best, sex-blind and at worst sexist. That is, there is, at best, no recognition that women's structural position and consequent experiences are not the same as men's and that sex is therefore an important explanatory variable, and, at worst, women's experiences are deliberately ignored or distorted. Furthermore, the ways in which men dominate and subordinate women are either ignored or seen as natural.

Anne Oakley (1982) has suggested that there are three explanations for this sexism in sociology:

1 that sociology has been biased from its origin;
2 that sociology is predominantly a male profession;
3 that the 'ideology of gender' results in the world being
  constructed in particular ways and in assumptions being made
  about how we explain differences between men and women.

It is evident that these three factors are interrelated. Sexist assumptions were built into sociology from its origins and these still underlie sociological theory and research. Sociology as a discipline developed in the nineteenth century, and sociologists were concerned with under-standing political and economic changes – including liberal theory, with its emphasis on the individual – capitalism and the consequent class relationships that developed, and the impact they had on people's lives. These changes included the growth of factory production, new class divisions and relationships, the growth of a politically conscious (male) working class, and the extension of political participation to more of the adult (male) population. A central aspect of this process for women was the increased separation of home from work, the separation of production from consumption and reproduction, and the development of an ideology that 'a woman's place is in the home'. Women became increasingly associated with the domestic (private) sphere of the home and domestic relationships, and men with the public sphere of politics and the market-place.

Sociologists concentrated on the public sphere of government and the workplace and ignored the private sphere of the home and domestic relationships. This was at least in part because the division of labour between the public sphere (men) and the private sphere, between the bases of male and female roles, was seen as natural – that is, as having a biological basis. This meant that there was no reason for sociology to explain gender divisions; it accepted biology as explanation and therefore had no need to consider gender as an explanatory variable. Women were consequently 'hidden' from the sociological gaze.

Sociology has ignored not just women, but the whole private sphere of domestic relationships; areas of interest to women have not been theorized and researched. Furthermore, sociology has failed to develop analytical tools that can be used to understand the public and the private sphere and the changing relationships between the two. While men have been seen as inhabiting both spheres and, indeed, as mediating between the two, women have been seen as inhabiting the private sphere, even when they have paid employment outside the home. Consequently, explanations for men's attitudes and behaviour are generally based on their position in the public world (social class), while women's are explained by reference to their role in the private sphere as wives and mothers and by their biology. Men are frequently said to influence the behaviour of their wives, while women are rarely seen as influencing their husbands (see Chapters three and nine).

Feminists have argued that theories and research that ignore the experiences of over half the population and the private sphere of domestic relationships are inadequate. What is needed is a sociology that investigates and theorizes these areas and treats the sex/gender system as important, along with class, race, and age. While sociologists have characterized as inadequate or wrong the theories that account, for example, for class divisions, crime, educational success, or failure, on the basis of biological differences, they have continued to accept them for explaining women's role in the domestic sphere. Feminists challenge this.

The ideology of masculinity and femininity

Malestream sociological theories underpin and justify the subordination and exploitation of women by men in modern Britain, while claiming to be 'factual'. Feminists argue that malestream theories in fact fail to meet the criteria for being accepted as adequate and valid knowledge because they are both objectionable and mistaken. They in fact serve as an ideological justification for the subordinate position of women.

By 'ideology' we mean a pattern of ideas (common-sense knowledge) – both factual and evaluative – which purports to explain and legitimate the social structure and culture of a social group or society and which serves to justify social actions which are in accordance with that pattern of ideas. Ideology also shapes our everyday feelings, thoughts and actions. However, the knowledge provided by an ideology is partial or selective and sometimes provides contradictory descriptions and explanations of the social world. Ideologies, especially dominant ones, also serve to construct certain aspects of the social world as natural and universal, and therefore unquestionable and unchangeable. Aspects of the social world that are created as natural and universal by an ideology are thereby protected from the charge of being socially produced. A dominant ideology is more easily able to present its ideas as natural and universal because it is produced and reproduced by those in a position of power. The exclusion of women from positions of power and from the production of knowledge has, feminists argue, meant that male ideology has been able to present itself as universal knowledge. However, feminists have challenged and continue to challenge male (patriarchal) ideology – that is, ideas that support male supremacy – arguing that it is partial and distorting, but because men are in the positions of power they are able to marginalize feminist knowledge.

Ideology as we are using the term, then, is seen as made up of a set of common-sense beliefs, practical knowledge – that is, it forms the basis for action. For example, familial ideology presents the nuclear family – of mother, father, and dependent children living as a household, with the man as economic provider and the woman as carer in the domestic sphere – as natural (biologically based) and universal as an institution. Alternative styles of living will break down because they try to change that which is inevitable. However, ideology conceals the fact that it is socially constructed by certain groups because it serves their interests. The nuclear family, with a gendered division of labour, was created in Britain in the nineteenth century, feminists argue, because it served the interests of men and/or capitalism (see Chapters four, six, and eight).

However, ideologies have changed and continue to do so, and they can be opposed by subordinate social groups. Feminists challenge and oppose patriarchal ideologies by demonstrating their partial and distorted view of the world. Feminists then seek to replace inadequate patriarchal ideologies by more adequate, more comprehensive knowledge. Patriarchal ideologies have the effect of disguising the actuality of male power. Men defined themselves as powerful because of their ability to master nature – to be dominant. Women, because of their biological role in reproduction, are defined as being closer to nature than men, thus justifying their domination by men. Male ideology confirms and reinforces men's dominant status by devaluing women's work and reproductive functions while at the same time presenting male work as of cultural importance and as necessary. Masculinity (man) is equated with the public sphere; to be a man is to be a person who does important things outside the domestic sphere – who does man's work.

Feminists argue that gender is a social construction; the roles that men and women occupy in society are not biologically given. It is accepted that sex itself is biologically given – there are anatomical differences between boys and girls – but what is important is the way these are perceived, the way boys and girls are socialized into what is seen as appropriate gender behaviour and what behaviour is valued. That is, parents, teachers, and society in general all treat boys and girls differently and have different expectations as to how they should behave. The expected behaviour of boys and girls is both encouraged and reinforced by the adults with whom they come into contact and the institutions of which they are members. Thus television programmes and school reading schemes both show appropriate role models. Boys and girls who do not conform to the appropriate role model are both chastised and ridiculed by adults and by their peers. Boys who display what are seen as feminine traits are referred to as 'sissies', and girls who behave in masculine ways as 'tomboys'. While some girls may actually welcome being referred to as tomboys, boys dislike being called sissies, which is seen as a term of derision.

However, historical and anthropological research suggests that what are seen as appropriate roles for men and women are specific to part-icular societies at particular times (Oakley, 1972). Different societies have different images of what is appropriate behaviour for males and females, and these have also differed over time in our own society. Explanations based on biological differences or biological factors are therefore inadequate. It is necessary for sociology to develop theories that are adequate both for explaining gender divisions and for taking account of gender differences.

A sociology for women: the way forward

Feminists are not agreed on what is required to fill the gaps in existing theory and research in sociology. We would suggest that there have been three broad responses:

1 integration;
2 separatism;
3 reconceptualization.

We will deal with each of these in turn.

Integration

This position sees the main problem as being the sexist bias in male-stream sociology. The task is seen as being to remove this bias by reforming existing ideas and practices in sociology, to bring women in and thereby to fill in the existing gaps in our knowledge. The way forward is to carry out research that incorporates women in samples and to reform existing theories by removing sexism.

The major problem with this approach is that women are likely to continue to be marginalized. They will become merely an addition to the syllabus and lip-service will be paid to incorporating women in research samples. Moreover, it leaves the basis of the discipline untouched, fails to challenge the assumption that the discipline is scientific and does not take into account feminist criteria of what counts as knowledge. For example, this approach would leave unchallenged malestream assumptions about the division between the public and the domestic, about the primacy of paid work, about class being the fundamental division in society, and so on.

Separatism

This position argues that what is needed is a sociology for women by women. Feminists should not be concerned with trying to change the biases of the existing sociology, but with developing a sociological knowledge which is specifically by and about women. Explicit recognition is given to the fact that the world is always seen from a particular position or site and that women's perceptions are different from men's. Furthermore, gender is seen as the primary division in society; all women share a common position because they are both exploited and dominated by men. Feminist scholarship should be concerned with developing theories and carrying out research on women that is of benefit to women.

The problem of this approach is that it perpetuates the marginality of women. Malestream sociology can get on with the 'real' theorising and research and continue to ignore women and feminist perspectives. Furthermore, feminist knowledge would not benefit from potentially valuable inputs from conventional sociology. Finally, by ignoring men, important aspects of women's social reality would be ignored, including the ways in which men exploit, dominate, and subordinate women in the public and the private spheres. Any analysis of women's oppression must analyse the role played in this by men.

Reconceptualization

This position recognizes the need for sociological research by women and for women, the notion that women have a different point of view from men and that it is essential that there be a sociology constructed from the position of women. It recognizes that it is necessary for women to carry out research on men and boys as well as women and girls and acknowledges that malestream sociological theories and research findings can have an impact on feminist sociology as well as vice versa.

However, it rejects the view that all that is needed is to integrate feminist sociology into existing sociological theory and research findings – that is, as it were, to fill in the gaps in our knowledge and to tinker with the edges of existing theories. Instead it is seen as necessary to reconceptualize sociological theories – revolution, not reform, is necessary. This is both because existing theories are sexist beyond reform by mere tinkering and because feminist research actually challenges assumptions and generalizations made from malestream research. What is needed is a total and radical reformulation of sociology so that it is able to incorporate women adequately.

The major problem is that many malestream sociologists are resistant to the view that there is a need for a revolution. Nevertheless, this is the position that we (the authors) accept, and while we recognize that this is an uphill struggle we think that it is a necessary one if we are to achieve an adequate sociology.

Feminist sociology

A feminist sociology is one that is for women, not just or necessarily *about* women, and one that challenges and confronts the male supremacy which institutionalizes women's inequality. The defining characteristic of feminism is the view that women's subordination must be questioned and challenged. This involves a critical examination of the present and past situation of women, and challenging the dominant patriarchal ideologies that seek to justify women's subordination as natural, universal, and therefore inevitable: challenging knowledge that is put forward as universal and demonstrating that this knowledge views the world from the perspective of men. What is necessary is a view of the world from the position of women, who have been excluded from the production of knowledge. Such a view will provide more adequate knowledge because it will seek to explain what patriarchal knowledge does not recognize as existing – the subordination and exploitation of women by men.

Feminism starts from the view that women are oppressed and that their oppression is primary. Women's freedom of action is limited by the power of men because men possess more economic, cultural, and social resources than women. The traditional emphasis in sociology on the state, economy, and other public institutions as the main sources of oppression ignore power and oppression in 'private' institutions such as the family and in personal relationships in both the public and the private sphere. Feminists have argued that the personal is political, that is, that it is active agents who 'do the oppressing' and that it is necessary to give credence to women's concrete experiences of oppression – ones occurring in personal, everyday encounters – as well as those at the collective and institutional level. Men and women, oppressors and oppressed, confront one another in their everyday lives; they are not just role-players acting out a pre-prepared script. Human actors in specific social contexts can and do oppose each other; men do exercise power and women do experience pain and humiliation. However, the power of men over women is collective; society's sexist assumptions advantage all men – patriarchal ideologies support and sanction the power of men over women. Feminist sociologists, then, are concerned to examine the relationship between individuals and the social structure, between women's everyday experiences and the structure of the society in which they live, between men's power in interpersonal relationships and the ways in which that power is institutionalized in British society.

Feminist perspectives

Theory is the basis of sociology. Theories determine the ways in which we make sense of the world – the questions we ask and the range of answers that are permitted. In this sense feminism is a theory; a world view. However, it is not a unified one; feminists do not agree on the ways in which we can explain women's subordination or on how women can be emancipated. There are a large number of feminisms, and any attempt to classify feminist theories is fraught with problems. Any system of classification is arbitrary and incomplete: arbitrary because we force women into a category, one with which they may not themselves identify, and describe a given position as if it were totally unified rather than representing a range of ideas that show some broad agreement. It is incomplete because our categories do not incorporate all feminisms. We have tried to provide a classification, however, that does cover the range of feminist theories that have made important contributions to British sociology, in order better to understand the differences between them.

We have identified four feminist perspectives (which we discuss in more detail in Chapter nine): liberal/reformist, Marxist, radical, and socialist. All of these perspectives address the question of what constitutes the oppression of women, and all suggest strategies for overcoming it. All argue that women are oppressed in British society, but they differ in their explanations of the oppression's cause and their suggested strategies for overcoming it. Liberal feminism is concerned to uncover the immediate forms of discrimination against women in Britain and to fight for legal and other reforms to overcome them. Marxist feminists argue that the major reason for women's oppression is the exclusion of women from public production and that women's

11

struggle for emancipation is an integral part of the fight of the proletariat (working class) to overthrow capitalism. Radical feminists see male control of women (patriarchy) as the main problem and argue that women must fight to free themselves from this control. Socialist feminists argue that women's oppression is both an aspect of capitalism and of patriarchal relations. An end to capitalism, they argue, will not lead automatically to the emancipation of women; women also need to fight to free themselves from control by men.

Feminist theories differ, then, in the ways they explain the subordination of women, and the different theories mean that feminists working in different perspectives tend to be interested in different aspects of women's lives, to ask different questions, and to come to different conclusions. This will become evident as you read this book, when we look at specific aspects of women's lives.

Radical feminists argue that women's oppression is primary and fundamental. Patriarchy, an elaborate system of male domination which pervades all aspects of culture and social life, is seen as trans-historical. All women are oppressed irrespective of historical, cultural, class, or racial differences. The family is seen as a key instrument of the oppression of women, through sexual slavery and forced motherhood – through male control of women's bodies. Radical feminists do not, on the whole, deny biological differences between men and women, but they challenge the meanings given to them. Women's oppression is seen as rooted either in women's biological capacity for motherhood or in the innate, biologically determined aggression of the male, as manifested in rape.

Marxist feminists argue that the oppression of women is integrally tied up with the capitalist mode of production, while socialist feminists maintain that the two systems, patriarchy and capitalism, combine to oppress women. Marxist feminists recognize that men do exploit women in capitalist societies, but see patriarchy and capitalism as closely related, while socialist feminists argue that the two systems are separate and often in conflict. Both argue that patriarchy needs to be seen as changing and dynamic, that the form that patriarchy takes changes historically and is not as static and unchanging as radical feminists suggest. Differences between men and women, both argue, are not biologically determined but socially produced and changing. The family is seen as a key site of women's oppression, but is viewed not in isolation but in a broader set of relations of work, leisure, and public life.

The main distinction between feminist theories, then, lies in their basic understanding of the causes of women's oppression. Radical feminists criticize Marxist and socialist ones for their view that patriarchy can be overcome; they argue that men have a psychological and even perhaps a physical need to coerce and dominate women whatever the economic conditions. Marxist and socialist feminists argue that radical feminists ignore the implications of the socio-economic system in shaping the ways in which patriarchy operates and point out that they tend to describe rather than to explain women's subordination. Socialist feminists argue that Marxist feminists place too much emphasis on the role of capitalism in explaining women's subordination and fail to recognize that the sex–gender system is independent of the class system.

While Marxist and socialist feminists have argued that it is necessary to analyse and explain class, gender, and racial subordination, black feminists have been critical of the lack of centrality given to issues of racism in feminist theory and research. They point out that racial ideologies that see it as natural and inevitable that white people are superior to black ones were developed to justify colonial exploitation and slavery. These pre-date the entry of black people to Britain and support and sustain institutional as well as individualized discrimination. Black people are portrayed as 'aliens' who bring 'problems' and who cannot or will not be integrated into British society. In sociology black women have been stereotyped, or the common-sense stereotypes of black women have not been challenged. Asian women are seen as passive and as being controlled within patriarchal family systems. Afro-Caribbean women are seen as dominating and running matriarchal family structures. This analysis is empty of class reference, yet black immigrants were imported into the class structure of British society – into the working class – to perform low-paid, low-status jobs. Feminist sociologists tend to have ignored the specific problems experienced by black women living in contemporary Britain in their research, and theories have paid only lip-service to incorporating racial oppression into analysis of gender oppression.

Women as a social class

All feminists agree that women's oppression is primary. However, radical feminists argue that women have shared interests because they are all exploited and oppressed by men. Women, then, are said to form a class that is in conflict with another class – men.

The radical feminist position has mainly been developed by the French feminist Christine Delphy (1977, 1981, and 1984). Delphy argues that while sociologists have regarded occupational class inequalities as primary, their own research demonstrates that sexual inequality is primary and more fundamental than occupational inequality. Thus women's oppression cannot be regarded as secondary to, and therefore less important than, class oppression. Delphy argues that women (or at least wives) form a class that is exploited by men (husbands):

> While the wage-labourer sells his labour power, the married woman gives hers away; exclusivity and non-payment are intimately connected. To supply unpaid labour within the framework of a universal and personal relationship (marriage) constructs primarily a relationship of slavery.
>
> (Delphy, 1977: 15)

Women then, according to Delphy, form a class in opposition to men. Women are exploited by men and therefore all women share common interests in opposition to those of men. Patriarchal structures are fundamental to our form of social organization, and therefore it follows that the main axis of differentiation in our society must be gender. While housewives may differ in their standard of living because their husbands are in different social classes, they share a common class position because they are exploited by another class (husbands) – their domestic labour is expropriated (taken away from them, in the same way that the goods produced by male manual workers are taken away from them).

However, Marxist and socialist feminists argue that what is necessary is a dual analysis that articulates Marxist class theory with the feminist theory of patriarchy: a theory that takes account of what unites all women – oppression by men – as well as the class divisions between them. While Marxist feminist theory continues to give primacy to class analysis, socialist feminists take as their question the relationship of women to the economic system as well as the relationship of men to women. The key question for socialist feminists is the cause of male exploitation and domination of women. Hartmann (1978) points out that the categories of Marxism are sex-blind and that patriarchal oppression preceded capitalism and will undoubtedly succeed it as well. In order to understand the subordination of women in capitalist societies, she suggests, it is necessary to articulate Marxist with patriarchal perspectives – that is, to show the specific form that female exploitation takes in capitalist societies.

Conclusions

In this chapter we have concluded that there is a need for a sociology from the perspective of women. We have argued that malestream sociological theory and practice is inadequate because it has either ignored or marginalized women or else accepted biological explanations as adequate for explaining gender divisions and women's social behaviour. We have suggested that biological reductionism is insufficient because it assumes that biological differences between the sexes can explain gender divisions. Gender divisions, we have argued, are socially constructed and cannot be explained by references to sex differences.

We have argued that it is necessary for there to be a sociology from the position of women and that if this is to become an integral part of sociology then sociology itself needs to be reconceptualized. 'Filling in the gaps' by carrying out research on women and tinkering with existing theories is not sufficient. Looking at the world through the female prism means that we need to rethink sociology and to challenge existing theories and research findings as at best inadequate and at worst wrong. In the rest of this book we demonstrate this, by not only explaining what feminist sociologists have found out but demonstrating how this requires a rethinking of existing sociological theories.

Summary

What is needed is a sociology, both theoretical and in practice, that recognizes:

1 the importance of gender as well as class and race as explanatory variables;
2 that the world needs to be seen through the female as well as the male prism;
3 that the public and domestic spheres are not separate worlds, but areas of mutual influence, and that the relationship between the two changes and need explaining; and
4 that the existing tools and theories of sociology need to be refurbished.

Finally, we want to point out that we have subtitled this book 'feminist perspectives', not '*the* feminist perspective' or '*a* feminist perspective'. This is because there are a number of distinct feminist perspectives, not just one. In sociology there are a number of competing perspectives – Marxist, Weberian, symbolic interactionist, ethnomethodological, and structural–functionalist, to name those most frequently encountered. Feminist sociologists are also divided among these schools; what they have in common is a commitment to looking at the world through the female prism.

Chapter two

Women and stratification

In all societies there are differences between people in terms of the amount of power and wealth which they command. The basis of stratification – the division of people according to a hierarchical system – varies from society to society. In very simple societies the divisions may be based on age and gender, older people having more power and prestige than younger ones and men more than women. In contemporary industrial societies such as Britain, sociologists argue, primary stratification is based on social class. However, as we have seen in Chapter one, feminists argue that the sex–gender system also provides a primary form of stratification, with men having more power and prestige than women. Racial differences are likewise a primary basis of stratification, with black people in Britain having less power and prestige than white people. While this form of stratification is most obvious in countries such as South Africa where the subordination of black and coloured people is *de jure* (legislated for), it exists *de facto* (in practice) in western societies, including Britain. Age is also a form of stratification, with young and elderly people having less power than those in the middle age groups (see Chapters three and eight). The division between the First World (western countries) and Third World countries also involves a relationship of exploitation and subordination and forms a principle of stratification.

In this chapter we will discuss the debates surrounding the exclusion of women from class research and the practice of determining a woman's class by the occupation of the (male) head of household. We shall also look briefly at sociological theories of racial subordination and black feminist criticisms of white feminists for ignoring the concerns of black women. Finally, we shall examine the exploitation of Third World women by western countries, including Britain.

Malestream theories of social class

In British sociology two main theories of social class dominate: those based on Marxist theory and those based on Weberian theory. They are often referred to as neo-Marxist and neo-Weberian, to indicate that the basic theories of Marx and Weber have been developed to enable an explanation for, and an understanding of, class divisions and relationships in modern British society. These theories are jointly referred to as European theories of class and see classes as distinct groups, each class comprising individuals with shared economic and social interests which are different from, and may be in conflict with, those in other classes. Members of a household are said to share a common class position, and generally the male head of household's class position determines that of all the members of his household.

Neo-Weberian theories of social class

Weberian theories of social class are based on the view that class position is determined by the job market. Occupations that share a similar market position – that is, ones in which employees have comparable conditions of employment – are said to be in the same social class. Weber argued that members of a social class would seek both to protect their advantages *vis à vis* other groups and to try to enhance their share of rewards and resources. A group would exclude subordinate groups from securing its advantages by closure of opportunities to those below it, which it defines as inferior and ineligible. Subordinate groups try to break through this closure and to bite into the advantages of higher groups.

Parkin (1979) and Murphy (1984) have argued that Weber's view of social stratification, and especially the concepts of market position and social closure, can be used to provide an adequate explanation of gender inequalities. Men, it is argued, have used strategies of social closure to exclude women from those occupations with the highest rewards and status.

Neo-Marxist theories

In Marxist theory social class is determined by relationship to the means of production – that is, basically whether one controls capital or has merely labour to 'sell'. Those who share a common relationship to the means of production – owners, and labourers – share the same class position. Marx argued that members of the same class should come to realize that they shared common interests and that these were in opposition to those of other social classes. The resulting class conflict would lead to the overthrow of the existing mode of production and its replacement by a new one. Marx argued that eventually there would be a classless society where no group exploited any other group.

According to Marx there are two main classes in capitalist society, the bourgeoisie and the proletariat. The former are the owners of the means of production and exploit the labour of the latter, who have to sell their labour on the market at market-determined rates in order to subsist. Exploitation comes about because capitalists pay workers less than the true value of their labour and thus make a profit. The price of goods on the market (the exchange value) is made up of two elements according to Marx: the costs of the raw materials, and the cost of labour. However, the worker is only paid for some of his labour: that amount he can demand as a wage; the remainder is kept by the capitalist as profit. Thus a worker produces surplus value. However, only use value is produced when the product is consumed by the producer (as, for example, when a housewife provides a meal for a family, knits a cardigan for a child, or grows vegetables for the table).

This distinction is important when when we consider the position of women. Women's labour in the home produces use value, not surplus value, because the goods that she produces are consumed rather than sold on the market in the same way as the products that factory workers make are sold. Given that class position is determined by relation to the means of production and that the basis for class identification is the production of surplus value, then women with no direct relationship to paid labour cannot have a class position other than via an association with someone in paid employment. It is evident that classes for Marx were predominantly made up of men and that women were seen as marginal. Furthermore, Marx saw class exploitation as the key issue and other forms of exploitation, such as gender and race, as secondary or derivative.

Feminist criticisms

Feminists have challenged the conventional view that stratification theory should only be about explaining class (economic) inequalities, and have suggested that it should be equally (or more) concerned with gender inequalities. Radical feminists have argued that sexual oppression is primary, while Marxist and socialist feminists suggest that gender, class, and racial inequalities have a mutual influence and cannot be analysed in isolation from each other (although Marxist feminists tend to give primacy to economic class) – see Chapters one and nine.

The malestream response to such criticisms has tended to be defensive: either to argue that stratification theory is not concerned with explaining gender inequalities or that existing theories are adequate.

However, neither of these responses is adequate, because explaining the location of women in the stratification hierarchy is essential (as we will show) to understanding that of men. This is a major theme of feminist sociology and is developed throughout this book.

The class system in Britain

Sociologists make use of social class in virtually all of their research; a person's social class is regarded as a summary variable which tells us about attitudes and values, standards of living, levels of education, and so on. Sociological research has shown that social class is an important determinant of life chances in terms of education, health, and so on (see Chapters four, six, and seven). While there are a variety of social class scales used by sociologists and others, probably the best known are the Registrar General's and the Hope–Goldthorpe scales. Broadly, sociologists identify three social classes – upper, middle, and working. The upper class forms a very small proportion of the population – about 10 per cent – and has received little sociological attention. It comprises the landed aristocracy and those who live on income derived from the ownership of land, business, property, etc. – what Marxists refer to as the bourgeoisie. Top civil servants, the heads of the armed forces, and members of the Government may also be classified as upper class. The middle class(es) comprises professional and managerial workers – for example, teachers, doctors, university lecturers, the clergy, factory managers, clerks, civil servants, and so on. The working class is made up of service personnel and manual workers – e.g. waitresses, cooks, car mechanics, bricklayers, dustmen, and so on – what Marx refers to as the proletariat.

The division between manual and non-manual workers was seen as an important class divide by Weber, who saw the skills that individuals brought to the market as the key determinant of the rewards they received for their work. Those with scarce skills could command higher pay and superior conditions of work. However, with universal schooling and the routinisation of clerical work (see Chapter six) the significance of the manual/non-manual divide has been eroded as the pay and work conditions of (male) routine non-manual workers have declined relatively to those of skilled manual workers.

The Registrar General's scale (the government-devised scale) divides the population into six social classes based on the occupation of the head of household:

I   higher professional or managerial;
II   lower professional or managerial;
IIIN   supervisory and lower/routine non-manual;

IIIM   skilled manual;
IV   semi-skilled manual;
V   unskilled manual.

A related scale frequently used in market research, the Social Grading Scale, has classes A, B, C1 and C2 as roughly equivalent to RG classes I, II, IIIN and IIIM, with a class D covering RG classes IV and V. A sixth 'class', E, is used for the unemployed, pensioners, housewives not in paid employment, and the permanently sick and disabled. This is generally excluded from sociological class analysis because, for example, the unemployed could formerly have been in any one of the other classes, so E constitutes the lowest stratum only in terms of spending power, not in class terms. The Hope–Goldthorpe scale, specifically developed for the Oxford Mobility Study, is similarly hierarchical, except that in the middle range, classes III-V are seen as distinct but of equivalent standing. The seven classes of the scale are:

I   higher professional and managerial, and large proprietors;
II   lower professional and managerial;
III   routine non-manual;
IV   small proprietors and the self-employed (petty bourgeoisie);
V   foremen and technicians;
VI   skilled manual workers;
VII   semi-skilled and unskilled manual workers.

As Heath (1980) has pointed out, there is general agreement among the various classifications as to who is at the top and who is at the bottom, but some disagreement about the ordering in the middle.

As the basis of classification is occupation, those who do not have paid employment cannot easily be classified. For men the difficulty of classifying the non-employed is overcome by allocation to class of former employment or by declaring a special class position/category for the unemployed/retired. However, these solutions are not considered for married women because they are assumed to share their husbands' class, being their husbands' dependents and therefore sharing their class position and interests. For this reason, even if women do have paid employment it is not thought to determine their class position.

Women in class theory

Feminists have challenged the practice by which many women (the majority) are said to have a derived class position, determined by the occupational experiences of the man with whom they live. Ann and Robin Oakley (1979) have pointed out that the instructions generally given to survey interviewers are such that if a man is living in the household it will be his occupation that determines the household's class. This is not just a coding device: it amounts to a theoretical statement that women's experiences, loyalties, and social action are determined by the occupational position of the man with whom they live and not by their own experiences. Acker (1973) suggests that there are five shortcomings to the conventional approach:

1 the assumption that the family is the rational unit of analysis, with complete class equivalence within it;
2 that the social position of the family is determined by the occupation of the head of the household;
3 that the male is necessarily the head of the household;
4 that women not living with a man none the less determine their own class;
5 the assumption that inequalities between men and women are inherent and inevitable.

Feminists argue not just that the classification of women by the class of male heads of household is sexist, but that the basic assumptions on which this position rests are false. Sheila Allen (1982) points out that a wife does not acquire her husband's education on marriage, nor does she automatically acquire a socially or politically powerful background (which can often be lost on divorce or widowhood). Feminists have gone on to demonstrate that the incorporation of women in research on social class necessitates at the very least a modification of existing theories and conclusions, if not a complete rethinking of them (see Crompton and Mann, 1986; Abbott and Sapsford, 1987a). Elizabeth Garnsey (1978) argues that taking the family as the only relevant unit of analysis obscures the inequalities between women and men within it (see Chapter four) and also the different market and work situations which they face outside it (see Chapter six). Women are at the bottom within each occupational class, and this pervasive inequality needs to be seen as central to the study of social stratification. The participation of women in the labour market affects the nature of that market for men. Women are concentrated in low-paid, low-status jobs, and this affects the range of jobs available for men. The ways in which female wage labour and domestic labour are combined and interact with each other and with the capitalist system also have complex consequences for class structure and class consciousness.

Michele Stanworth (1984) argues that assimilating a woman's class position to that of her husband is not justified by the evidence, and that doing so closes off some of the most interesting issues in class analysis. She points out that John Goldthorpe (e.g. 1983), who argues for the conventional approach, rests his case on three key assertions: that husbands are more involved in the labour process than wives (being more likely to have full-time, continuous employment), that wives' patterns of employment can largely be explained by the class position of husbands, and that contemporary marriages are largely homogeneous with respect to class (i.e. that husbands and wives have the same class of occupation when both are in paid employment). She demonstrates that Goldthorpe's own evidence does not support two of these claims and that none of them has the logical consequences which he implies. It is true that most women do take time out from the labour market at some point, but Martin and Roberts (1984), for example, demonstrate that they none the less show a substantial and lifelong commitment to paid employment. That women's labour-market participation is dependent on husbands' class receives little support even from Goldthorpe's own data (the 'Oxford mobility study'), and the timing of a woman's withdrawal from the labour market seems to be less affected by husband's occupational class than by the class of her own job. Finally, if female routine non-manual workers are to be reclassified as working class, as Goldthorpe suggests, in an attempt to 'solve' the problem of cross-class marriages, this does indeed abolish one kind of cross-class marriage; but only at the expense of creating another kind, where a routine non-manual woman (now classified as working class) is married to a non-manual man. In addition Heath (1980; see also Heath and Britten, 1984) demonstrates that cross-class marriages are in fact qualitatively and quantitatively different from other households on most criteria associated with social class.

Abbott and Sapsford (1987a) argue that their analysis of the data on the female respondents in the Open University 'People in society' survey demonstrates that women do have a subjective class identification and that this is no better predicted from the husband's or the head of household's occupation than from a woman's own occupation and/or personal and 'pre-marital' attributes such as class of origin (determined by father's occupation) and educational level. Women's overall social imagery, whether they saw society as conflictual or harmonious and divided or homogeneous, was again no better predicted by a head of household's class than by a woman's own attributes. They conclude that the view that a woman's class sentiments are solely and necessarily determined by the occupation of the man with whom she lives is not sustainable.

On the basis of the research to date it is evident that there is a need for women to be included in social class research. It is equally evident that women's class placement should be determined by their own occupations, or that the household's class position should be determined by reference to the occupation of both husband and wife. In sociological research generally, however, the most common approach is still to use the husband's occupation to determine the social class of wives.

Women and social mobility

Social mobility studies are concerned to describe movement from one class to another either intergenerationally or intragenerationally. Intergenerational studies are concerned with movement between generations, and intragenerational studies with movement in an individual's own lifetime. Mobility studies are not solely or mainly concerned with description, but with testing theories about the (non)changing class structure of British society. Since the Second World War sociologists and politicians have been much concerned with the question of the extent to which Britain has become a more open society – that is, one in which an individual's own talents determine his (*sic*) class rather than birth. The major English mobility studies (Glass, 1954, and Goldthorpe, Llewelyn, and Payne, 1980), as well as the Scottish Mobility Study (Payne, 1987a and b), were concerned to examine how open Britain is and to determine the extent to which British society has become a meritocracy.

The Oxford Mobility Study (Goldthorpe, Llewelyn, and Payne, 1980) was concerned in addition to test three theories of social mobility and class formation:

1. the 'social closure' thesis, which argues that those who occupy 'superior positions' may be presumed to be strongly motivated to retain these positions for themselves and their children and to close off access to them by those from lower social classes, and that they have command of the necessary resources to do so;
2. the 'buffer-zone' thesis, which argues that the existence of a high degree of mobility around the manual/non-manual boundary will serve to block off wider range mobility;
3. the 'counterbalance' thesis, which argues that with the increased professionalization, bureaucratization, and technological complexity of work, education is the main route to social mobility, and that intragenerational work progress is of little significance. That is, it is no longer the case that the sons of middle-class men are able to enter the labour market in working-class jobs, achieve significant mobility via achievement at work, and regain the class position of their fathers; rather, placement in the occupational market is primarily determined by educational qualifications.

On the basis of analysis of data drawn from an all-male sample Goldthorpe, Llewelyn, and Payne reject all three hypotheses. They argue that there is mobility into the highest social classes from below, that a buffer zone no longer exists, and that counter-mobility does still take place.

Social mobility studies have been criticized from a range of theoretical perspectives (see Abbott and Sapsford, 1987a). The main criticism from feminists concerns the virtual exclusion of women. While the Glass study (Glass, 1954) did collect data on women, they have never been analysed. The Oxford Mobility Study excluded women, while the Scottish Mobility Study included only a sub-sample of wives. The major justifications for excluding women have been that the family is the unit of stratification and that the class position of the household is determined by the occupation of its (male) head. Other reasons cited are financial constraints, the need to be able to compare results with previous research, and the fact that, for the period under consideration, the majority of women have not been economically active (and that those who have, have only been intermittently employed, generally in part-time employment).

Abbott and Sapsford suggest three major points which challenge these arguments:

1 If the concern is with the openness of society and the extent to which individuals can be mobile within the class structure, then it would seem just as important to examine female as well as male mobility. By not including women, sex-related occupational demarcations are ignored, as are the interactions between class background, gender, and education in individual mobility.

2 The mobility of women is also of fundamental importance if the concern is with class formation, whether the individual or the household is seen as the fundamental unit of stratification and independently of how a women's class is determined in practice (by her own occupation or that of her husband). Marital mobility, for example, is relevant: how many women marry men higher, or lower on the class hierarchy, or at the same level, and how this influences class formation given the possibility of familial ties across classes. A wife's occupational role may be of interest in that it may enable a family to enjoy a materially higher standard of living and influence the attitudes and values of all members of the family – including the mobility of children.

3 Female mobility is relevant to understanding class formation – married women who are themselves intragenerationally mobile may have just as much influence on the attitudes and values of the household as their non-mobile husbands.

Abbott and Sapsford point out that there are a number of problems with incorporating women into social mobility studies:

1 not all married women are in paid employment;
2 many or those that are, are in part-time, low-status work, taken to fit in with domestic responsibilities, which could be a poor indicator of their class;
3 married women move in and out of the labour market as the demands of their family changes – they tend not to have a career in the sense in which at least some men have one;
4 labour market segmentation means not only that women tend to be concentrated in a narrow range of occupations, but also that the 'class' distribution of women's jobs is different from that of men's; women are concentrated in routine non-manual and unskilled manual occupations and are under-represented in high status occupations and in skilled manual work.

Intergenerational occupational mobility

The Scottish mobility study included a sample of wives, and Abbott and Sapsford have analysed the data for the female sample of the 'People in society' survey. The conclusions from both of these studies seriously challenge the findings from the all-male studies about class movement across the generations.

Chapman (1984), analysing figures from the Scottish Mobility Study, found that men were more likely to be upwardly mobile than women, and women were more likely to be downwardly mobile than men, so that overall the rates of social mobility were much the same. In terms of origins (father's class), there was considerable similarity between the male and female sample, but in terms of destination (own occupational class), there were considerable differences.

Abbott and Sapsford (1987a) compared their analysis of patterns of female mobility with those of male mobility in the 'Oxford mobility study'. The Oxford study demonstrated that there is a considerable amount of upward mobility combined with upper-class stability. Seventy-two per cent of the study's sample could be described as mobile, and the significance of the manual/non-manual divide as a barrier to both upward and downward mobility seemed to have declined since the Glass (ed.) study in the 1950s. There was considerable mobility from the working class to the middle class and much of this was long-range. Thus, 12.7 per cent of men in social class I had an unskilled/semi-skilled background and 18.1 per cent of those in social class II. In total, 34.4 per cent of men in professional and managerial occupations (social classes I and II) came from manual backgrounds. However, this was combined with considerable middle-class stability; few sons of men in middle-class occupations ended up in working-class jobs. Only 4.1 per cent of manual workers came from professional and managerial backgrounds. Furthermore, 60.9 per cent of the sons of professional and managerial workers ended up in the same classes. Male inter-generational mobility was mainly explained by structural changes, an expansion of middle-class jobs, and a decline in manual ones. Thus, there had been considerable upward social mobility without cor-responding downward mobility (see Table 2.1).

Table 2.1 Male occupational mobility in the 'Oxford mobility study'

Father's occupation	Total		Respondent's occupation						
			I	II	III	IV	V	VI	VII
			Percentaged by class of origin – father's class						
I	582	%	48	19	9	8	5	5	6
II	477	%	32	23	11	8	9	9	8
III	594	%	19	16	11	9	13	15	18
IV	1223	%	13	11	8	25	9	15	20
V	939	%	15	13	9	8	17	20	17
VI	2312	%	8	9	8	7	12	30	25
VII	2216	%	14	11	9	10	12	21	23
			Percentaged by destination (own) class						
			%	%	%	%	%	%	%
I			24	12	8	6	3	2	2
II			13	11	7	5	4	3	2
III			9	10	9	6	8	5	6
IV			13	14	13	37	11	10	12
V			12	13	12	9	16	11	8
VI			16	22	27	20	29	39	30
VII			13	18	24	18	29	30	40

Note: Occupations are classified according to the Hope–Goldthorpe scale.
Percentages may not add exactly to 100 because of rounding errors.

Analysing the mobility of the female respondents in the 'People in society' survey, Abbott and Sapsford found similar rates of mobility but a dissimilar pattern. The daughters of professional and managerial workers were much more likely to be downwardly mobile than their sons and the daughters of manual workers were less likely to be upwardly mobile than their sons. Women who were upwardly mobile from manual backgrounds tended to end up in routine non-manual occupations – 44 per cent of the women were upwardly mobile and 31 per cent ended up in routine non-manual work. Fifty-six per cent of the women were downwardly mobile from professional and managerial backgrounds, but only 12 per cent ended up in manual occupations. From their analysis Abbott and Sapsford conclude that there is considerable female intergenerational mobility, that downward mobility occurs more frequently for women than for men, and that women of whatever origin are more likely than men to end up in routine non-manual jobs. The majority of women who cross the manual/non-manual divide end up in routine non-manual work (see Table 2.2).

Table 2.2 Occupational mobility of employed women in the 'People in society' survey

Father's occupation	Total		Respondent's occupation				
			A	B	C1	C2	D
			Percentaged by class of origin – father's class				
A	200	%	8	38	44	8	4
B	354	%	2	41	44	8	5
C1	310	%	2	24	46	10	19
C2	693	%	< 1	14	32	19	35
D	253	%	< 1	12	27	13	48
			Percentaged by destination (own) class				
			%	%	%	%	%
A			50	17	13	5	2
B			24	35	23	12	4
C1			15	17	21	13	13
C2			9	23	33	56	54
D			3	7	10	14	27

Percentages may not add exactly to 100 because of rounding errors.

Intragenerational occupational mobility

We would expect women to show less upward mobility within their life-span than men (intragenerational mobility), given women's involvement in childbirth and childcare and their consequent tendency to move in and out of the labour market. Indeed, this has been shown in one British study (Harris and Clausen, 1967), in which most of the mobility which did occur appeared to be downwards from skilled to semi-skilled or unskilled manual work.

Studies of men tend to show a fair amount of intragenerational mobility. The 'Oxford mobility study' found that a full half of the class I and II men who appeared occupationally stable intergenerationally (that is, in comparison with their fathers' social class) had been downwardly mobile earlier in their careers. On first entry to the labour market 75 per cent of men from working-class homes had manual jobs, but by 1972 only half of these were still in manual occupations (see Goldthorpe *et al.*, 1980). The 'Scottish mobility study' (see, for example, Chapman, 1984; Payne, 1987a, 1987b) found that 75 per cent of men experienced downward mobility on their first entry to the labour market, but men tended to recover their position after a period of years. Of sons of professional/managerial fathers who were downwardly mobile at first job, nearly 40 per cent eventually achieved professional status. The argument put forward in both studies to explain these figures is that such mobility is a routine part of career progression involving a start below the father's level but a progression back via career advancement.

The pattern is very different for women. In the 'Scottish mobility study' (Chapman, 1984) 77 per cent of women were downwardly mobile on entry to the labour market, and many remained there. Of the daughters of professional/managerial men, only 12 per cent achieved professional status; of the daughters of men in the intermediate class, 72 per cent showed initial downward mobility, and only 15 per cent eventually achieved professional or semi-professional status. Seventy per cent of the daughters of manual workers remained in manual occupations. Jones (1986), analysing 'National child development study' data, concluded that women are more intragenerationally stable than men up to the age of 23, and that for young women both the initial and the eventual class of job are far more likely to be determined by initial educational qualifications than is the case for men – there is less mobility through career advancement for women than for men (see also Greenhalgh and Stewart, 1982).

A more complex picture emerges from the detailed study of women's life-span work histories carried out by Martin and Roberts (1984). The study involved interviews with 5,588 women of working age in Great Britain in 1980, of whom 60 per cent were currently in paid employment (rather more than half in full-time employment), 10 per cent described themselves as unemployed or students; and the remaining 30 per cent were described as economically inactive. Martin and Roberts found that marriage as such did not affect labour market participation, but that having children – particularly young children – was the main reason for withdrawal from the labour market; only 4 per cent of women continued in employment when they first had a child. However, most women were economically active for the majority of their employable years; the older women in the sample had spent 60 per cent of their employable years in employment, and the data suggested that the percentage would be larger for the younger women, as they tended to return to work sooner after having a child. (For those who have dependent children, however, part-time work continues to be the norm.) Childless women were more likely to be in non-manual occupations than women with small children, and older childless women were far more likely to be in the professional or semi-professional categories. Childless women were also more likely to be upwardly intergenerationally mobile, though not as much so as men.

A question of key interest is the fate, on return, of the women who leave the labour market to have children. Martin and Roberts found that just over half of these change occupational class on return to work, 37 per cent moving down and only 14 per cent moving up; those who take part-time work on return are more likely to be downwardly mobile than those who take full-time work (45 per cent, compared with 19 per cent). There was some evidence for eventual upward mobility among returnees – more were upwardly mobile eventually than downwardly mobile – though the effect of movement from part-time to full-time work or vice versa was more influential. Thus there was some evidence for recovery over time, but interruption of work history and the taking of part-time jobs were definite inhibitors of upward social mobility for women.

Conclusions: women's mobility

Looking at women's social mobility, Britain is seen as a very mobile society. Education is an important factor in occupational mobility, as with men, and in the case of women it appears a crucial variable for upward mobility. However, women are overall more likely to be downwardly mobile than men and less likely to be upwardly mobile, because of labour market distortions – the excess of jobs for women at the bottom of the non-manual classes and at the bottom of the manual ones (see Chapter six). Daughters are somewhat less likely than sons to be employed at the same occupational level as their fathers if this was a 'high' one, and less likely than men to be counter-mobile (to move up from an initial decline in status). The manual/non-manual divide acts as a barrier for women in a different way from its effects on men because of the high concentration of women in routine non-manual work: it blocks downward mobility into the working class to some extent, but the considerable upward mobility from the working class is largely confined to movement into this 'routine' class. In other words, the daughters of manual workers who are upwardly mobile into middle-class occupations tend to end up in the routine non-manual category, as do the daughters of professional men or managers who are downwardly mobile.

Women's intragenerational mobility is a complex issue. Domestic responsibilities, and especially the care of young children, have a marked effect; women leave the labour market at least temporarily, and if they return then downward mobility is very likely. Even single women, however, show less intragenerational mobility than men, and initial level of educational qualification appears to be a far more important determinant of eventual occupational level for women than for men, with fewer women rising through 'on the job' promotion.

What such analyses show is that concentrating on the mobility of men provides a false picture of the society in which we live, because women form over 40 per cent of the working population and their experience of Britain as an 'open society' is very different from men's. Goldthorpe *et al.* (1980) claimed on the basis of the 'Oxford mobility study' to have disproved notions of social closure and 'buffer zones' as explaining the current distribution of class positions in Britain. Analysis of women's mobility suggests that both are very important explanatory factors: men operate closure against women with respect to the highest classes of occupation, the concentration of women in routine non-manual jobs constitutes a buffer zone limiting women's mobility, and within each class of occupation women occupy the lower levels and act as buffers against men's downward mobility.

However, while women have all this in common, they are also divided by class (see Goldthorpe and Payne, 1986; Abbott and Sapsford, 1987a). Women are not equally likely to end up in the same class of job irrespective of class origins; there is a tendency to gravitate towards routine non-manual work, but women in professional and managerial jobs are highly likely to have come from a similar background – this holds particularly for the highest class of occupations – and women in manual jobs are likely to have come from a working-class background. Gender inequalities do not abolish the need to look at class inequalities; however, they exist, and they are demonstrably important.

Measuring women's social class

The research we have discussed so far uses the existing class scales, measuring women's social class as if the scales used for classifying men's occupations can equally be used for women. However, some women – for example, full-time housewives – are currently without paid employment outside the home. Others may be in paid employment but not at a level compatible with their qualifications or with the place they could achieve in the labour market if free from domestic responsibilities. Even the apparently simple case of single women is not so simple in practice because labour-market segregation means that women tend to be clustered in particular occupations (see Chapter six) which are themselves clustered into relatively restricted ranges of the occupational scales which have been developed with men's jobs in mind. This makes fine discrimination difficult and tends to suggest that women are more homogeneous with respect to occupational class than women's own views and experiences would suggest. For example, an airline stewardess and a waitress end up in the same social class, as do a shop assistant and a personal secretary.

Four basic positions have been taken on how to cope with these problems:

1 to retain the household (family) as the unit of analysis, but to take women's occupational position and/or other characteristics into account when determining its class position;
2 to locate women in the class system on the basis of their own paid employment, without reference to the remainder of the household, but to develop more adequate measures of social class;
3 to attempt to develop a measure of 'consumption class' for families which will take account of the influence of all family members on life-style, and to look in parallel at an occupation-based measure of individuals' market position, one which more adequately distinguishes between women's occupations than the conventional scales;
4 to locate women in the class system by taking into account both their paid employment (if any) and their role as unpaid domestic labour.

The position that the household should remain the unit of analysis, but taking account of women's employment in assigning it a class, has resulted in two distinct 'solutions'. One, the 'dominance principle' (Haugh, 1973; Erikson, 1984; Goldthorpe and Payne, 1986) would in practice make very little difference to conventional analysis. It involves taking as the class of the household the occupational class of whichever partner has the highest class of occupation, provided that this person works full time and is fully committed to the labour market. In practice, then, husband's class will determine the class of most households, but in a (non-trivial but relatively small) minority of 'deviant' households the class would be taken from the wife's occupation. The other solution is to compute a joint social class for the household as a whole by combining the classes of husband and wife, if the wife is economically active (Britten and Heath, 1983; Heath and Britten, 1984; Pahl and

Wallace, 1985). A variant which goes further, by giving some weight to personal characteristics of full-time housewives, would combine a number of possible indicators – education, housing tenure – with occupational levels (Osborne and Morris, 1979).

If we are to look at women's social (occupational) mobility then it is necessary to classify women on the basis of their own occupations. If women are classified by their own occupations, market and class inequalities are available as topics of investigation for both men and women in a way that they are not if we aggregate men and women together into a household class. Doubts have been raised, however, about the adequacy of existing class scales for this purpose, because of the concentration of women in certain occupational groups that are much more rarely filled by men. A number of attempts have been made to develop an alternative social-class scale that more adequately reflects the class position of women. In some cases the scales have been developed for use on both men and women, and in others for women only. We will examine an example of each.

The 'Surrey occupational class scale'

In a recent paper, Arber *et al.*, (1986) report on the development of a scale intended for the categorization of both men and women but discriminating between the occupational sectors in which women are most employed more finely than the conventional scales (noting, however, that the current occupation of women in part-time employment may be a doubtful indicator of true market position, given the tendency of returnees to the labour market to take part-time work at below their previous level). This 'Surrey occupational class scale' divides jobs into the following nine categories:

1 higher professional
2 employers and managers
3 lower professional
4 secretarial and clerical
5 foremen and self-employed manual workers
6 shop and personal service workers
7 skilled manual workers
8 semi-skilled manual workers
9 unskilled manual workers.

The scale does not assign a class directly to those currently unemployed – for example housewives – but Arber *et al.* follow Martin and Roberts (1984) in suggesting that the best indicator would be last full-time occupation prior to the birth of the first child, or failing that then just last full-time occupation.

They admit that despite their attempts at disaggregation, 39 per cent of working women still fall in a single one of their classes, SOC 4. They argue, however, that:

> The two main advantages of [the 'Surrey occupational class scale'] for women are, first, it provides a distinction...between employers and managers (SOC 2) and lower professional (SOC 3). SOC 2 is predominantly male, containing 13 per cent of full-time men compared to five per cent of full-time women and under two per cent of part-time working women, and SOC 3 is predominantly female, containing 13 per cent of full-time women compared to only five per cent of men. Secondly, it separates shop workers (SOC 6) from secretarial/clerical workers and sales representatives (SOC 4) and separates personal service workers (SOC 6) from semi-skilled factory workers (SOC 8). These two changes highlight the concentration of part-time women in shop and personal service work, 35 per cent compared to 14 per cent of full-time women and a bare three per cent of men. They also show clearly the smaller participation of part-time women in clerical and secretarial occupations, which is masked in other classifications. Under 20 per cent of part-time working women are in SOC 4.
>
> (Arber *et al.*, 1986: 68)

This classification distinguishes occupational categories which are distinct in terms of work and market situation and which can be used for both men and women. If men and women appear in the same 'Surrey occupational class', however, this does not necessarily mean that they have the same experience of and rewards from work; gender inequalities could still be concealed (see Chapter six).

The 'City University classification'

One major feminist criticism of scales so far developed is that they fail to take account of the unpaid work of full-time housewives. Helen Roberts and her colleagues (Roberts: 1985b, 1986, 1987) are attempting to construct a scale for women which would distinguish between women's jobs and between full-time and part-time work, taking account of domestic as well as paid labour, and allocating a class position to full-time housewives. The advantage of this classification will be that it will enable all women to be allocated a class position on the basis of *their* characteristics, and on the basis of a relatively small number of questions. A problem with the scheme's use is that it is likely that it will mask inequalities between full-time housewives, who are all in the same class irrespective of any measure of household class as determined by the occupations of other members of the household. This means that

33

women with very different standards of living will share the same class position on this scale. Also, the initial ranking using husbands' class is based on the assumption that husbands' contributions to life-style can be averaged, which may not hold true; the sort of man a woman marries, depending on her occupation, may be an important class marker. (Some evidence for this is provided by Prandy (1986): air hostesses, for instance, marry 'higher class' husbands than waitresses, although both share a Registrar General's class category.) Finally, the scale is for use only with women and thus cannot be used to explore gender inequalities. None the less, this appears another promising scale for some research purposes.

Conclusions: social class

There is increasing empirical evidence to suggest that women's social class position cannot be ignored or treated as derivative from the social class position of husbands or fathers; not only does this fail to explain their social and political behaviour, but it often leads to mistaken conclusions about the social mobility of men and the structure of British society for both genders. For example, the social mobility of men and the openness of the occupational structure to upward mobility cannot be fully understood without taking the mobility and occupational distribution of women into account. Women's preparedness to 'have a job' rather than following a career is certainly important in explaining male mobility; few 'dual career' families actually have two partners following careers – more often the male has a career and the woman fits her work into the demands of that career (Crompton and Sanderson, 1986). Janet Finch (1983a) has demonstrated the importance of a wife's unpaid labour for many men in enabling them to follow their occupations, and Chapman (1984) has suggested that most upward mobility depends on the wife being able to take on the 'higher' life-style.

The study of women's social class convinces us at least of the importance of studying family members in their own right and not making common-sense assumptions about shared family norms and interests or shared experience of the social world. It may be, contingently, that there are considerable shared interests and a considerable amount of shared experience. It may be that class is a more important principle of stratification than gender in our society. That this is the case must be demonstrated, however, not taken for granted in the untheorized way which has been typical of malestream sociologists, and for this we need adequate tools and unblinkered theories so that women can be fully incorporated in sociological research.

Summary:

1 The study of social class has been a key issue in sociology, and women have traditionally been excluded from it on the grounds that they are not permanent in the labour market and that their social class is determined by their husbands' jobs. Recently some have argued that this tradition should be continued.

2 Feminists have argued that this treatment of women in class theory is not only sexist but leads to a distortion of our understanding of social class, particularly in matters such as social mobility, the openness of society, and the question of class identification.

3 Feminists have offered a number of alternative ways of working. Some have attempted to incorporate an understanding of women into existing social class schemas. Others have tried to develop new forms of classification which take both men and women into account. Finally, others have argued that men's classifications are totally inadequate for accounting for women's social class and have developed classifications based upon women alone.

Black women in Britain

In this section we want to examine the situation and life experiences of women who have come to Britain as immigrants from Third World countries, and their daughters. We refer to them as 'black women' because of the problems associated with other possible terms. The use of the term 'coloured' has distasteful connotations because of its use in South Africa. 'Ethnic minority groups' tends to suggest that the majority of the population do not have an ethnicity – or that one is shared by all those we are meaning to include in our designated group – and to carry overtones of inferiority, whereas 'black' is a term that has been reclaimed by those struggling for the emancipation of oppressed people: hence the slogan 'black is beautiful'. The term 'black' would not be accepted by all the women we mean to encompass, but it has been used as a term of self-definition by many of them, especially Afro-Caribbean women. We use the term as the best available, in our view, but recognize its limitations.

In the period after the Second World War, Britain encouraged New Commonwealth citizens to immigrate to fill the job vacancies in the growing economy. The initial immigration in the 1950s was mainly from the West Indies, and the Asian immigrants (from India and Pakistan) came in the late 1950s and the 1960s. Immigrants were expected to come and fill the growing number of job vacancies and to take on the low-paid, low-skilled jobs that the native population were reluctant to fill. These immigrants were often met with hostility by the native white population, who regarded them as inferior and a threat to the British way of life. They were often seen as in competition for the scarce housing, educational, and health services, and were blamed for the deteriorating state of the inner cities. While many, especially West Indians, had thought that coming to Britain would be like coming home, returning to the mother country, they have experienced hostility from the native population, a low standard of living, poor educational facilities for their children, and unemployment. The daughters of immigrants have experienced even greater problems. Some are critical of the low-status, poorly paid jobs, the treatment from white society that their parents experience, and the poor education that they frequently receive. Problems of finding employment often mean that their hopes and aspirations have been shattered.

Black women experience subordination and exploitation as women, as members of the working class, and on the basis of their colour. Sociologists have been concerned to reject biological and psychological explanations for the subordinate and inferior position of black women in Britain. Instead they have explored the social and structural aspects of social inequalities and examined how black women became socially constructed as subordinate. They have considered differences in power, both in social and in economic terms, and examined the ways in which ideologies have come to construct black women as inferior and to justify their inferior status.

The status of black women has been explained by reference to biological factors – for example, that black people are inherently less intelligent than white people, a proposition to which the work of psychologists such as Eysenck (1971) and Jensen (1973) has given some scientific credibility. An alternative explanation is one in terms of norms and values – that they do not share the values of white society and that this explains why they do not 'get on'. Similarly, racial prejudice has been explained in terms of the blind and irrational prejudice against 'outsiders' of bigoted individuals, or the inability of groups to cope with the 'unusual' cultural character of a different racial group – that is, the group's way of life, including language, religion, family customs, clothes, and so on. All of these explanations tend to present non-white people as 'deviant', or as 'strangers', and seek to explain reactions to this status. This leads to a tendency to study the characteristics of ethnic groups themselves and to make a problem out of these very characteristics. Hence Asians are seen as too tied to tradition, hampered by 'arranged marriages', or too passive; West Indians are seen as disruptive, or criminal, too active, or militant. More recent work by black writers has attempted an alternative approach: to analyse the institutional structures within white society – and this includes white sociology – which serve to oppress non-white people and to present 'the problem' in terms of them rather than in terms of white racist society (Centre for Contemporary Cultural Studies, 1982).

Two major theories of ethnicity and race have emerged in sociology. Marxists argue that racial disadvantage can be explained by reference to the class structure under capitalism. Ethnic minorities are an integral part of the proletariat, the working class who are exploited by capitalists. Racial prejudice can be explained by reference to Britain's colonial past and the development of ideologies during the nineteenth century that justified Britain's exploitation of the black inhabitants of the colonies by suggesting that they were inferior, less than fully human. The waves of immigration in the 1950s and 1960s must be seen in the context of the needs of international capitalism. The immigrants came to a country where ideologies of racial inferiority/superiority already existed. As the economic situation has changed and a shortage of jobs has arisen, prejudice has increased to some extent. Furthermore, Marxists argue that the ruling class is able to exploit the ideologies of racial prejudice to maintain its position of dominance. Thus, conflict between black and white working class people is based on the whites blaming the blacks for their bad housing, lack of hospital resources, etc., while the black population blame their plight on the prejudice of the whites with whom they come into contact. This, it is argued, deflects attention away from the 'real' causes of the problems, the lack of adequate provision for the working class as a whole.

Weberian sociologists reject the Marxist theory of racial divisions. They argue that racial disadvantage arises out of competition between groups for scarce resources – such as housing, employment, and education. A group seizes on identifiable social and/or physical characteristics of potential or actual competitors and use them to exclude them from the competition. (We have already seen in this chapter how men use social characteristics to exclude women from higher-class occupations.) In modern Britain the white native population have used social closure against ethnic minority populations, especially those from the New Commonwealth and their descendants.

Weberian sociology better explains the diversity of ethnic divisions, but without adequately explaining why those particular characteristics, rather than others, should have been chosen. Marxists have provided a better historical framework, but they have to discard most of what is distinctive about the problem of race in order to explain it.

Black feminists have criticized both theories for taking no adequate account of gender differences and for not realizing that the experiences of black women and the ways in which they are exploited are different from the case of black men. As Bryan *et al.*, (1985) say of their own experiences: '...We have seen the women's movement ... documenting 'herstory' from every angle except our own.' This criticism is now widely accepted by white feminists and one with which we agree. As two white women, we cannot write fully about the experiences of black women, and studies of ethnicity have ignored the specific position of black women. This limits the analysis we are able to provide.

Black women are disadvantaged on a number of dimensions. The 1982 Policy Studies Institute Survey (see Brown, 1985) compared the situation of New Commonwealth settlers and their families in 1974 and in 1982, and found that there had been little improvement in their situation. In terms of employment, ethnic minorities are highly concentrated according to their ethnic origin: West Indians in the National Health Service and in transport industries, and Pakistanis and Bangladeshis in the clothing and textile industries – the very industries for which they were recruited in the 1950s and 1960s. West Indian women are more likely to be found in service industries than are other ethnic groups, and West Indian men and Indian women are more likely to be found in manufacturing and mining than either white women or Indian men. Only 1 per cent of West Indian women were recorded in RG social class I, as against 7 per cent of Asians and 9 per cent of white women. On the other hand, very large proportions of West Indian women (42 per cent and 45 per cent) were recorded as unskilled or semi-skilled manual workers, as against only 30 per cent of white women. Unemployment was unevenly distributed, only 10 per cent of white women being recorded as unemployed as against 16 per cent of West Indians and 20 per cent of Asians. (However, in interpreting these statistics we need to take into account the problems of measuring women's unemployment discussed in Chapter six: many of those women who are seeking work are not registered as unemployed.) Taking into account the employment position of black women as well as men highlights their extremely disadvantaged labour-market position.

Black girls and young women are also disadvantaged in the schooling system, in housing, and in the health service (see Chapters three and five, and Bryan *et al.*, 1985). Black families are more likely to be seen as inadequate or incapable of caring for their children, and black women are over-represented in the prison population, where they make up 40 per cent of female inmates (Bryan *et al.*, 1985).

Sociologists have argued that this situation is not just a result of individual prejudices, but of institutionalized racism:

> The policies of institutions that work to perpetuate racial inequality without acknowledging that fact.... Camouflaged racism...[is]

concealed in the routine practices and procedures of organisations such as industries, political parties and schools.

(Cashmore and Troyna, 1983: 60)

Examples of this would be the ways in which West Indian English becomes seen as 'broken' English, and the ways in which Immigration Acts have operated to exclude black immigrants while still permitting white immigration.

Black feminists have argued that white feminist models of oppression are inadequate for accounting for the experiences of black women. By setting up theories of women's oppression as applying to all women they have contributed to institutionalized racism. Black feminists have pointed out how women from Commonwealth countries are perceived as dominated and oppressed by their traditional cultures. Assimilation into western mores is therefore portrayed as a form of liberation, allowing them to rebel against their families, wear western clothes, cut their hair, and so on. This exaggerates the stereotype of 'traditional' society just as it exaggerates the 'liberation' of western society. For white women, the nuclear family is the central site of oppression because of the way in which it defines women's sexuality in terms of monogamy and 'respectable' femininity and situates women in the privatized domain. Some black women, on the other hand, have argued that the family – threatened by slavery, indentured labour, and migration for work – was often something to be defended, a source of support and resistance in a racist society (Brah, 1986). Rather than the family being a marginalized and privatized domestic prison, in many ethnic households it remains the central area of subsistence and is less likely to consist of an isolated couple and more likely to consist of a supportive network of kin.

Access to paid employment was seen as the way forward for many years in the women's movement, reflecting the aims of white middle-class feminists. Black women, by contrast, are more likely to *have* to go out to work and to define this as part of their role. The kind of work they are likely to do exploits them both as women and as workers, since they make up the lower-paid workers who also do the longest hours. The sexist assumption that employment cannot be combined with good mothering has not applied to black women, who are often expected to work full time for most of their lives.

Black women are often perceived as sexually exotic by white men. Wealthy western visitors are sold packaged holidays in Asia on this basis, and this imagery is hinted at in the advertizing of airlines. Third World women are seen as more submissive, obedient, and feminine than western women. Thus, for Third World women, their sexuality is often shaped by racist assumptions. Carby (1982) has questioned whether the whole notion of 'patriarchy' is really appropriate to the experiences of black women. Black West Indian men never possessed 'patriarchal power' over their women in the way that white men did.

What is evident is that it is very difficult to generalize about all ethnic groups, which have very different histories and traditions. While black West Indian women came to Britain explicitly as workers, some Asian women came to join families but later became workers as part of the economic strategy of survival.

Summary

1 Studies of ethnicity have ignored the very different experiences of different women.
2 White feminist accounts of women's oppression have ignored the distinctive experiences of black women. The sources of oppression of white women – for example, the nuclear family – are not the same for black women.
3 Black women are oppressed not only by their gender but by the intersection of class, race, and gender. On the whole, they suffer the worst of all groups in terms of disadvantage.

Women in the Third world

'The Third World' refers to countries outside of the 'core' of western industrialized nations; they are also referred to as 'the developing nations', or 'underdeveloped', or 'non-industrial nations'. They include areas such as Latin America, much of Asia, and much of Africa. We have chosen the term 'Third World' because although it lumps together a large variety of cultures and countries it can be used as convenient shorthand for countries existing in a state of economic dependence upon the west – a state of dependence that has been created by imperialistic economic policies of capitalist countries and multinational firms.

In Third World countries there is a large pool of cheap labour available and prepared to work for very little money – far less than workers in Britain. This potential labour pool has been exploited by western capitalism in two ways: first, western firms have moved factories to Third World countries, and second, western countries have encouraged immigration from Third World countries to remedy labour shortages in their economies. In the Third World taxation is very low as there is no welfare state, no pensions, and no social security system for the majority of the people. Employers can get away with production processes which are much more dangerous to people and the environment than would be allowed in the west. These methods of production are therefore cheaper, since the industrial safety and environmental protection legislation is less stringently enforced than in western nations.

While the situation of the Third World generally receives little attention in the west, the position of women within it receives even less attention. However, gender serves to structure social relationships in all societies, and just as western economic and cultural relations have penetrated Third World countries, destroying traditional ways of life and creating dependent economies, so western notions of femininity and the family have likewise been imposed upon other models of gender and rendered them 'peculiar', 'heathen', 'unliberated', or sexually exotic. On the other hand, the adoption of western life-styles and gender roles is often seen as evidence of 'progress'.

Sociology has concentrated on explaining why the poor countries of the world have not industrialized in the same way as the richer nations. Theories have tended to stress the lack of motivation or the inappropriate attitudes of the Third World, or suggested that they lack the economic foundation on which to build, or that they have been systematically exploited and underdeveloped by First World countries. Less attention has been paid to the role of women in Third World countries, and what happens to them as countries attempt to industrialize and develop. In this section we shall attempt to look briefly at women in the Third World, illustrating our arguments with a few examples. It is not possible to make generalizations, because women's experiences in Third World countries differ according to their role prior to the beginnings of change. Many Third World women working in agriculture or industrial production in their own countries are exploited both by the men of their own country and by the capitalists of the First World, as women are seen as a source of cheap and docile labour, to be used to provide goods for First World markets.

Seager and Olsen (1986) suggest that we need to understand the ordinary lives of women and to recognize their common everyday experiences:

> They are the providers of food, fuel, water and often the whole family income – the sustainers and developers of their families, communities and countries ... the fate of women is a critical determinant of the fate of whole societies.
>
> (Margaret Snyder, U.N. Voluntary Fund for Women, quoted in Seager and Olsen, 1986:7)

Third World women are everywhere worse off than their men, have less power, less authority, do more work but earn less money, and have more responsibility than men. In most societies women shoulder the primary responsibility for housework, nursing children, and meeting the needs of their families, and in many countries women are also responsible for farming. According to the United Nations (see Brown, 1985) women constitute half of the world population but do nearly two thirds of the world's work, receive 10 per cent of the world's income and own less than 1 per cent of the property. It has been estimated that women's unpaid labour adds a third to the world's economic product (Seager and Olsen, 1986).

Development is usually assumed to be 'a good thing' despite the enormous human costs. One area of interest to feminists has been the effects of socio-economic development on women. Susan Tiano (1987) has suggested that there are three competing perspectives on the impact that economic development has had on women:

1 the Integration Thesis, which argues that development results in female liberation and sexual equality as women become more centrally involved in economic and public life;
2 the Marginalization Thesis, which holds that with capitalist development women become increasingly excluded from production roles and confined to the private sphere of the home – in the process losing their control over resources and becoming economically dependent on men;
3 the Exploitation Thesis, which argues that modernization results in the creation of a low-paid female labour force – women become more central to industrial production but are exploited because they are seen as a secondary labour force.

In order to understand the impact of economic change on women it is necessary to have some understanding of women's lives in pre-/non-industrial societies. However, there is considerable controversy over the position of women in such societies. There is some agreement among anthropologists that gender inequalities were less prominent in hunting and gathering societies, and in simple horticultural societies, than in peasant-based agrarian ones. However, cultural factors, especially religion, are also important.

Furthermore, the effects that economic change has on women also depend on class, as well as ethnic status. As a society undergoes economic change, so does the nature of work, and so does the distinction between men and women. There is an increase in the sexual division of labour, and this occurs in a way which perpetuates female subordination. In areas where men and women work for wages, employment is segregated into industrial sectors, and women are typically in lower-paid work than men, and in work that is defined as less skilled than the work men do. In unwaged work women are increasingly seen as the domestic workers, and in many areas they lose the land they farmed, to produce food for the family, to men who produce crops for cash. Thus women's economic dependency is increased. Often these changes are actively encouraged by aid agencies and First World employers, who work with western ideologies of the family, the division of labour between men and women, and the appropriate role for each gender (see Chapter four). Thus, in parts of Africa where women generally farmed to produce food for their families, aid agencies have trained men in farming and encouraged them to produce cash crops. In the process women have often lost control of their land or been edged out into more marginal land, which they till with no access to modern farming technology (Obbso, 1980). The very low pay of women employed in manufacturing industry can similarly be said to be based on the assumption that women either have only themselves to support or are partly supported by some man. Rae Lesser Blumberg (1981) suggests three reasons why economic development results in the marginalization of women:

1 there is an increase in women's real workload;
2 there is a decrease in women's resource base;
3 there is a decrease in women's well-being and their opportunities as people.

As men are drawn into the cities of Third World countries to participate in the cash economy, women often have less control over resources. Men are less likely to help out as they are freed, by the demands of regular paid work, from traditional male domestic responsibilities. However, women are often expected to continue to grow crops, to feed the family, and carry out all the domestic work.

The impact of economic change on agriculture varies between regions. In Africa south of the Sahara, and some of South-East Asia, and Central America, the 'slash and burn' technique has traditionally been used. Men cleared the land while women did most of the cultivation. Women had a central role in food production and therefore some influence in decision-making (Blumberg, 1981). European settlers, however, brought in the idea that farming is man's work and that crops should be produced for the market. Men took over control of the land from women and began to produce cash crops. Women continued to be expected to produce crops for home consumption, often on smaller plots of more marginal land. Women were also excluded from agricultural education; in Africa less than 5 per cent of trained agricultural personnel are women.

In India the 'Green revolution' – the introduction of modern farming methods – began in 1964 (Beyres *et al.*, 1983), the goal being for India to become self-sufficient in the production of food grains. The changes this brought about had a considerable impact on women's roles. In India prior to the 'Green revolution' women were economically dependent on men in all classes, although the dependency varied in form and intensity between classes. In landowning and peasant households it was always men who owned the land and the means of production. In the dominant classes the dependency of women was further intensified by purdah (the concealment of women), which made it difficult for them to move outside their own homes, preventing their participation in the public sphere. Peasant women did work the land owned by their husbands, but only the wives of poor peasants and landless labourers worked for wages. In all households women would have been responsible for all domestic duties, including the processing of grain, and looking after the poultry, cows, buffaloes, and sheep.

The introduction of new technology has not affected all parts of India alike, but where it has been introduced it has resulted in a decline in employment for women. In rich peasant households women have been withdrawn from direct participation in farm work – labour has been hired to do the work previously done by women. This has reinforced women's economic dependence on men. In poor peasant and landless labourer households, women have not voluntarily withdrawn from labour – their wages are essential for survival – but in many cases they have been squeezed out of employment by the new technology. Male labour is employed to use the new machinery.

Only a very small proportion of Third World women are employed in factory work, but when they are, they are employed in 'female' jobs. Most production in Third World countries is mass production for developed countries who have located some manufacturing in the Third World but control it from the west. The work exported is generally standardized, repetitive, calls for little technical knowledge, labour-intensive, and often uses assembly-line operations which would be difficult and/or costly to mechanize still further. The aim is to exploit a suitable labour force – that is, one that is lower in costs of employment and/or higher in productivity. The wages in Third World factories are often as little as a tenth of those in the developed countries, and working hours up to 50 per cent higher, while productivity is as high as that of the First World or higher.

Female labour is cheaper than male labour, female productivity is higher than that of men, and women are thought to be naturally better at some tasks than men. The First World owners do not have to bear the cost of training the female work-force. The work is seen as unskilled, not because it does not require skill, but because the girls have already learned these skills in the home. Much of the relocated work is women's work or becomes seen as such because of the perceived advantages of female labour.

Summary

1 Women are generally worse paid and suffer worse conditions of employment compared with men, the world over.

2 'Development' has often worsened the situation of women because:

   a western ideas of gender are imposed through the introduction of new forms of industry and through aid programmes;

   b women are primarily responsible for subsistence and household needs – maintaining the family economy and bearing and raising children – whereas men working as migrant labour may have to leave home altogether;

   c where women are engaged in production their wages are generally lower.

3 We have found little evidence to support the integration thesis; women do not seem to be liberated and to achieve equality with men as societies develop. There is some evidence for the marginalization thesis – that is, that women are excluded from production roles and confined to the private sphere of the home, and this seems to be especially true in some rural areas. However, it seems that in urban areas and some rural ones modernization results in the exploitation of women in new ways as they come to be seen as a cheap, expendable labour force, whether in the factory or on the land.

Conclusions

We recognize that women's experiences are structured by class and race – that black women in Britain suffer discrimination, exploitation, and subordination because they are black as well as because they are women. While middle-class women are more advantaged than their working-class sisters, this does not prevent them becoming poor if they become a head of a single-parent family or from suffering relative poverty in old age. Third World women's subordination and exploitation are based not only on ideologies of women's role but also on ideologies of racial inferiority developed to justify the First World's use of black slaves, and exploitation of Third World peoples. Nevertheless all women's lives are structured by expectations of role-appropriate behaviour, the idea that women are – and should be – dependent on men, and the notion that women's fulfilment comes from marriage and caring for a husband and children. These assumptions are a key to women's subordination and exploitation – why women lack control over

45

resources. This is equally as true in the Third World as in the First World.

Further reading

Abbott, P.A. and Sapsford, R.J. (1987) *Women and Social Class*, London: Tavistock.
Centre for Contemporary Cultural Studies (1982) *The Empire Strikes Back: race and racism in 70s Britain*, London: Heinemann.
Crompton, R. and Mann, M. (1986) *Gender and Stratification*, Cambridge: Polity Press.

Chapter three

Girls and young women

Age is usually seen as a natural or biological status, yet historical and cross-cultural research has shown that the way in which different societies divide up the life course is highly variable, as is the behaviour associated with different age groups. Age status is of particular importance to women, who are more often defined in terms of ascribed biological characteristics than of social achievements. For example, a sexually attractive woman is usually assumed to be a young woman, whereas an attractive man can be of any age. In this chapter we look at feminist work on girls and young women – including their education, which is an integral part of their socialization into femininity and feminine roles.

Childhood

Children are perceived to be not quite fully social beings – for example, they are seldom questioned in sociological surveys, presumably on the assumption that they are incapable of making rational responses in the same way as adults. But children also have a privileged status as representing the future hopes and aspirations of a society or social group and as such are accorded particular help and protection. This has not always been the case. For Rousseau, the eighteenth century French philosopher, children were primitive savages waiting to be civilized through education.

It was generally argued that there were no distinctive phases of childhood and adolescence; rather, from the age of about 7 years children became part of adult society, expected to undertake work roles and contribute to the maintenance of the family (Aries, 1962). Children were punished for crimes in the same way as adults, being deemed morally responsible for their actions from the age of seven. By the nineteenth century they had come to have a special status between 7 and 14 years. Nevertheless, children of this age were still usually prosecuted in the same way as adults:

On one day alone in February 1814 at the Old Bailey sessions, five children were condemned to death: Fowler aged 12 and Wolfe aged 12 for burglary in a dwelling; Morris aged eight, Solomons aged nine and Burrell aged 11 for burglary and stealing a pair of shoes.

(Pinchbeck and Hewitt, 1973, quoted in Muncie, 1984: 33)

Children in pre-industrial Britain, whether they remained at home or went into service, had little freedom. Working-class children as young as 6 or 7 years of age were sent away to work in other households. The rising middle class frequently sent their sons to be apprenticed, and from the sixteenth century increasingly to boarding-school, although the main growth of these came in the nineteenth century. Middle-class girls were mainly kept at home, while the small number of girls' boarding-schools trained girls for domesticity. Girls were controlled either by their fathers or by their masters. Wages were nominal, and many girls would have been expected to send things home to their parents.

In the early nineteenth century working-class children provided cheap labour in the factories. However, from the 1830s, Factory Acts limited the age from which children could be employed (to 10 years) and the hours that young people could work, making children under the age of 10 economically dependent on their parents. However, young people continued to be in paid employment well into the century; young girls were frequently sold into prostitution, and child chimney-sweeps were not outlawed until late in the nineteenth century. Families were often dependent on the wages of their young, and this situation continued up to the First World War, and beyond (Humphries, 1981). Girls would also have been expected to help their mothers with domestic tasks and to help in the care of younger siblings.

By the twentieth century childhood had become identified by psychologists and the medical profession as a crucial period of language and identity formation. As the welfare state developed, children were singled out as particular objects of welfare intervention needing special diet, dental, and medical assistance. The expanding social services were concerned with the moral and social welfare of children, and the education system began to concern itself not only with their erudition but increasingly with their well-being more generally.

Other trends served to change the status of childhood. The decline in infant mortality and the decline in the birthrate more generally after the Second World War meant that families were able to invest more in their children in the reasonable certainty that they would survive (Gittins, 1985). Under these circumstances, children became objects of fun and pleasure for adults, a sort of household luxury, objects of conspicuous consumption.

Also, from the late nineteenth century, children began to be recognized as having rights of their own. Various legislative measures were designed to protect the child from his or her own family, and from exploitation or neglect by other adults. However, the welfare of children was also linked to their social control, and the 1908 Childen's Act was intended both to protect children from becoming criminal adults, and to separate them in 'reformatories'. 'Problem' children were to be both protected and reformed. The young offender was handled differently from adult offenders, tried in 'juvenile courts', and schools were supposed to monitor the progress of children in order to identify 'problem' cases. This was partly because it began to be argued that disturbed children would become delinquent adolescents. Hence, childhood came to be associated with developmental and psychological stages which had to be correctly negotiated (Rose, 1985). Recent public interest in child physical and sexual abuse following the deaths of Maria Caldwell and Jasmine Beckford from neglect and injury by their parents, and the setting up of telephone 'childlines' for the victims of sexual abuse, have once more resulted in intervention to protect children from adults and a renewed debate about the status of childhood.

Summary

  1 Childhood is not simply a biological category but was constructed as a social category, one of particular concern, from the sixteenth century onwards. This process continued in the late nineteenth century and later with the growth of the welfare state and education.
  2 Childhood gradually became identified with a special psychological process of development.
  3 Children then started to become objects of special attention within families, the focus and purpose of family life rather than an economic resource.

Educating girls

The sociology of education has been concerned primarily with examining class inequalities in educational achievement, and especially the relative failure of working-class children in obtaining educational qualifications. Sociologists have overlooked other important dimensions of educational differentiation – for example, gender and racial differences in achievement. Feminists have argued that girls are not only disadvantaged in the educational system, but that it is there that they learn to be subordinate and to accept dominant ideologies of femininity and masculinity. Girls, for example, come to see themselves as less able than boys and specifically as 'no good' at mathematics and sciences. Girls are channelled into particular subjects that are seen as suitable for them and thus have their opportunities in the labour market severely reduced. What needs to be explained is how girls come to accept this.

Table 3.1 Education and economic activities of 16-year-olds in 1982 and 1986

% of 16-year-olds	1982			1986		
	Girls	Boys	Total	Girls	Boys	Total
a) in FT education						
School	33	30	32	33	30	31
F.E.	19	12	16	18	11	14
Total	52	42	48	50	41	45
b) in Employment						
(not YTS)	22	30	26	16	15	15
c) On YTS	13	14	14	24	31	
d) Unemployed	12	14	13	10	13	
% in PT education [1]	4	11	8	3	7	
Total (000s)	453	479	932	419	441	860

Note 1: Public sector PT – excludes those on YTS. The majority are in employment, but some are receiving unemployment benefit.

Table 3.2 School-leavers: highest qualification by sex, 1985/6

% with	Boys	Girls
2+ A or 3+ H Grades	14.9	14.2
1 A or 2 H grades	3.6	4.3
5+ O A–C grades/CSE grade 1	10.0	11.9
1-4 O A–C grades/CSE grade 1	24.4	28.7
1+ O D–E grades/CSE grades 2-5	34.0	30.9
No GCE/SCE/CSE pass grades	13.2	10.0

Girls' educational achievement

Girls generally do better than boys in the primary school and the early secondary years. Girls have tended to gain better O-level results than boys, and the gap is very narrow at A-level (Table 3.2). It is increasingly true that a higher proportion of girl than boy school-leavers are gaining good grades at O-level/CSE, though there are differences by subject taken. More girls than boys stay in full-time education after the age of 16 (see Table 3.1), although boys are more likely to have day release from an employer – reflecting the small number of girls who are taken on as apprentices. Women are more likely than men to take evening classes. However, boys are more likely than girls to go on to higher education (see Table 3.3). The major difference, however, is in subject taken. In 1986/87 girls were more likely than boys to have gained a higher-grade O-level result (GCSE Grades 1-3, SCE Grades 1-3, CSE Grade 1) in English, biology, French, history and/or the creative arts. Only a tiny number of boys gained passes in commercial or domestic studies (though substantially more than in 1976/7, perhaps reflecting the growing number of 'business studies' courses). In physics, where 22 per cent of boys achieved a higher grade of pass, only 9 per cent of girls did so. Boys are more likely than girls to take and pass mathematical, scientific, and technological subjects, and girls are more likely to take and pass the arts and domestic subjects.

This same pattern emerges in higher education. While in 1985 the same number of men and women gained a first degree in arts subjects, nearly three times as many men as women gained one in a science subject. Education itself was very much a minority subject of study, but over twice as many women as men were awarded a first degree in education – a teaching qualification. At postgraduate level nearly twice as many men as women obtained a postgraduate qualification in an arts subject and nearly four times as many in a science subject. Table 3.4 shows that only in education – mainly Postgraduate Certificates in Education – did women outstrip men.

Table 3.3 Full-time students (000s) in 1985-6: educational sector

		Men	Women
Universities	*Postgraduate*	21.0	12.6
	Undergraduate	134.4	99.9
	Other	1.5	1.2
Public sector H.E.		143.5	132.2
Total		300.4	245.9

51

Table 3.4 Higher education qualifications obtained in 1985, by subject group

Type of qualification	Male (000s)				Female (000s)			
	Arts	Science	Educ.	Other	Arts	Science	Educ.	Other
Postgraduate	10	11	5	–	6	3	6	–
First degree	36	38	2	4	36	14	5	4
Below first degree	22	30	2	–	15	7	2	–

It is also necessary to look at what happens to non-academic girls. Here it is evident that the main education is preparation for 'women's jobs'. Their aspirations are 'cooled out' not just by educational failure but also by the expectations of their future roles in the family. Many parents, teachers, and employers ask what the point is of girls striving for success at school when they will only get married and become dependents of men. Such expectations filter through to the girls, and domestic roles are seen as the alternative to academic success for them. However, in reality they are likely to spend much of their lives in paid employment – see Chapter six – so this experience in the education system leaves them ready to accept lower-paid, lower-status jobs without promotion prospects.

Just as gender differences in educational achievement have been neglected, so have ethnic differences. What is evident is that Asian and West Indian women tend to have fewer academic qualifications than white women. West Indian women are more likely than West Indian men to have reached GCE O-level or CSE standard and to have vocational qualifications (a large percentage in nursing). But Asian women in the 16-24 age-group are much more likely than Asian men to have no academic qualifications (Brown, 1985).

Educational failure has tended to be explained in malestream sociology in terms of material and cultural disadvantage. However, feminists have suggested that women's educational experiences are the outcome of sexism and that black women's experiences are also the outcome of institutional racism (see Chapter two).

The history of education for girls

Middle-class Victorian girls were inculcated from an early age with ideas of self-sacrifice and service while boys were encouraged to be independent. Middle-class Victorian boys and girls were separated at puberty, and girls were forced to cease any vigorous exercise, to dress in a more feminine way, and to cease educational activity. This was because it was assumed that women were inherently weak and needed to reserve all their energies for their natural function of bearing children (see Chapter five). At this time boys entered the all-male world of work or the public school, were encouraged to increase their physical and intellectual activities and to become more active and independent. Thus middle-class young people had a prolonged period of education, but while young men went to boarding school or into employment, young women were kept at home and prepared for domesticity.

Schooling for working-class children, by contrast, was not made compulsory till 1880, although the state permitted local school boards to build schools for them, by an Act of Parliament passed in 1870, and had required that factory children be educated for 2 hours per day by an Act of 1834. The main aim of education for working-class children was seen as teaching them to be obedient, punctual, clean, and deferential to authority – to compensate for what were seen as the deficiencies of the working-class family. Literacy skills were taught, but there was more concern with moral education and discipline. While boys were taught gardening and carpentry, girls were instructed in needlework, cooking, and other domestic skills. The aim was to produce a skilled and docile male work-force and more domesticated wives, mothers, and domestic servants. However, education was regarded as less necessary for girls than for boys by both parents and employers. Truancy was treated with greater leniency when committed by girls since it was felt that if they were at home helping mother this was probably a useful education for them (Dyhouse, 1981).

Generally, it has been argued that schooling was made compulsory for economic and political reasons, but Anna Davin (1979) has argued that, in fact, since women were not able to vote it is difficult to see why they were included in mass education at all. The explanation, she argues, is that this was a way of furthering the ideology of domesticity, since education was the way in which the middle-class model of the family could be imposed upon the working class. Education was designed, then, to prepare girls for mothering, so that they would bring up a healthy, properly socialized future generation.

During the slow process of introducing education for girls in the nineteenth century, two alternative models of female education emerged. In the first model, based on the traditional view and embodied in the work of Miss Beale at Cheltenham Ladies' College, girls were equipped for their role in life as wives, mothers, and companions to middle-class men. An education was supposed to make them more attractive to a potential partner by training them in domesticity and the feminine arts. This helped to foster the nineteenth-century ideology of middle-class domesticity. The second model was developed by Frances Buss at the North London Collegiate School. Miss Buss argued that girls often had to earn a living if they did not get married, and the usual career for a middle-class spinster was as a governess. The girls of Miss Buss received the same academic education as boys. However, girls were barred from higher education; Oxford did not allow them to become full members of the university until 1920 and Cambridge until 1947. After feminist campaigns in the nineteenth century they were finally admitted to special women's colleges – such as Girton at Cambridge. Some colleges gave them the equivalent education to that which was available at the men's colleges, but in others they received a different, less academically demanding intellectual diet.

The emphasis on differentiated curricula for boys and girls continued into the twentieth century. In the debates over education in the 1920s and 1930s, arguments concerning biological differences between boys and girls were used to strengthen the view that their curricula should be different. The 1927 Hadow Report accepted the evidence from teachers that girls were more passive, emotional, intuitive, lethargic, and pre-ferred arts subjects, despite alternative evidence from academic experts that natural differences in mental/physical capacity and educability were small and not relevant to the design of the curriculum. The 1943 Norwood Report accepted the view that while a boy's destiny was to have a job and be academically successful, a girl's was marriage and motherhood, and for this she did not need academic success.

The 1944 Education Act was the first formal recognition of the concept of equality of educational opportunity – that ability should determine the type of education that a child received. However, boys were (and are) admitted to the selective grammar schools on the basis of a poorer academic performance in the 11+ examination than was required of girls. If selection were accurately tied to ability at that age, then 30 per cent more girls than boys would have gone to grammar schools (Weiner, 1986). As far as less academic girls were concerned, official reports continued to emphasize the importance of education for motherhood. The 1959 Crowther Report argued that the curriculum for 'less able' girls should take account of their 'natural' domestic specialization, and the influential Newsom Report *Half Our Futures* (1963) argued that:

> We are trying to educate girls into becoming imitation men and as a result we are wasting and frustrating their qualities of womanhood at great expense to the community.... In addition to their needs as an individual, girls should be educated in terms of their main function – which is to make for themselves, their children and their husbands a secure and suitable home and to be mothers.

Two models of girls' education continued to exist in the early post-war period. A small minority of middle-class girls received a grammar-school education, while for the majority of so-called 'non-academic' girls the emphasis was still on education for domesticity.

In the 1960s and 1970s there was a general move towards comprehensive, co-educational schools, and this is the way in which most children are now educated. The comprehensive schools were introduced as a response to research that had demonstrated that the school system advantaged children who had fathers in non-manual occupations. However, subsequent research has indicated that comprehensive schools do not necessarily overcome class inequalities (Ford, 1969), and feminists have questioned whether the strategy has benefited girls. In secondary co-educational schools the choices made by boys and girls become even more sex-stereotyped – girls are even less likely to take science subjects than in the single-sex girls' schools. Furthermore, it has been reported that girls are academically less successful in co-educational schools (National Union of Teachers, 1980; Harding, 1980; Kelly, 1981). It seems that in mixed classes girls are less able to develop an 'ethic of success', are less likely to have female teachers and heads as role models and are more likely to come under the influence of stereotyped images of femininity which are antithetical to academic attainment (Shaw, 1976). Consequently, some feminists have argued for a return to single-sex schooling.

Once educational equality was codified in the Sex Discrimination Act 1975 and the Race Relations Act 1976, the concept of equality of educational opportunity had been broadened to include race and gender as well as class.

However, feminists have argued that processes within the school, the 'needs' of the economy, and the pressures on women to take up domestic roles, mean that ensuring that boys and girls have the same curricular choice or even an identical curriculum will make little difference to patterns of inequality and that this is because of factors quite apart from whether boys and girls, working class and middle class, are educated together in the same classroom.

Explaining girls' continued disadvantage

On the surface it would appear that girls have equality of access to education, and indeed, the gap between girls and boys in terms of their educational qualifications is narrowing. However, girls are still channelled into 'feminine' subjects and are not fulfilling the educational potential which they display prior to puberty. If they did, we would expect to find more women in the higher education system than men. We may advance five reasons for girls' continued disadvantage.

First, the academic hierarchy remains very firmly masculine. As illustrated in Table 3.5, the higher up the academic ladder we go, the more dominated it becomes by men. Primary and infant schools are more likely to have women teachers and women heads. At the other end of the spectrum, there are far fewer women professors than male ones and hardly any female vice-chancellors or college principals. Women are concentrated at the bottom rungs of the professional ladder within colleges, and this applies equally to any level of the educational system at which we choose to look. In Table 3.5 we have chosen primary schools as our example to show that even where women predominate they are less likely to be in positions of authority than men, but we could equally have chosen any educational sector to illustrate the same point. This means that the role models which boys and girls have available are ones suggesting that positions of high educational prestige are taken by men, reinforcing roles elsewhere in society.

Table 3.5 Male and female nursery and primary school teachers in England and Wales, 1978

Grade of employment		Total	*Women*	*Men*
		%	%	%
Head teachers		12	7	29
Deputy heads		10	8	17
Senior teachers		0.3	0.3	0.5
Assistant teachers on scales 3 or 4		6	5	10
Assistant teachers on scales 1 or 2		72	80	44
All teachers	%	100	77	23

Second, feminists have demonstrated that teachers have stereotyped attitudes to boys and girls and that the school reinforces rather than challenges gender divisions in the wider world. Ann-Marie Wolpe (1977) has argued that girls are encouraged to behave in a feminine way, and teachers see it as part of their duty to inculcate properly feminine standards of behaviour. Michelle Stanworth (1983) found in her study of a humanities department in a further education college that in an A-level class there was a tendency for both boys and girls to underestimate girls' academic performance and to regard the boys as more capable and more intelligent. Male teachers, when asked what they thought their pupils would be doing in future, tended to see even the most able female pupils' futures in terms of marriage, children, and domesticity. When careers for girls were mentioned they tended to be sex-sterotypical – personal assistants and secretaries – even when these were not what the girls themselves wanted. However, the male pupils were seen as having careers ahead of them, with marriage hardly mentioned. This expectation of the teachers was in turn reflected in the expectations of pupils. She found that teachers seemed to be heavily influenced by the verbal contributions that pupils made in the class when making judgements about their academic ability, as were the pupils when making judgements about each other. The teachers agreed with the opinion of boys that they were more able than the girls and based this judgement on verbal contributions in the class, as the boys rarely had access to the girls' marks. This was despite the fact that some of the girls consistently got better marks for the written work than the boys.

Third, textbooks embody various assumptions about gender identities. Children's reading schemes have been show to present boys and girls, men and women in gender-sterotyped roles. They also present far more male than female characters (Lobban, 1975). Science textbooks are also more likely to portray men than women, and where women are portrayed it is again likely to be in a stereotyped way (Kelly, 1985).

Fourth, although most schools are now co-educational, gender differentiation is nevertheless reflected in the organization of the school – the different sports boys and girls are expected to play, for example. There are still subjects originally introduced as 'feminine' or 'masculine': crafts for the less academically able, such as childcare, domestic science, home economics, woodwork, metalwork, technical drawing, and so on, which although they are often available now to the opposite gender are seldom taken up in this way. Indeed, in many schools the timetable is constructed in such a way that there is not a genuine choice between such subjects. Katherine Clarricoates (1980) has demonstrated, from her observation study of a primary classroom, that the key to understanding the way in which teachers organize and structure classroom life is to recognize that their central concern is to maintain control. Discipline is an important factor for teachers – both because it is necessary for them to carry out their teaching role and because of the expectations of their colleagues. The outcome is that boys receive more contact with teachers than girls because boys need more controlling. Teachers actually select material in lessons that will gain the attention of boys; this is both to help in the control of boys and to encourage them to work because girls score higher on tests. Not only the teachers but also the girls and boys recognize that certain subjects are 'boys' things' and others girls'. All of these are based on masculinist assumptions, which results in boys identifying with science and girls seeing it as a 'boys' subject'.

These processes of differentiating subjects into 'boys' ones' and 'girls' ones' take on a reality in the curriculum choices that girls make in the secondary school, as do parental and teacher expectation (Kelly, 1982) and the ways in which the timetable and subject choices are organized (Pratt *et al.*, 1984). These choices in turn prepare girls for domesticity and also determine the occupations which are open to them, both in terms of having the necessary qualifications and in terms of what they see themselves as being able to do. Traditional careers advice and teachers' attitudes tend to mean that girls do not choose science subjects; it is often suggested that girls are uneasy in handling science equipment and that they lack the familiarity with it that boys often have.

Fifth, there are different kinds of classroom interaction associated with the different genders. Detailed analysis of the moment-to-moment interaction in the classroom indicates that boys talk more and are allowed to dominate the classroom interaction, and this continues even when teachers are consciously trying to overcome it (Spender, 1982). Feminist researchers have pointed to the importance of language in the classroom. They have drawn attention to the tendency of women to take a back seat in the classroom and to be more hesitant in making contributions than boys. Girls are often reluctant to speak in class and diminished in the discussion which takes place. The classroom becomes seen as a man's world and girls are marginalized. Furthermore, teachers often use sexist remarks and sexist language in controlling girls. Katherine Clarricoates (1980: 161) noted that:

> If boys get out of hand they are regarded as 'boisterous', 'rough', 'aggressive', 'assertive', 'rowdy', 'adventurous', etc. For girls the adjectives used were 'funny', 'bitchy', 'giggly', 'catty', 'silly'. It is obvious that the terms applied to boys imply positive masculine behaviour, whereas the categories applied to girls are more derogatory.

Taken together, these indirect forms of socialization are sometimes called 'the hidden curriculum'. While the overt message may be that girls should perform in the same way as boys, this is subverted by a different message underlying the curriculum.

Summary

1 Until recently girls were disadvantaged in the educational system because they were not provided with an education equivalent to that of boys.
2 Although there now appears to be more equality in terms of co-education and equal access, in practice girls are still disadvantaged in that they are channelled into particular subject areas and their participation is not taken seriously. They are 'cooled out'. This is on account of the 'hidden curriculum'

which, in the case of girls, includes such factors as the organization of the school, the expectations of teachers, the content of textbooks, the gender balance in the academic hierarchy, and the way in which classroom interaction takes place.

3 Several competing models exist as to how girls should be educated. The first model argues that they should be equipped with domestic skills for their lives as wives and mothers. The second argues that they should compete on equal terms with men by receiving the same education as boys. The third model argues that girls should be educated separately as a way of better enhancing their academic performance.

Feminist perspectives on education

Liberal feminists

Liberal feminist perspectives have been very influential in education, and indeed it was campaigns by liberal feminists that created opportunities for girls within the educational system. They argue that girls should have an equal chance to be educated in the same way as boys and that this will lead to equal opportunities elsewhere. They measure their 'success' in terms of the higher achievements of girls: better examination results and a higher proportion of girls entering polytechnics and universities. However, these are only successes when seen from a middle-class perspective, and although more girls may be in the educational system this does not mean that they enter jobs as 'good' as those of boys (see Chapter six). They simply enter feminine jobs at a higher level. Moreover, dominant expectations of femininity also follow them through the educational system. Hence, radical and Marxist feminists argue that equality of opportunity is not enough and more fundamental changes need to be sought.

Radical feminist analyses of schooling

Dale Spender (1980) has argued that knowledge taught within the educational system is not neutral, but rather that it reflects masculine assumptions about the world – for example, about the role of 'objective' interpretations rather than subjective, intuitive ideas, and about controlling nature through science rather than trying to live with it, and about the importance of political leaders as opposed to ordinary people. The school system, likewise, sets up teachers as 'experts' who pass on knowledge to others and who have authority over others, who determine what is a 'right' answer and what is a 'wrong' one. This also reflects a masculine view of the world – boys and girls learn that the 'great' artists, scientists, writers, and sociologists were men. Men are portrayed as superior to women in all areas of knowledge, and women rarely find their experiences reflected in this knowledge. Knowledge, in this model, is packaged into discrete 'subjects' which become either masculine or feminine, and students are not encouraged to see the connections between them or to question these classifications. The importance of competitive striving for success in an individualistic way, which is embodied in the educational system, is for radical feminists an example of a male approach to the world.

Marxist and socialist feminist perspectives

Marxist and socialist feminists would both argue that this ideology of gender has to be seen in the wider context of a capitalist society. The school in capitalist society is the major ideological state apparatus that ensures that the relations of production are reproduced – that is, that the next generation of workers graduate not only with skills appropriate to the position they will take in the labour market but also with appropriate attitudes. Thus, it is necessary to understand how schools provide different experiences for girls and boys so that gender as well as class relations are reproduced. This takes place through cultural reproduction, including the way in which those who develop anti-school attitudes and values and overtly resist the authority of the school nevertheless end up accepting low-paid 'women's' jobs.

Michelle Barrett (1980) has suggested that in relation to education three key questions need to be answered:

1 how is education related to the reproduction of the gender divisions of labour in capitalist societies?
2 what is the relationship between class and gender in schooling?
3 what role does education play in preparing men and women for a particular social order – one structured by class and gender?

In answering these questions Marxist/socialist feminists have adapted the Marxist theory of social class to analyse the question of gender relationships by examining patriarchal and class relationships within capitalist society. The aim is to provide an analysis of the role of education in creating a sharply sex-segregated labour force and to explain the processes involved in this. To do so they have adapted theories of social reproduction, such as those developed by Bowles and Gintis (1976), and of cultural reproduction such as that developed by Willis (1977). In the process they have challenged the political neutrality of education, arguing that its structures and ideologies are already linked to the needs of capitalist society and dominant class interests.

Bowles and Gintis have analysed the way in which the school acts as a selection and allocation device for the social reproduction of the class structure. The major function of the education system, they suggest, is to produce a stratified and conforming work-force. Experiences at school prepare pupils for the labour market; for example, pupil/teacher relationships and the hierarchy of authority in the school prepare pupils for supervisor/manager/worker relationships. Different forms of education provided by different streams in the school system prepare children for different levels of occupation. Middle-class pupils are encouraged to develop the autonomy necessary for middle-class jobs, and working-class children are prepared for their subordinate position in the division of labour. Thus, for Bowles and Gintis the school reproduces the relations of production.

In England, Paul Willis moved away from simple 'reproduction' to examine the cultural way in which divisions are reproduced. He asked not just why working-class children finish up in working-class jobs, but why they see them as desirable jobs to take on. In other words. he argued that working-class boys were not forced into unskilled manual work but positively opted for it – seeing it a 'real men's work'. The study focused mainly on a group of twelve 'lads' in a school in Birmingham who constituted a small 'sub-culture'. It was evident that the lads experienced school not as a process of enlightenment but as a source of oppression. They reacted against teachers' authority by escaping from supervision and doing the things they valued most: smoking, drinking, swearing, and wearing their own variation on the school uniform. While the teachers saw these lads as trouble-makers, the lads themselves were effectively driven by their experiences in the school to embrace male working-class culture. The lads were proud of their actions and saw those who conformed to school as passive and absurd 'ear'oles'. The lads looked forward to starting work, their subcultural values and expectations reflecting those of the factory subculture.

Marxist feminists have argued, in the same way, that school repro-duces gender divisions; it prepares girls not only for their place in the workforce but also for the sexual division of labour. Ann-Marie Wolpe (1977) argues that the family and the school prepare women for low-paid work in the secondary labour market and for domesticity. Michelle Barrett (1980) has pointed out that women have a dual relationship to the class structure. The education and training women receive by virtue of their class background prepares them for the places they will occupy in the labour market, but this is moderated by the expectation that all women will take on domestic labour and childcare and become economically dependent on a man. Thus working-class girls are prepared for low-paid secondary sector jobs, while middle-class girls are prepared for semi-professional 'female' jobs (see Chapter six).

Marxist feminists have criticized Marxist models of work-role reproduction for not including any account of the reproduction of gender roles. They have examined the experiences of female working-class pupils in order to understand the ways in which they interpret and mediate the structures and ideologies transmitted by the school. The aim has been to understand how working-class girls come to have a particular definition of femininity which is constructed and negotiated in a competitive education system in which they 'lose out'. It is argued that the particular version of schooling that working-class girls get puts them in a position where they freely choose their own subordination – that is, they choose marriage and domesticity. The form of resistance that working-class girls develop is different from that of working-class boys. They form a subcultural ideology of love and romance – an exaggeration of the feminine stereotype. Most girls experience school as dull and boring, and their hopes for the future focus on romance, marriage, and motherhood. Their ambitions are not focused on achievement and qualifications but on leaving school, 'getting a man', and setting up a home of their own. Girls also signify in other ways their opposition to a school system which aims to control expression of femininity in the interests of discipline and management. Girls use their sexuality to control the classroom; for example, flirting with male teachers, can be used to undermine the teachers' authority and control. Refusal to wear school uniform, or adapting it to the current fashion, wearing costume jewellery or certain kinds of shoes, are all forms of the same strategy.

However, some feminists have questioned the Marxist feminist emphasis on class-based resistance. Meyers (1980) has argued that all girls resent wearing school uniform and flout the rules on jewellery. Therefore the division between 'conformist' and 'resister' on the basis of academic performance found in the research on boys is not useful, she argues, for describing the differences in girls' responses to schooling. Lyn Davies (1984) found that girls' responses to schooling in a mixed comprehensive school were similar to those of boys in the same stream in terms of attitudes to teachers, anxieties over achievement, the tedium of school assemblies, homework, and so on. However, she found that girls had common attitudes to school uniforms regardless of ability group, and that irrespective of ability girls were pushed towards the same school subjects.

Black feminist perspectives on education

Black feminists have been critical of the way in which educational theories are assumed to apply to black as well as white women (e.g. Carby, 1982; Bryan *et al.*, 1985; Amos and Parmar, 1981). They argue that racism is a more central aspect of their experience than sexism. The differences between black women, especially between Afro-Caribbean and Asian girls, who have very different cultural backgrounds, complicates this argument. Indeed, the cultures of Asian girls also vary considerably depending on the country from which their parents came and the religion of their family. However, Valerie Amos and Pratkha Parmar (1981) argue that all black women share a history of subordination and of being treated in Britain as second-class citizens. They suggest that black culture is blamed for the problems of black people – that is, the educational failure of black children is said to be because of their religion, their language, their communities, rather than being seen as a result of a racist society. In Britain, to understand the experience of black girls in school it is necessary to understand the racist, class and sex/gender system of which school is a part. Black girls experience racism in school not only from white pupils and some white teachers, but also from a racist and Eurocentric curriculum.

Thus Bryan *et al.* (1985) quote the experiences of a number of black girls; for example:

School became a nightmare for me. They poked and pulled at me. 'Is your hair knitted, then?' 'Do you live in trees?' (p. 62).

I remember my early schooldays as being a very unhappy time....There was a time when this teacher pulled me up in front of the class and said I was dirty and that she was going to make sure that my neck was cleaned – and she proceeded to do, with Vim (p. 63).

My memories of school are of being laughed at and everyone calling me golliwog (p. 63).

They point out that the curriculum is racist and Eurocentric. Not only do reading books present women in sex-stereotyped roles; the majority of children and adults in reading schemes are white. History is taught from the perspective of white Britain. English books are selected on 'literary merit', which is judged from a white perspective. Black people are often portrayed as inferior:

You will be getting deep into a story and suddenly it will bite you – a reference to black people as savages or something. It was so offensive....Sometimes you would sit in class and wait, all tensed up, for the next derogatory remark to come tripping of the teacher's tongue: Oh yes it was a 'black' day today, or some kid had 'blackened' the school's reputation (p. 65).

While few educationalists overtly accept the view that black children are genetically less intelligent than white children, nevertheless teachers often expect less of them and black children consistently underachieve at school. On the other hand, Afro-Caribbeans are expected to do well at games and are encouraged in this area of the curriculum. The result is that black women underachieve at school and leave with few qualifications and are propelled into the very same jobs that their mothers were encouraged to come to Britain to take up in the 1950s and 1960s – dirty, low-paid jobs in the secondary labour market.

However, as with white working-class girls, some black girls do resist the white culture. Mary Fuller (1980) has argued that some Afro-Caribbean schoolgirls' anger and frustration at the way they are treated at school leads them to a positive self-image – an acceptance of being black and female. They aim to achieve good educational qualifications, get decent jobs and move out of the subordinate position that their parents are in. Gaining educational qualifications gives them a sense of their own worth. However, this does not necessarily result in conformity to the norms of the school. They conformed to the ideal of the 'good pupil' only in so far as they did their school work. Apart from this, their behaviour was designed to exasperate the teachers. In the classroom they gave the appearance of inattention, boredom, and indifference; they expressed opposition to what they regarded as boring and trivial features of school by, for example, reading magazines or doing homework in class. They accepted the relevance of the school only in terms of academic benefit; they were able to exploit the school system without becoming subordinate to it.

Summary

1 Liberal feminists argue for equality of educational opportunity, and it is increasingly evident that more girls are found at different levels of the educational system than was the case in the past. The fact that girls are actually out-performing boys at some levels would be taken as a sign of success by liberal feminists.

2 Radical feminists argue that in a patriarchal society the forms of knowledge processed at school reflect patriarchal assumptions. The educational system is set up in a masculine form and merely serves to reproduce gender differences. There can be no equality within the present educational system and women need to seek out their own forms of knowledge and styles of learning.

3 Marxist and socialist feminists have argued that schooling is essential to the maintenance of a capitalist society. They show

that gender is part of the process of the reproduction of the work force, serving to create a docile, low-paid labour-force of women and a private sphere for which women are responsible.

4 Black feminists have argued that white feminists have ignored the experience of racism suffered by black girls as a distinctive form of subordination. They have shown that education is not just androcentric but also Eurocentric, denying black women's experiences.

Adolescence

Just as childhood is a socially and historically specific phenomenon, so too is adolescence, although it too is usually assumed to be biologically defined. 'Adolescence' is sometimes portrayed as a phase in which people have to make difficult psychological adjustments to the physical changes in their bodies. For boys and girls it is associated with the development of secondary sexual characteristics – breasts, body hair – which are also thought to cause particular problems.

In legal terms the status of adolescence is ambiguous. Young people are seen as responsible for their criminal activities from the age of 10. However, a girl cannot give consent to sexual intercourse with a man until she is 16, although a doctor may give her advice on contraception and prescribe the contraceptive pill before she reaches that age. Young men and women may marry at the age of 16 but need their parents' consent. A young man may be conscripted into the armed forces at the age of 16, but the age of voting for members of Parliament is 18, and this is also the minimum age for standing for election. The legal point of transition from childhood to adulthood is 18 years – reduced from 21 in 1970. However, homosexual relationships between men are not legal unless both parties are 21, but not illegal at any age if both parties are women. It is already evident from this that young men and young women have a different status in law reflecting different assumptions of masculinity and femininity.

Adolescent rebels?

The idea of adolescence as a period of storm and stress is part of common-sense ideology. However, the anthropologist Margaret Mead challenged this view. In her study of adolescent girls in Eastern Samoa (1943) she found no evidence of role confusion, conflict, or rebellion. On the basis of this study she suggested that adolescence was not universal and biologically determined but culturally variable, and that the stresses of adolescence are socially determined and relate to the ambiguous status to which young people find themselves consigned by particular societal forms. Whether adolescence is a period of strain, stress, and conflict even in the western world is questionable. Coleman (1980), in a review of a number of studies, suggested that difficulties between young people and their parents have generally been overstated by academics and the media because of almost exclusive concentration on 'bizarre' behaviours and spectacular youth cultures. This view is supported by a 1982 NOP survey of 1,800 15–21 year olds. Most of these lived with their parents and reported generally good relations, 95 per cent claiming to get on well with their mothers and 86 per cent with their fathers. Young people tended to be conformist rather than deviant or radical. The majority disagreed with taking drugs, did not drink much alcohol, believed themselves to behave responsibly, and mainly turned to 'Mum' when in trouble (cited by Springhall, 1983, p. 34).

Girls in teenage culture

In the period after the Second World War, with increased affluence in the 1950s and 1960s, considerable attention was paid to youth. They were portrayed as the 'affluent consumers' who were able to stimulate the pop music, magazine, and fashion industries with their new-found spending power (Wallace, 1989). Media, political, and sociological attention has always focused on specific 'problem' groups such as muggers, football hooligans, and drug-takers. These groups of young people are seen as deviant, as holding antisocial values and as challenging adult society. In the 1950s it was the 'teds', in the 1960s the 'mods' and 'rockers', followed by the 'punks' in the 1970s. During the 1960s the 'hippies' – a more middle-class subculture – and the student movement rejected middle-class ideas of the Protestant work ethic and 'respectability', in a consumer society. The problems with these groups were portrayed as problems of 'the youth of today' in general. In this way the idea of adolescence as a universal phenomenon was reinforced. However, Marxist sociologists at the Centre for Contemporary Cultural Studies (e.g. Hall and Jefferson, 1977) analysing these subcultures, argued that they were not examples of 'universal' problems of youth but rather of particular class factions. Thus the 'teds' and 'skinheads' were examples of working-class youth subcultures and the hippies of a middle-class one, rather than a reflection of the behaviour, attitudes, and values of all young people.

The 'subculture' literature does not take girls into account; it focuses entirely on male subcultural activity. McRobbie and Garber (1977) wondered whether this was because girls are really not active in subcultures, or because they are rendered 'invisible' by male researchers. They answer their own question by arguing that girls are not present in male subcultures, except as girl-friends and hangers-on, because they have their own cultural forms of expression based upon the retreat from male-defined situations into an alternative culture of 'femininity' based around the girls' bedrooms and being a 'fan'. This subculture is therefore negatively defined in the literature:

> They are marginal to work because they are central to the subordinate and complementary sphere of femininity. Similarly, marginality of girls in the active, male-focussed leisure subcultures of working-class youth may tell us less about the strongly present position of girls in the 'complementary' but more passive subcultures of the fan-club.
>
> (McRobbie and Garber, 1977: 211)

Teenage girls are the main consumers of a variety of romantic magazines which give instruction on hygiene and behaviour and provide romance cartoons and stories as well as information about favourite popstars and actors. Main features in such magazines are articles about fashion and appearance. Through these strictly age-graded magazines, it is argued, young women learn their roles in life, and this encourages them to see romance as normal and desirable and to see the ultimate goal of romance – to get married or have a steady relationship with a male companion – as their hearts' desire. For these girls the main interest of their teenage years is in getting a man, and to this purpose they become absorbed into the ideology of romance – 'falling in love with love'. This preoccupation with appearance and boyfriends appears to be more important for working-class girls than middle-class ones (Sarsby, 1983; Sharpe, 1976).

The behaviour of teenage girls is at least in part an outcome of the ways in which they are treated differently from boys. Because girls are seen as more in need of care and protection, parents 'police' their daughters' leisure more strictly than that of their sons. This is linked to to the dominant ideological definition of 'appropriate behaviour for women'. Sue Lees (1986) has also shown how boys control girls in the public sphere through the threat of labelling them as sexually promiscuous. It is expected that boys will 'sow wild oats', but similar behaviour attracts censure in girls and is likely to lead to derogatory labels such as 'slag', 'slut', 'scrubber', and 'easy lay'. Indeed, this sexual labelling has less to do with the actual sexual practices than with the extent to which young women's behaviour deviates from the popular ideas of femininity – for instance by the use of swear-words or loud behaviour. To remain desirable – a 'nice' girl – girls must suppress any real sexual desire and conform to expectations of romantic love and monogamy. This double standard serves to constrain the private and the public lives of young women to ensure conformity based on a model of sexuality which ultimately takes its form from the ideology of the nuclear family.

Criticisms of the sociology of youth by feminists have raised issues of gender in a new way. Feminist sociologists' arguments showed that ideas of 'masculinity' and 'femininity' which had been taken for granted as natural were in fact social in origin: these roles had to be learned by young people. Feminist critics such as McRobbie and Garber argued that girls did not 'rebel' in the way that young men did, but rather used romantic fantasy as a source of escapism. By contrast, other studies such as those of Sue Lees (1986), Christine Griffin (1985), and Claire Wallace (1987) have argued that the ideology of romantic love plays a more complex role in the lives of young women. In many respects girls are not deceived by the images of life portrayed in women's literature but have very realistic ideas of what married life might hold in store for them. Second, they argue that young women do have a number of strategies of resistance, such as becoming tomboys or even getting pregnant, both of which flout the 'nice girl' sterotype. Third, these studies have emphasized the importance which jobs hold for young women, as a source of status and independence both outside and within the family. Marriage and motherhood are not their only goal in life.

Young women entering work

Given this emphasis on romance and courting, jobs are expected to have a lower priority in young women's lives. However, one may validly question the extent to which the assumption is in fact true.

The early literature about the transition from school to work was concerned mainly with 'occupational choice' (see Williams, 1974). This was later replaced by a model which emphasized class socialization and considered the roles of parental background and school career in determining the destination of school-leavers (Ashton and Field, 1976; Willis, 1977). What all these studies have in common is a focus upon waged employment – and most of them focus explicitly or implicitly on young men. Feminists, by contrast, have tended to emphasize the role of the family in feminine socialization. Young women, for example, may have to take care of housework or dependent relatives in a way seldom required of young men (Griffin, 1985). Once out of school, girls' occupational roles are circumscribed by the structure of opportunities for them in the labour market and by their anticipatory socialization which leads them to think in terms of a very narrow range of careers. Their future roles in the home serve to limit both their own perceptions of the situation and the ways in which they are viewed by employers.

Girls are more likely than boys to continue in education and less likely to go into youth training schemes. Girls who do not go into higher education tend to enter different sectors of the labour market from boys. Those with educational qualifications are likely to take up clerical work. Shop and distributive work also absorbs a large proportion of girls, and the remainder enter unskilled assembly work, mostly in the engineering and textile industries. Those who do pursue some sort of extended education are likely to enter the 'semi-professions' of nursing, teaching, and social work. There are a number of possible reasons for this pattern. First, there is discrimination by recruiting managers, who consider girls and boys appropriate for different jobs (Ashton and McGuire, 1980; Kiel and Newton, 1980). Second, there is the belief that girls are more nimble-fingered and patient than male workers (Pollert, 1981; Ashton and McGuire, 1980). Third, those entering traditional male jobs have had to contend with pressure and ribald commentary from male peers (McRobbie and McCabe, 1981; Cockburn, 1987). Fourth, informal and familial recruiting networks tend to have a conservative influence in that boys are recruited for boys' jobs and girls for girls' jobs (Kiel and Newton, 1980).

However, differences between boys' and girls' experience in the labour market are not limited just to their initial point of entry. As they grow older these differences are likely to widen, for girls are less likely to receive any training, and such training as they do receive is of the 'sitting next to Nellie' sort (Pollert, 1981; Keil and Newton, 1980). In addition, girls are less likely to be promoted once in a job (Downing, 1981; Abbott and Sapsford, 1987a).

The labour market destinations of girls are also structured by their own preferences, formed well before they enter the labour market. In the literature about girls' decision-making two bodies of opinion have emerged. One argues that girls simply enter the jobs available in the local labour market and adjust their expectations accordingly (Youthaid, 1981). The other argues that girls' preferences are unrealistic, reflecting ideas of glamour rather than labour market realities. Clerical and office work is seen as very desirable and 'feminine' by many girls, because it is clean, respectable, and allows girls to 'dress up' (Griffin, 1985; Sharpe, 1976; Downing, 1981). Parents, too, feel that office work would be a 'nice' job for their daughters, and it sometimes gives the appearance of upward mobility . Other glamorous jobs mentioned by Sharpe's sample included air hostessing and modelling – all extensions of feminine roles.

Marriage and motherhood cast a long shadow over their lives at this stage. Girls tend to regard marriage as a main concern and to find their expectations shaped entirely by marriage, which for them is a career (Sharpe, 1976). In the context of the 1980s, the fact that girls expect to get married need not necessarily mean that they also expect to give up work, nor that they structure their ambitions entirely around men. In

Sharpe's sample of Ealing girls the majority expected to stop work for only a few years when their children were small. Fuller's West Indian girls, by contrast, were very determined to continue working whatever their domestic responsibilities and exhibited high aspirations in career terms. These sentiments were reinforced by the belief that it was not good for a girl to be too dependent on a man. In the words of one of her respondents: 'I want a proper job first and some kind of skill so that if I do get married and have children I can go back to it; don't want just relying on him for money, 'cause I've got to look after myself' (Fuller, 1980: 57).

The calls of the public and the private sphere may nevertheless remain in conflict for women. Anna Pollert (1981) found that working in a factory was not a 'nice' job for girls, as they were at the bottom of both the sexual and the occupational hierarchy. Romance offered an ideology of escape, but at the same time there was acceptance of the reality of manual labour as an inevitable part of their lives.

In the 1960s and early 1970s young women leaving school could look forward to employment – though this would in many cases have been an interval between dependence on parents and dependence on husbands. However, by the mid- and late 1970s there was rising unemployment which hit young people particularly hard. The Government response to rising youth unemployment was to introduce training schemes to prepare young people for work and equip them with skills. Initially the Youth Opportunity Programme was instituted, then it was replaced by the Youth Training Scheme (YTS). In 1986 the YTS period was increased from one to two years and was opened to 16- and 17-year-olds. From 1988, changes in the state benefits system meant that all young people under the age of 18 were forced into YTS unless they found employment or went into full-time education and continued to be supported by their parents (the alternative being no economic support whatsoever from the state). Trainees on YTS are paid a training allowance, which increases in the second year. While the Government argues that the scheme provides training, preparing young people for the world of work, it has been argued by many young people, and by trade unions and others, that its main effect is to provide a source of cheap labour and keep the unemployment figures artificially low. However, even critics recognize that the places offered to young people are variable in the training they provide and that some do lead to 'real' jobs. In many areas the YTS has become the main route by which people enter particular kinds of work – for example, the construction industry.

In 1986, one in four young 16-year-olds were on the YTS, and just under 50 per cent of these were women. Given that YTS is presented as a period of training it might be thought possible for the sex-typing of jobs to be broken down and girls trained for employment in non-traditional occupations – that is, that it would provide opportunities for girls to train for jobs that are traditionally seen as male. However, despite YTS having been set up with a commitment to equal opportunities, Cockburn (1987), in her research in London, found that this was not happening. Trainees were segregated by gender, girls taking up traditional female jobs and boys male ones. She suggests a number of reasons for this. The main one is what she calls the 'reality principle' in occupational choice – that is, that young people know how jobs are gendered. Other factors are the role models of parents, parental expectations, education, and the demands of employers. Furthermore, her research into workshop YTS schemes suggests that even when girls choose to train in non-traditional areas, the attitudes of the other trainees, and specifically the way they are treated by the young men and male instructors, mean that it is difficult for girls actually to pursue their chosen area. In the words of one girl:

> When I was at school this youth opportunities thing came up, I thought 'Great! Great! I can do my mechanics job', you know, but girls don't do that sort of thing. I thought 'Right, if anyone can do it, equal rights and all that' I thought 'I can get in there'. 'Cause, a garage wouldn't take me on. But I got talked out of that. After that I went mainly for shop work, but really, you know, I would have been much happier working in a garage.

> (Wallace, 1987: 193)

Cockburn also found that girls on YTS were much less likely to be offered places in the higher-status employer-based schemes and more likely to end up in workshop schemes that were less likely to lead to a job or to be seen as providing a 'proper' training. West Indian girls found more problems than white ones because their colour was used as a screening device by employers, while Byrne (1978) argues that West Indian girls are likely to end up on training schemes that do not adequately prepare them for the jobs they want.

Thus, young women are trained for women's jobs – low-paid work that is seen as suitable for women. While the specific experiences of young women may have changed, nevertheless they have always been, and continue to be, conditioned by the assumption that a woman's major role in life is to be a wife and mother.

Summary

1 The issues looked at among youth – such as youth cultures, youth rebellion, or labour market destination – have been masculine ones, and the respondents questioned and the investigators, have been mainly males.

2 The interests of young women – such as their role within the family – have been ignored until recently. Feminists have indicated the importance of the ideology of the family in socializing young women and in structuring other aspects of their experience, such as their attitudes to work.

Conclusions

In this chapter we have argued that the experiences of girls and young women are conditioned by ideologies of femininity and especially by their acceptance that their major role is to be a wife and mother. While, formally, girls have equal educational and training opportunities with boys; the ways the curriculum is structured, the ways in which girls make sense of their experience of schooling and work, and the assumptions of teachers, parents, and employers, all serve to 'encourage' girls to select subject options that propel them into 'women's jobs' and prepare them for domesticity.

Further reading

Deem, R. (1978) *Women and Schooling*, London: Routledge & Kegan Paul.
Sharpe, S. (1976) *Just Like a Girl*, Harmondsworth: Penguin.

Chapter four

The family and the household

The family is a concept that is familiar to all of us. Most people regard themselves as members of one or more families. We are constantly bombarded with images of a particular type of family – what the anthropologist Edmund Leach (1967) has called 'the cereal-packet norm family' – consisting of husband as head of household and children being cared for by a smiling wife. We come to think of this as the normal, natural, and inevitable family form. In fact only one in twenty households in Britain at any one time consists of a father in paid employment, a dependent wife, and two children. Consequently we need to distinguish 'the family ' – a group of relatives – from 'the household' – a technical term used to describe all the people living in one home, who may or may not be related. The nuclear family (the cereal-packet family) is often the unit which is assumed in advertising, housing, and social policy when we talk about 'the family', and it is to this that we shall mainly be referring here. However, this is an ideal; an ideal of a happy family which does not often fit the reality and one which is not descriptively neutral but value-laden.

Politicians have seen the family as extremely important. Both of the major political parties have expressed their support for the family and argued that state policies must strengthen it. The Conservative Party, since its election in 1979, has stressed that it is 'the party of the family' and argued that people must be discouraged from choosing alternative life-styles such as cohabitation or homosexuality. They argue for the traditional patriarchal nuclear family; that is, one in which the father sets and enforces standards of behaviour. In this type of family there is assumed to be a gendered division of labour such that the man takes on the major responsibility for earning a wage and the woman for caring for the 'bread-winner' and the children. This view of the family is one that is widely shared by the British public as an ideal. Hence, although other family forms such as single-parent families, extended families, or re-formed families are increasingly common, they are not seen as normal or desirable. Indeed, these and other families in which no father exercises control are often seen as the cause of many social problems; especially crime, juvenile delinquency, and people's inability to take on responsibility for their own economic and social support.

Sociological perspectives on the family

Sociologists studying the family have claimed that it is a central and necessary institution in society. However, they have tended to take the domestic division of labour for granted. Feminist sociologists, by contrast, have highlighted the position of women in families and argued that the family is the main way in which women are oppressed in modern Britain. Sociological theories of the family have been dominated by the structural-functionalist school of sociology and in particular the work of Talcott Parsons. In this perspective the co-resident nuclear family with a gendered division of labour is seen as the one most suited to the needs of industrial society. Marxists challenged this picture to the extent that they suggested the family met the needs of capitalist society – that is, that it served the interests of the ruling class by helping in the maintenance of the capitalist system. These traditional sociological theories of the family have tended to look at the relationships between family and society and have not examined relationships *within* the family, nor how these relationships both structure and are structured by external social, economic, and power relationships. The domestic sphere has tended to be regarded as a private area – not only outside public concern, but also outside the concerns of sociologists.

The symmetrical family

One of the most influential studies in the sociology of the family was undertaken by Willmott and Young in the 1960s (Young and Willmott, 1973), building on previous studies they had carried out in London into families in the 1950s (Willmott and Young, 1957). This study was carried out in a period when rehousing policies and increased affluence meant that most young people, when they married, could set up home independently, and more geographical mobility meant they often did so at a distance from kin. It was argued, partly as a consequence of this and partly because more married women (including those with children) were taking paid employment, that the division of labour between men and women in the domestic sphere was changing: men would take on more domestic work and women would be more likely to work outside the home. Willmott and Young argued that the family would become more democratic, with both partners sharing decision-making and financial resources. It was suggested that rather than having segregated conjugal roles, where husband and wives did different jobs within the house and had separate activities and friends, husbands and wives were increasingly spending their spare time together and had friends in common. The main conclusion of the Willmott and Young study was that the British family was becoming increasingly symmetrical – that is, that the roles of husbands and wives were becoming more alike and would eventually become identical. Willmott and Young were careful to argue that this was the *coming* family form – the way that the family was developing, not the way that it was already – but argued that in Britain there was a definite progression in this direction.

Feminist approaches to the family

Feminists have challenged the view that the family is becoming more egalitarian and symmetrical. Feminists argue, by contrast, that the family is a site of inequality where women are subordinated and women's roles perpetuated. It is suggested that there are two inter-locking structures of subordination of women in the family:

1 women's position as wives and mothers;
2 socialization processes in the family during which children internalize male and female attitudes and transmit them to their own children, thus perpetuating male domination and female subordination.

While Marxist feminists stress that women's exploitation in the family serves the interest of capitalism, radical feminists stress that it serves the interests of men, who benefit from the unpaid labour of women in a system of patriarchy. They are agreed, however, that the family oppresses women and that women are exploited and sub-ordinated within it. Feminists argue that women's position in the family as wives/mothers results in a position of subordination to men/fathers, at least in part because of economic dependency, but also because of widely shared ideologies of the family. Thus feminists have questioned not only sociological assumptions concerning the family, but common sense ones as well.

Barrie Thorne (1982) has argued that four themes are central to the feminist challenge to the conventional sociology of the family:

1 The assumptions concerning the structure and functioning of
the family. Feminists challenge an ideology that sees the
co-resident nuclear family with a gendered division of labour as
the only natural and legitimate form of the family. Feminists
argue against the view that any specific family form is natural –
that is, based on biological imperatives. Rather, they would

claim that forms of family organization and ideology are based on social organizations and assumptions about people's roles held by the individuals of a given society. For example, there is no inherent (biological) reason why men cannot do housework; it is just that people in our society believe that it is not the right thing for them to do and thence that they are incapable of it.

2 Feminists have sought to claim the family as an area for analysis; this challenges the gender-based categories of analysis in malestream sociology.

3 Feminists argue that different members of families experience family life in different ways. They argue that women's experiences of motherhood and family life have demonstrated that families embody power relationships that can and do result in conflict, violence, and the inequitable distribution of work and resources.

4 Feminists question the assumption that the family should be a private sphere. While women and children are often cut off from outside contact in the modern nuclear family, this is partly an illusion at the level of public policy. The form that the family takes is heavily influenced by economic and social policies and the family is permeable to outside intervention.

It is argued that common-sense beliefs about the nature of the family deny women the opportunity to participate in the wider society and gain equality with men. It is in this way, also, that we can explain women's exclusion from the labour market, youth cultures, political life, and other areas of social life discussed elsewhere in this book.

Industrialization, the family, and the origins of the family wage

Feminists have examined the history of family life and changes in the organization of families, from the perspective of women. There is some disagreement as to whether or not women have always been subordinated and exploited in the family, or whether their subordination is a result of the growth and development of capitalism. Radical feminists argue that patriarchy (the domination of women by men) in the patriarchal mode of production (the family) existed long before the development of capitalism. Marxist feminists argue that the economic dependency of women on men which enables them to be dominated and exploited in the family is a result of the growth of industrial capitalism. Socialist feminists suggest that the ideology of patriarchy pre-dates capitalism but that the way in which women are exploited and subordinated in modern Britain is the result of the interaction of this ideology with the material relations of production (the way in which goods and services are produced and the relationship between the workers and the owners of the means of production in capitalist society).

For feminists the great change that has occurred in the family since the seventeenth century has been the institutionalization of the 'housewife and mother' role. Before industrialization, the product of labour was regarded as the joint property of the family and not seen as the property of individuals to be divided up. Every member of the family worked to produce what the family needed – there was no distinction between production and consumption. With industrialization the home became separated from the place of work – consumption from production. Gradually women became associated with the domestic sphere, the care of the home and children, and men with the public sphere, earning a wage and participating in politics. These changes were gradual and affected different classes at different times. However, most middle-class women accepted the housewife role by the beginning of the nineteenth century, and the number of working-class women in officially recognized paid employment (as recorded by the Census) declined rapidly after 1850. Roberts' 1981 research demonstrates that by 1900 the majority of working-class women thought that ideally a wife should stay at home to care for her husband and children, although there were regional variations. The change that occurred was summed up in a satirical gibe by John Roby (quoted in Pinchbeck, 1977: 37):

1743	1843
Man, to the plough	Man, Tally Ho
Wife, to the cow	Miss, piano
Girl, to the yarn	Wife, silk and satin
Boy, to the barn	Boy, Greek and Latin
And your rest will be netted	And you'll be gazetted.

The changes brought about by the Industrial Revolution altered not so much the type of work that women did as the context in which that work was carried out. Women became economically dependent on the wages of their husbands and no longer had direct control over economic resources. The legal subordination of women to men continued, women had limited rights in property, and the ability of women to participate in public life was very limited. Until 1884 a married woman had no right to her own property – this passed from her father to her husband – nor did she have any right to custody of or access to her children. It was not until the passage of the Marital Causes Act 1928 that women could divorce their husbands on the same ground as the husbands could divorce them, and not until 1892 that an Act was passed instituting maintenance for women from the husband in case of legal separation, and even then only on the grounds that he had committed aggravated assault on her.

The Industrial Revolution resulted in the growth of towns and cities, in a vast increase in population, in the development of new and better methods of transport (roads, canals, and railways), and in new class relationships – the emergence of a working class (factory workers), a middle class (clerks, administrators, and professionals) and an upper class (the owners of factories and productive land). As well as the new economic and political structure that developed as a result of industrialization, changes in the relationships between men and women, husbands and wives, and parents and children also took place.

In the pre-industrial period middle-class women helped their men in productive roles. An example is the Cadbury family. Before the nineteenth century they all lived above the chocolate shop and the wives and daughters were actually involved in the running of the business. However, when with the growth of the town the Cadburys moved to the suburb, the men went to work at the shop and the women stayed at home. Mrs Cadbury and her daughter undertook domestic tasks and the supervision of domestic servants, and the daughters were instructed in feminine graces. The women became involved in religious and philanthropic activities. The Cadburys wanted to have a different kind of home life. With increased affluence they no longer needed the labour of the female members of the family and could afford to bring in labour. They also valued the domestic ideal – the home as a retreat from work and a view of women as delicate and needing protection from the world as a place of danger and sin. The Cadburys did not have to move from the shop, but for other middle-class families new methods of production meant that the factory was separated from the home, and the home – the domestic sphere – became seen as the place for women.

For the working class the changes were very different. In pre-industrial Britain the family had been a unit of production. There had been a division of labour by gender, and men were generally seen as having a dominant role, but women were not regarded as the economic dependents of men. In the early stages of industrialization, men, women, and children all worked together in the factories. Men generally managed to secure for themselves the jobs that were seen as the most skilled. Gradually during the course of the nineteenth century women and children were excluded from factory jobs and became increasingly dependent economically. The working class came to share the domestic ideals of the middle class and to see a non-working wife as the ideal – a wife who could care properly for her husband and children and provide a home for them. The reasons why this happened are complex, and feminists do not agree on them precisely, but two factors do emerge as very important:

1 Middle-class philanthropists attempted to shape working-class life to fit their ideas of what family life was like, and put pressure on Government to implement reforms that reinforced these conceptions. The 1834 Poor Law assumed that a woman was dependent on a man, for instance. Factory legislation restricted the hours women and children could work, lessening their worth as employees. Women were assumed to be responsible for caring for their husbands and children, and middle-class women set out to teach working-class women how to do this. Towards the end of the nineteenth century and into the early twentieth the poor health of the working class was blamed on negligent mothers, especially those who worked.

2 From the mid-nineteenth century sections of the male working class began to argue that a man should be paid sufficient to support a wife and children, so excluding the necessity of his wife or children taking paid employment. Most feminists argue that the 'family wage' principle resulted in the exclusion of women from paid employment and their economic dependence on men, thus giving men power over their wives. Women performed domestic and other duties in exchange for being maintained by their husbands (see Chapters six and nine).

Barrett and McIntosh (1980b) argue that women were disadvantaged by the growing idea that a man should earn a family wage, and that the capitalists and the organized male working class benefited from this concept of the family wage. Capitalists benefited because women at home caring for their husbands and children helped to maintain a fit and active work-force, and working-class men because they gained the unpaid services of their wives. It also enabled men to have economic and social power in the home. They argue that this ideology of the family wage is still powerful and is a major aspect of inequality for women – not only because married men are supposed to support wives and children, but because men are thought to be entitled to earn a 'family wage' while women are not. This justifies the low pay that attaches to 'women's jobs' (see Chapter six) and restricts women's choices and reduces their economic power within marriage.

Women's experience of family life

To understand the feminist criticisms of the family it is necessary to examine the disjuncture between ideologies of domesticity and women's personal experiences as wives and mothers. Betty Friedan (1963) referred to the distress suffered by middle-class American mothers in the 1960s as 'the problem that has no name', while Liz Stanley and Sue Wise (1983) have argued that many women distinguish between the family as an institution and their own family. The former is seen as desirable, while the latter is often experienced as not meeting their expectations of family life.

Girls grow up expecting and wanting to get married, seeing the wedding day as the supreme moment of their lives. Married life rarely turns out to be what they had expected, however – the reality is very different from the dream. Jessie Bernard (1973) has suggested that there is 'her' marriage and 'his' marriage, two different things, and that men benefit more from marriage than women do. Married women are more likely than single women or than single men to suffer from mental illness, while married men are the least likely to do so. Women often get married from economic necessity, because they cannot earn sufficient to live on and therefore it is only through marriage that they have potential access to a decent living wage. Single women are thought to be in need of the protection of a man, and this is an additional pressure towards marriage. Men, on the other hand, gain both economic and social advantages from marriage – they are cared for, they enjoy the 'unpaid' domestic labour of their wives, and often receive 'unpaid' help with their employed role as well. Women 'help' their husbands by entertaining colleagues and clients, by doing unpaid clerical work, by acting as a telephone-answering service, and in some cases a wife is seen as essential, or nearly essential, for a man to be able to carry out his work role (Finch, 1983a). Most wives are expected to organize their lives around the demands of their husbands' jobs – preparing meals and other activities to fit in with their partners' working hours – and to tailor what they do to his 'needs'.

Housework, the 'unpaid' labour of a wife, is worth quite a lot if it had to be paid for at market rates. In 1987 the Legal and General Life Assurance Company estimated that a 'dependent' wife was worth £19,253 a year in earnings (quoted in the *Sunday Times* 29 March, 1987). The company located on a computer the 'average' wife, a 37-year-old mother of two named Rosalind Harris. Her work was found to start at 07.00 on Monday, when she began to prepare the breakfast, and to end at 21.00 that day (a 14-hour working day). During the week she worked as a shopper, a window-cleaner, a nurse, a driver, a cleaner, a cook, and a child-minder. Her total working week was of 92 hours' duration. (This excludes periods 'on call', with the children in bed.)

Feminists have suggested a number of reasons why married life does not turn out to be the ideal that is portrayed for women. Ann Oakley (1982) has suggested that women experience four areas of conflict in family life:

1 The sexual division of labour means that women are expected to be responsible for domestic work and child care. This means that women become economically dependent on men and have no access to money that they see as their own.
2 Conflict arises over the different emotional needs of men and women. Women are expected to deal with the frustrations and anger of husbands and children but have no one to whom they can turn themselves.
3 Economic and physical differences in power between husbands and wives mean that women can experience lack of control over financial resources, an inability to engage in social activities, and even physical violence from their husbands.
4 Male control of sexuality and fertility means that men's needs are assumed to be the more important. Women are expected to 'please' their husbands, to give in to their sexual demands, and to have and to care for their children. At the extreme a man can rape his wife, because a married woman is assumed to have given her consent to her husband to have sex.

Indeed, it could be argued that married women do not have a separate identity either in their own eyes or the eyes of others. Married women generally put the needs of their families before their own needs and desires and they are identified by others with their families. In Britain married women generally take their husbands' name and often become seen as an appendage of their husbands and children, being 'John Smith's wife' and 'Jean and Billy Smith's mother' – having no separate social identity of their own. This identification with the family often carries over into paid employment (see Chapter six). Men, on the other hand, tend to take their main identity from their employment. Wives are frequently asked what their husband does for a living, as if that were a major source of their identity, and seldom what they do themselves.

Familial ideology

Ideas about women's role are reinforced by the mass-media presentation of women in a narrow range of roles, with an emphasis on the wife/ mother role. This is especially noticeable in television commercials and popular soap operas. What is equally important is the range of roles that women are not portrayed as playing, or seen as exceptional if they are so portrayed. Even in programmes such as 'The Gentle Touch' and 'Cagney and Lacey' the 'tough' women not only have male bosses but are portrayed in domestic roles as well. Similarly, children's reading schemes have often been shown to portray men and women, boys and girls in typically segregated masculine and feminine roles (see Chapter three).

Beechey (1986a) has suggested that two assumptions underlie familial ideology:

1 [that] the co-resident nuclear family...is universal and normatively desirable;
2 [and that]...the form of sexual division of labour in which the woman is the housewife and mother and primarily located within the private world of the family, and the man is wage-earner and bread-winner and primarily located in the 'public' world of paid work, is universal and normatively desirable. (Beechey, 1986a: 99)

She suggests that the assumption is that the family is biologically determined and argues that this view of the family is part of our taken-for-granted common-sense assumptions. This family form is reproduced by social institutions in modern Britain because it is assumed that this is both how people do live their lives and how they should live their lives. For example, these assumptions about families underlie patterns of schooling, labour markets and, ways in which the social security system is organized, as well as the type of housing that is provided in both the private and the public sector. Their force is three-fold: to set up the role of housewife and mother as an available life-style for women, to declare it a life-style which is inherently satisfying for women and one with which they ought to be satisfied, and to place on women as individuals any blame for the life-style's failure to satisfy them. In other words, like any ideology, the familial ideology has the effect of converting the interests of a dominant group into the self-perceived interests of a subordinated one and making the dominated group responsible for any consequent failures – in this case by individualizing a set of discontents which might otherwise be thought to have their base in collectively experienced structural pressures rather than in individual failures.

Boys and girls, and men and women take it for granted that men are strong, and tough, and should be 'bread-winners', and that women are submissive, and gentle, and should stay at home and care for men and children. Even when people's own experiences do not live up to this idea, they still see it as how things ought to be. It is also assumed that this type of family best serves the interests of its individual members and of society generally. Feminists question the assumption that a particular set of living arrangements is natural and universal and that this form of living arrangement necessarily best serves the interests of women.

The diversity of family forms

Feminists have argued that while the nuclear family may be the moral norm in Britain, anthropological research has demonstrated that there are a wide variety of living arrangements throughout the world, as well as kinship systems. Ann Oakley (1972) concludes from a review of the anthropological evidence that while in all societies there are rules about what is suitable for men and women to do, there is also a wide variation between societies as to what is considered suitable for each gender.

Even within contemporary Britain, there is a diversity of family forms and ways of organizing roles within the family. Nevertheless, families that do not conform to the nuclear family norm are seen as deviant, strange, and a less desirable form of living arrangement. This applies not only to those who choose not to get married, but to families of Asian origin who choose to live in extended family form or to retain close family connection, to West Indian families which are often ass-umed to be matrifocal (mother-headed), and to those families in which the mother chooses to work full time, especially when the children are young. It extends also to families where the father takes a considerable responsibility for domestic work and child-care, or where the mother is 'the bread-winner' and the father the home-maker.

More and more households do not conform to conventional norms. More people are cohabiting (living together without formal marriage); the proportion has risen from 2.7 per cent of couples aged 18-49 in 1979 to 5 per cent in 1985. (This probably underestimates the incidence of cohabitation; a study by Wallace (1987) found it a normal prelude to marriage for almost all young couples.) Illegitimacy rates are rising, as more people have children without being married. Whereas only 6 per cent of all live births in 1961 were illegitimate, the figure now is 21 per cent. Perhaps some of the stigma associated with illegitimacy has vanished. Also, the fact that these births are also increasingly registered in the father's as well as the mother's name implies that they are taking place within stable relationships, perhaps to couples who are cohabiting. Many of the respondents in Walllace's study reported that they might have children and then see how well they got on with their partners, rather than getting married: 'What's the point of getting married to someone if you haven't lived with them? You don't know what they're like, do you?' (Wallace, 1987: 161).

However, these *de facto* relationships are of a form which mirrors the conventional nuclear family, including its sexual fidelity. Children may now be born outside of marriage, but traditional roles of motherhood are usually the same, and, indeed, children are now more likely to be brought up by their biological mothers than to be sent away for adoption as in the past. The result of increasing divorce and increasing illegitimacy, however, is that more children grow up for at least part of their childhood in lone-parent families, and these are almost invariably headed by women. They have risen from 8 per cent of all households in 1972 to 13 per cent in 1986. Many people have argued that the trends cited here are evidence of the breakdown of the family.

Despite all the arguments about the decline of marriage, the increase in illegitimacy, and so on, it continues to be the case that most people in Britain grow up, get married, and form a nuclear family for part of their adult life. Nine out of ten people get married at some time in their lives; 90 per cent of women are married by the age of 30 and over 90 per cent of men before the age of 40. In 1981 only 6 per cent of women and 10 per cent of men aged 35-44 had never been married. Most couples who get married (or have stable cohabitation relationships) have children. Thus nine out of ten married women have children, and four out of five children live with their two natural parents. Eighty-seven per cent of families with children are headed by a married couple and 13 per cent a lone parent. The majority of lone-parent families (90 per cent) are headed by a woman, and the major reason is separation or divorce from the male partner, although some female family heads are single or widowed (Family Policy Studies Centre, Fact Sheet 1, 1988).

In some respects marriage is more popular than ever; people marry younger and more often. The age at which people marry has fallen during this century, so that in the 1960s one bride in three was a teenager, although it is now rising again – the comparable figure for the 1980s is one in five. There are both gender and class differences in age of marriage, with working-class couples marrying, on average, at a younger age than middle-class ones. The average age of first marriage in 1988 for all men was 26.3 years, and for all women 24.1 years. People are also marrying more than once, and the percentage of remarriage has risen from 14 per cent in 1961 to 35 per cent in 1986.

However, it is important to examine household structures as well as familial relationships, given the continuing emphasis on the moral superiority of the nuclear family. It is also important to note that there are a variety of family forms in modern Britain: single-parent families, extended families, role-swap families, dual career families, and re-formed families as well as conventional nuclear ones. Furthermore, while the ideal may be that (married) women with young children should not be in paid employment, an increasing number are. Indeed, as Martin and Roberts (1984) point out, it is the norm for mothers of school-age children to have paid employment, and most non-employed women with young children expect to work when the children grow older.

Power and the division of labour in families

The choices about who works in the family and who stays at home to care for the house and children are based on an ideology of appropriate gender roles. However, this is reinforced by labour market factors; men can generally earn more than women, so that it is generally the case that men have the paid employment and women care for the children. This traps women in a situation of financial dependency. Employment, taken to fit in with domestic responsibilities, rarely pays sufficient to give a woman financial independence, and most women do not feel they are entitled to control the spending of the 'family wage'. The family wage is supposed to be large enough to support a man, his wife, and his children. The man's need to earn a family wage is used in wage bargaining by trade unions, and a wife's earnings are seen as supplementary – money with which to buy luxuries. Hunt (1980) found that the husband's money was spent on the essentials and the wife's on extras, so it was the man's employment that was seen as essential and the wife's as something that could be given up if necessary. However, not all married men with a family earn a 'family wage', and many men and some women without familial responsibilities do earn one. In 1977 the Equal Opportunities Commission estimated that the number of families living in poverty (i.e. below the supplementary benefit level) would have been three times greater if it had not been for married women's earnings. Women without a male head of household are more likely to be living in poverty than those with one.

The 'family wage' is not paid to the family, but to the (male) wage earner. How this money is distributed within the family depends on power relationships between husband and wife, and who is seen as having the right to decide how and where the money is to be spent. Jan Pahl (1980) has described the different ways in which husbands and wives manage their income. In some cases the husband hands over the wage packet and the wife gives him back his 'pocket-money'; in others the husband gives the wife housekeeping money; in a third type of case resources are pooled and spending decisions made jointly. Pahl has pointed out that in some cases the husband does not maintain his wife. Graham (1984) and Pahl (1983) have also found that women with children whose marriages have broken down have sometimes found that they are better off on supplementary benefit than they were when they lived with their husbands.

Furthermore, research shows that resources are not shared equally within families. Women tend to put their husbands and children first and their own needs last. When money is tight, women go without food, clothes, and other necessities. Women rarely have personal spending money in the way that men do, and they feel that if they spend housekeeping money on themselves they are depriving their children. Even where, in theory, women have control over resources, or joint control, men expect to be consulted and have the final say over the purchase of large household items such as washing machines, refrigerators, or cars (Hunt, 1980; Edgell, 1980). When the household has a car, it is generally the husband who has the use of it, even if the wife can drive. In many cases the car is a perk of the job, and the wife has no claim over it in any case (Graham, 1984). Within the home, men tend to have more space that they regard as their own – a den, a study, or even a garden shed.

Women accept the lack of control because they are not the bread-winners. However husbands and wives handle their money, it is unusual for a married woman to have money for her own personal use. As Lee Comer has said:

> If any sociologist...had inquired into the financial arrangements in my marriage I would have lain my hand on my heart and sworn that we shared money equally. And in theory I would have been telling the truth. In fact, it would no more have occurred to me to spend money on anything but housekeeping as it would for him...not to...a reality in which a husband can spend money however he wishes but a reality...in which she makes do because to do otherwise is to encroach too far into the man's rights. The only money she spends guiltlessly is on food for the family and clothes for the children.
>
> (1974: 124)

Obviously women's lack of power over financial resources relates not just to ideologies concerning the appropriate roles of men and women but also to the realities of who is seen as earning the money and who is seen to be 'not working'. Women's domestic labour is not seen as 'real' work because it does not bring in money, and women are not paid for it. They are maintained by their husbands in exchange for the labour. However, it is men's control over financial resources that gives them such power in marriage and makes it difficult for a wife to leave her husband even if he is mentally or physically violent to her or she is just unhappy in her marriage. Again this is compounded by the kind of job that she would be able to get if she left, and if she had children.

The division of labour in the home

To understand the division of labour within the family we need to examine not just who does what job, but who is seen as responsible for ensuring that a particular job is carried out, and to challenge the view that there is an equitable division of labour between 'man the bread-winner' and 'woman the carer'. The imbalance comes about partly because women increasingly have paid employment as well as doing housework, cooking, and child care, and partly because women's domestic labour requires far more hours of work than men's paid labour (see Chapter six). Feminists often point out that it is women who are generally responsible for the necessary, repetitive jobs that *have* to be done on a regular basis, while men do those that are creative and can be done when convenient. Often this division is based on what men and women are thought to be naturally good at. Women are said to be naturally good at cleaning, sewing, washing up, shopping, washing, caring for children, cooking, and so on.

Ann Oakley (1974a,b) was the first feminist sociologist to examine seriously the division of labour in the household and to look at domestic labour as work (see Chapter six). She has also challenged the view that women have a private domain of their own – a domain which they rule and where they make the decisions. In fact, she suggests that as men spend more time in the home, take more interest in their children, and have more joint activities with their wives, so women's power is diminished.

Young and Willmott (1973) have suggested that men and women now share child care, domestic tasks, and the 'bread-winner' role and make decisions jointly, but Ann Oakley (1982) has argued that even when conjugal roles are shared, men are generally said to be 'helping' their wives. Women are held responsible if essential tasks are not carried out, and men will frequently 'make do' for meals if their wives are absent. Stephen Edgell (1980) has argued that wives are left to make the more minor decisions, about meals or purchasing children's clothes, while the major decisions such as moving house are made by the husband. However, even in the more minor areas of decision-making, a husband's wishes may be paramount. Pauline Hunt (1980) has suggested that women prepare meals that are the ones their husbands like and discount their own preferences.

As Martin and Roberts (1984) have shown, the majority of married women are economically active for most of their employable years. The jobs that women take are often designed to fit in with their domestic duties and they may continue to do most of the domestic work – to take on the dual role. Martin and Roberts asked the husbands and wives in their sample if they shared housework equally. Twenty-six per cent of wives and 27 per cent of husbands considered that they shared equally, but 73 per cent of wives and 72 per cent of husbands said that the wife did all or most of the housework. The reported division of labour did change when the wife was in paid employment; 43 per cent of wives in paid employment and 44 per cent of husbands whose wives were in paid employment said they shared domestic tasks. However, this still left a majority saying that wives did the majority of the domestic work. (When the wife was in part-time employment only 23 per cent of wives and 24 per cent of husbands reported an equal sharing of household duties.)

Similarly, Audrey Hunt (1975), in a study of female managers, found that they did not get much help at home. Anna Pollert (1981) found that even married women working full time in a factory regarded themselves primarily as housewives and their husbands as workers. Even if they said their husbands 'did a lot', they still seemed to do most of the domestic labour:

> A closer look showed that Sheila still did most of the daily drudgery of cooking and housework and with most of the women it became apparent that 'sharing' meant a limited delegation of specific tasks to their husbands, while they bore the responsibility for the endless, undefined, niggling work.
>
> (Pollert, 1981: 198)

On a larger scale, the British Social Attitudes Survey (1984) found that the majority of married people thought that women should be responsible for most domestic and child care tasks. Eighty-eight per cent of respondents thought that women should do the washing and ironing, 77 per cent thought they should prepare the evening meal, 72 thought they should do the cleaning, 54 per cent thought they should be responsible for the shopping, and 54 per cent thought they should have the responsibility of looking after a sick child.

While it is evident that men are not sharing domestic work with their wives, even if their wives are in full-time employment, it is even more clear that they are not taking on responsibility for tasks. Men seem to be able to choose what domestic tasks they undertake and often take on those that women find more enjoyable, such as bathing children, rather than tidying up the toys or cooking the meal. The division of labour is considered 'natural' by both men and women.

Motherhood and mothering

For many feminists, women's subordination and exploitation arises because women have children. It is this biological fact which enabled men to subordinate women, with women thereby placed under the protection of men. Firestone (1974), for example, has argued that women will be able to free themselves from men's control only when they are freed from reproduction (see Chapter nine). Not all feminists accept this biological argument as an adequate explanation for the subordination and exploitation of women in modern Britain. Nevertheless, the assumed centrality to women's lives of having and rearing children is an important aspect of women's lives. It is generally assumed that women will get married and have children. Women who choose not to do so are seen as strange, as unnatural.

Feminists have pointed out that there is a need to distinguish between the biological capacity to have children and the social role of motherhood. It is assumed that because women have children they will look after them. But, as Miriam David (1985: 32) has pointed out: 'Motherhood is a social concept, fatherhood barely recognised. To father a child refers only to the act of procreation.' Not only is motherhood a social construction, it is also a historically specific concept, in terms of being seen as a woman's chief vocation and primary identity. It developed among the middle classes during the Industrial Revolution as part of the new ideology of domesticity and womanhood. By the end of the nineteenth century a woman's primary duty was seen as having and caring for her children.

Mothering is seen as a full-time vocation for women. It is regarded as something that women are naturally good at and derive great emotional satisfaction from. Women are seen as responsible for the care and control of their children. When something goes wrong, the mother is blamed; she is seen as inadequate or negligent. In the early part of the twentieth century women were blamed for the high infant mortality rates and the poor health of their children. While there was considerable evidence that the 'real' underlying causes were poor housing, poverty, and appalling environmental conditions, women were blamed for not being hygienic in the home and for not providing adequate nutrition (see Chapters five and eight). In the period after the Second World War the popular interpretation of psychoanalysts such as Winnicott and Bowlby led to an emphasis on the need for mothers to care for their pre-school children full time. Mothers who did not do so were in danger of raising delinquents and badly adjusted children. These ideas continue to have widespread popular appeal despite considerable evidence that it is the quality of care and not the quantity nor the biological identity of the person giving it that is important, and indeed that young children need to form attachments to a variety of adults and children. Interestingly, upper-class parents who employ nannies and send their children away to boarding-schools at a young age are rarely accused of neglecting them.

The ideal of motherhood as a full-time vocation has shaped our thinking about women and mothering. Women's primary identity is as a wife and mother – a vocation that 'enables them to fulfil their emotional needs'. However, feminists have pointed out that there is a wide gap between the ideal and the reality. Mothering is hard work – children require constant care and attention – and is generally carried out in isolation. Ann Oakley has suggested that, given the disjuncture between the ideal and the reality of mothering, we should not be surprised at how many women suffer from post-natal depression, but at how few do so. A response in Boulton's 1983 interview study expresses the immediacy of the mothering role:

There are times when I feel like saying, 'I will feed you twice as much today so tomorrow I can just have a break'. Before, I could say 'The fridge badly needs to be cleaned but I can leave it'. With children they need feeding when they need feeding. Their nappies have to be washed every day. It's as simple as that. When they cry, you cannot say 'Well, I'll see you in an hour'. That is when it hits you. The fact that it's seven days a week, twenty-four hours a day, and they make the rules.

(Boulton, 1983: 69)

Research by Brown and Harris (1978) found that women at home with pre-school children stood a high risks of suffering from clinical depression. A recent report to the Government by the Women's National Commission suggests that women are twice as likely as men to suffer from stress because 'they are the buffer and absorber of stresses of the other members of the family'. They suggest that women often cope by turning the stress in on themselves, and this can result in alcohol or cigarette addiction. Hilary Graham (1984) has argued that working-class mothers with young children smoke cigarettes as a way of coping – sitting down with a cigarette is the one peaceful time they have. Despite all this evidence the myth persists that motherhood is a satisfying and fulfilling role for women. Helen Roberts (1985a) found that general practitioners could not understand why the married women who came to them were dissatisfied and that a married woman with a good husband, lovely children, and a nice home was not necessarily happy.

It is important, however, to separate out mothering from the conditions of isolation under which it is practised, and indeed from the associated drudgery of housework that accompanies it. Anne Oakley, in her study (1974b), found that the housewives enjoyed child care more than the other work. Nevertheless, many of them felt isolated and missed the company of other adults during the day. Feminists have suggested, given the amount of time women spend with children and the ideologies of mothering, that it is hardly surprising that some women do physical harm to their children. It is a result of frustration and desperation, not of individual pathology. Ann Oakley (1982) quotes a letter from a mother, in the *Sunday Times*:

When I read a study of baby battering I can't help thinking, 'There but for the grace of God go I'.... If all mothers who have ever shaken a screaming baby, or slapped it, or thrown it roughly into its cot, stood up to be counted, we would make a startling total.

Because motherhood is presented as a natural and desirable role for women, abortion of unwanted pregnancy is often seen as unnatural and even horrific. Feminists have campaigned for many years to defend the right to abortion, although it is still difficult for married women to get abortions, since it is thought that they *should* want children (MacInytre, 1977). The assumptions about women's natural roles structure women's lives, not only in families, but in education and the world of work. Girls are educated for motherhood. Women are seen as 'natural' carers because of their maternal role. Furthermore, women's employment opportunities are limited because employers argue that motherhood is more central to women's lives than a career. This affects all women, and indeed the limited job opportunities and the low pay that women receive may actually push women into marriage and motherhood. Ann Oakley (1974a) found that many of the housewives she interviewed reported that when they got married they wanted to have children in order to escape from boring jobs. (Interestingly, many of them found being a housewife even more boring and could not wait to get back to work!) It could also be argued that because most women have to get married, to have access to a living wage, having children is the price they have to pay. Other women may, on the other hand, regard marriage as the price they have to pay to have children.

Black women and families

Some black feminists have argued that the family has been an important resource in the resistance of the working class and ethnic minorities. Hazel Carby (1982) argues that not all married Afro-Caribbean women are dependent on a male, and she suggests that black men have not held the same power as white men (see Chapter two). Sally Westwood and Parminder Bhachu (1988a) have also pointed out the importance of the family as a source of strength and resistance in the fight against racism for Asian families in contemporary Britain. They suggest that although there is a trend towards nuclear families among the Asian communities, none the less there continues to be a commitment to the family, shared across generations and households. Despite the view that there is a cultural chasm between the generations – traditional versus modern – they argue that young Asians are no more alienated from their parents than other groups of young people. The comparison that most young Asian women make is a gender-based one, between the freedoms that their brothers enjoy and the restraints on their own lives.

Sexuality

The idea of the family as the natural and normal place where sexual relations take place has tended to privilege heterosexual relations and to render deviant any sexual relations which take place outside this context. Although more people now accept pre-marital sexual relations as normal, this also means that courting has become sexualized and the 'norm' of sex between a man and a woman, sanctified by romantic love, has been reinforced. In Victorian England women were not supposed to enjoy sex at all and it was only men who were thought to have an uncontrollable sex drive which impelled them to the many prostitutes who patrolled the streets. From the 1920s the 'sexologists' such as Havelock Ellis (1910–1928) started to argue that sexual satisfaction was important for both partners, and this became incorporated into ideas of of what an ideal marriage should be – a satisfying sexual partnership. However, this companionate sexuality was defined according to masculine norms: women should enjoy penetrative sex with men; if they did not then they were 'frigid'. Frigidity is assumed usually to be the woman's problem rather than her partner's. Furthermore, this whole discourse reinforced the idea that heterosexuality was the natural biologically determined human relationship.

Sexuality more generally, however, continues to be defined in male terms. Women's bodies, conveying sexual promise, are presented as desirable and are used to sell anything from cigarettes to spare parts for cars. We are constantly presented with the idea of woman being sexually passive but attracting the man and thus needing to beautify herself by, for example, purchasing exotic underwear. Men are presented as sexually active and predatory, at the mercy of their 'uncontrollable lust' which can be satisfied only by penetrating women, whether the women are willing or not. Radical feminists have argued that unwanted sexual advances by men could be construed as a form of rape and that our society condones and indeed institutionalizes rape (see Chapter seven). The sexual abuse of women and girls in the home is likewise a product of the presentation of men as having uncontrollable sexual appetites and women as victims of this, since most of the abusers are men and most of the victims are female. Many feminists have thus argued that constructions of sexuality serve to define women's identities and that this derives from the ideology of the family and experiences of family life.

Summary

1 Feminist sociologists have explored women's role in the family critically, seeing the family as the central area of oppression for women, whether it is capitalism, men as a class, or both that benefit from this.
2 They have looked at various factors associated with women's position within the family: mothering, the domestic division of labour, and economic dependency.

3 These things which characterize women's position within the family also characterize their position outside in the labour market, the education system, and political and public life.
4 In reality there is a wide variety of household arrangements and feminists have been concerned to endorse these. However, there is also a strong familial ideology which is reinforced through state legislation, advertising, and institutional structures. This ideology represents the patriarchal nuclear family as the natural and normal way to live.

Further reading

Barrett, M. and McIntosh, M. (1980) *The Antisocial Family*, London: Verso.
Gittins, D. (1985) *The Family in Question: changing households and familial ideologies*, London: Macmillan.

Chapter five

Women, health, and caring

Health is an issue of central concern to women. Women form the majority of workers in the health service and are, in the family, responsible for the health of others. However, until the development of feminist sociology, little attention was paid to gender as a key variable. Feminists have re-opened the history of women healers, explored the roles that women play in the health care system, analysed the ways in which health inequalities affect women, pointed to the ways in which medical power is used to control women and the ways in which doctors have taken away control over pregnancy and childbirth from women and medicalized what women have perceived as a natural process. More recently, feminists have focused on the informal health care work done by women, pointing out that much of the caring work women do in the domestic sphere is concerned with promoting the health of household members. Women also play a key role in the lay referral system – the system in which decisions are made about whether to visit the doctor or not, or what other action should be taken. In the process of highlighting the key role that women play as unpaid health care workers, feminists have also highlighted ways in which conflicts develop between informal and paid providers, and the extent to which paid providers are unaware of the needs of the unpaid carer. The unpaid carer is often invisible, the focus of attention being the patient, so that the needs of a woman caring, for example, for 24 hours a day, seven days a week for a disabled relative are completely ignored. A key point here is that the paid providers are themselves often women, yet because they work within the dominant medical paradigm they fail to identify with the unpaid carers and assume that women are ready, willing, and able to provide the constant care demanded of them.

Feminists have also pointed out that the multiple roles that women play affect their physical and mental well-being. However, most research into work and ill health has focused on male-dominated occupations. Little attention has been paid to the health hazards of work roles where women predominate, and even less to those of the housewife. Similarly, research into health inequalities has focused on differences between social classes or between deprived and non-deprived households; little attention has been paid to differences in the health experiences of women and men, nor has account been taken of the ways in which resources are distributed within households, often meaning that some members are deprived while others are not. There is evidence to suggest that when resources are limited women do without in order to ensure that their husbands and children are adequately provided for (see Chapter four), while Brown and Harris (1978) suggest that women at home with young children are more likely than others to suffer from clinical depression.

The discourse of health assumes that women will care for the members of their family when they are unwell and takes for granted, as natural, the health care work that women do in the domestic sphere. It also assumes that mothers will prioritize the needs of their children, putting their needs and care above their own needs – that women will, if necessary, sacrifice themselves for their children. It also, paradoxically, defines as health care the formal health care provision supplied by the state and private paid medicine. Health care is seen as provided by doctors, nurses, health visitors, and so on; the health care provided by women in the home is not defined as such but is seen as an integral aspect of their caring role in the family.

Women and medicine

During the course of the nineteenth and twentieth centuries, scientific medicine has come to dominate health care in the western world and doctors have achieved a high social status and considerable power. In Britain the National Health Service provides health care free at point of delivery to all citizens, and we generally regard this as 'a good thing'. We regard medicine as something good that has improved the health of the nation and alleviates pain and suffering. We tend to argue that what we want is more: more hospitals, more doctors, more nurses, more research and so on; then there would be improvement in health. Historically, however, improvement in health has often come from raised living standards, changes in behaviour and general public health reforms rather than from specific advances in medical knowledge. Jane Lewis (1980), for example, suggests that the decline in the maternal mortality rate in the 1930s and 1940s was as much due to improvement in the diet of pregnant women as to medical advances. Today, a decline in female deaths from lung cancer, for example, is much more likely to come from women stopping smoking, and indeed from the elimination of pressures in women's lives that led them to smoke, than from advances in treatment. This is not to deny that medical advances improve health and reduce mortality (death) and morbidity (illness), but to point out that preventive measures are often more effective than curative ones and indeed less costly in the long run.

Western scientific medicine is said to be objective and value-free, and doctors are seen as medical scientists who are objective about their patients in much the same way as any other scientists are about their subject matter. Medical science progresses via the scientific method (the experiment), resulting in the acquisition of certain, objective and unchallengeable facts and an autonomous and value-free body of knowledge. However, there are problems with this view of science, which sociologists have challenged in general (see Chapter nine) and specifically with respect to medicine. Sociologists argue that all scientific activity is inevitably influenced by the society in which it is carried out and that the scientist often plays a major role in explaining and ultimately justifying various aspects of the way in which a society is organized.

Furthermore, feminists regard medical knowledge as part of the means by which gender divisions in society are maintained. Medicine not only reflects discriminatory views of women but serves to reproduce these views by actively stereotyping and controlling women who deviate from them. The way in which women were seen as weak and in need of constant rest by the medical profession in the nineteenth century, thus justifying, for instance, their exclusion from higher education, is one example. Helen Roberts (1985a) also shows in her research how doctors stereotype female patients and fail to understand the problematic nature of the housewife role. She gives an example of a middle-aged woman who woke up one morning and decided she no longer wanted to do housework. She went to the doctor with her husband and the doctor had her admitted to hospital for psychiatric treatment.

Women experience the health care system as paternalistic, and their own experiences and knowledge are ignored or downgraded. This has been especially highlighted in the area of pregnancy and childbirth and it is also true with respect to contraception. In terms of women's informal caring roles their own knowledge and understanding of the patient is dismissed as irrelevant. Often, feminists argue, medical intervention does more harm than good, and in other cases it offers palliation rather than a cure. In childbirth, for example, it has been suggested that many procedures that have become routinized, such as routine episiotomy, are of dubious benefit to mother or child. They do, however, justify the role of the medical doctor in controlling delivery. The giving of tranquillizers to housewives with depression only renders the intolerable more tolerable; it does nothing to alleviate the underlying causes of depression.

Women and health inequalities

Gender inequalities in health care provision, and the ways in which the specific health care needs of women are ignored, have been highlighted by feminists. So also have the ways in which medical intervention is used as much to increase the power and prestige of medical men as to improve the health of women, and the questionable benefits of much medical intervention to its receivers. Marxist feminists have highlighted inequalities in health care and the ways in which the health care system serves the needs of a capitalist society. A 'cultural critique' has questioned the view that medicine, as a science, is value-free and objective, that doctors as professionals are knowledgeable and concerned with meeting the health care needs of clients, that medical intervention is always of benefit to clients and that the dramatic reductions in ill health and general improvements in health achieved in industrial countries in the last 100 years are due to advances in medical knowledge. The concern that feminists have expressed, then, is not just that women's health needs are ignored, nor that medicine is sexist, but that modern medicine itself may be less valuable than is claimed. The actual technical competence of doctors and of modern medicine is scrutinized. It is argued that doctors exhibit massive ignorance on such subjects as birth control, menstruation, breast feeding, the management of childbirth, the menopause, vaginal infections, which are the dangers that women face across the life-course.

The publication of the Black Report on health inequalities in 1979 stimulated investigations into the existence, extent, and causes of health inequalities. The main focus of attention has been on social class differences, and sociologists have developed materialist and structuralist accounts to explain these. They have argued that the major causes of health inequalities are material inequalities – that the reason why the working class has higher mortality (death) rates and higher levels of morbidity (illness) is material deprivation. Research by Townsend *et al.* (1987), Abbott (1988) and others has found that there is a high correlation between local government wards that have high levels of material deprivation and wards that have poor health experience relative to the rest of the wards in a defined area.

However, the priority in such research has been on investigating men's health, and specific studies of work hazards have concentrated on male-dominated occupations. Little attention has been paid to the health hazards of women's paid and unpaid work. Furthermore, women are expected to look after the health of men and children. While it is recognized that men and women do have different health experiences, little account has been taken of the sex/gender system in examining the pattern of health and illness. Thus the research has failed to explain why

97

it is that although men die on average at a younger age than women, women appear to suffer more ill health than men. In 1984 the life expectancy of a British man was 71 years, and the life expectancy of a woman was 77 years. However, there are social class differences between women in this respect. Women married to men employed in semi-skilled or unskilled jobs are 70 per cent more likely to die prematurely than those whose husbands are in a professional or managerial occupation (OPCS, 1986). (Unfortunately, data classified by married women's own occupations are not published.) Furthermore, women in social classes IV and V have higher mortality rates than men in social classes I and II, despite the overall tendency for women to live longer than men.

Table 5.1 Social class, gender, and GP (NHS) consultations in Great Britain, 1980

Socio-economic group	Average consultations per person	
	Males	Females
Professional	2.9	4.1
Employers/managers	3.5	4.4
Intermediate/junior non-manual	3.7	4.6
Skilled manual	3.7	4.9
Semi-skilled manual/personal service	4.0	5.4
Unskilled manual	4.3	5.5

Source: adapted from Hilary Graham (1984).

Women of all social classes consult their general practitioners more often than do men (Table 5.1). Again there are social class differences. Women married to men in the lowest social classes suffer three times more longstanding illness than do those in the highest social classes. However, it is not the case that we can determine the relative health experience of different groups from the amount that they consult doctors or make use of the health services. Women of the lowest social classes, for example, make more use of the health services than the more affluent, but not to the extent that their much greater health problems would suggest that they should (LeGrande, 1982). The preventive services are used least by the women who suffer most from the problems that these services are intended to forestall (Doyal, 1987). A good example here is screening for cervical cancer. Although women married to men in social class V are four times more likely to die of cancer of the cervix than women married to men in social class I, they make much less use of the screening facilities than middle-class women; the difference in death rate between working-class and middle-class women is not fully explained by differential use of the preventive services. There is also a marked social class gradient in the use of services connected with fertility control. Women married to men in middle-class occupations are much more likely than women married to manual workers to attend Family Planning Clinics or discuss fertility control with general practitioners. Inequalities are also evident with regard to abortion. While working-class and black women argue that they are pressured into having abortion, other women point out how difficult it is to get one – especially on the NHS. Fifty per cent of abortions are in fact performed outside the NHS (Doyal, 1987).

It is necessary to consider, if women's greater use of health services suggests that women are sicker than men, why working-class women make less use of preventive services than middle-class ones, and why working-class women make less use of the health services than their health problems would suggest they need. Some feminists have suggested that women's life experiences mean that they suffer more ill health than men. Others have argued that this is an artefact – that women's greater use of health services is due to factors other than that they are suffering more ill health than men. Explanations that stress the different life experiences of women are:

1 that women suffer more problems with the reproductive tract than do men;
2 that the isolation of women in unpaid domestic labour seems to be linked with a higher incidence of depression among women (Brown and Harris, 1978).

Those that stress the artefactual nature of the difference suggest:

1 that women often visit the doctor on behalf of others, especially children (Graham, 1984);
2 that female socialization in western cultures makes it more acceptable for women to adopt the 'sick role';
3 that women are subject to the 'medicalization' of normal childbirth (Leesen and Gray, 1978; Oakley, 1980);
4 that women live longer than men (the ratio of women to men aged 75+ is 2:1), and older people tend to have more health problems than younger ones (Leesen and Gray, 1978).

Indeed, Leesen and Gray (1978) report that the hospitalization rate is higher for men than for women, if maternity and disorders of the breast and reproductive tract are excluded. For example, in Britain in 1972, 816 per 100,000 men were hospitalized compared with 710 per 100,000 women, counted on this basis.

99

Other research suggests that consultation rates are a poor guide to the amount of illness suffered in the community, and that women are more likely than men to 'suffer in silence'. Scambler and Scambler (1984) found that women do not necessarily visit the doctor when they are unwell (see Table 5.2). Helen Roberts (1985a) found that women differed in the extent to which they visited the doctor and divided them into the frequent attenders and the infrequent attenders. She did not find that the latter group suffered less ill health than the former, but rather that they differed in their views as to when the doctor should be consulted. The infrequent attenders argued that the doctor should only be visited when this was essential, the frequent attenders that the doctor should be visited when one was unwell, before things became too bad. Both groups were concerned with not wasting the doctor's time, but while the former group argued that this meant only going when it was essential, the latter argued that the doctor should be visited at the first signs of illness to prevent his having to spend a lot of time treating a serious illness.

Table 5.2 Ratio of symptoms noted at consultations with medical practitioners (*based on health diaries kept by 79 women aged 16–44*)

Symptom	Ratio of consultations to occurrences
Tiredness, lack of energy	No consultations
Nerves, depression or irritability	1:74
Headache	1:60
Back-ache	1:38
Sleeplessness	1:31
Aches or pains in muscles or joints	1:18
Cold or influenza	1:12
Stomach pains	1:11
Women's complaints (e.g. period pains)	1:10
Sore throat	1: 9

Source: adapted from Scambler and Scambler (1984)

Scambler and Scambler found that women differentiated between illness that required a visit to the doctor and illness where alternative methods were indicated. Thus women often experience suffering but do not regard themselves as ill. A similar situation was noted fifty years ago in the Workers' Health Enquiry into the lives of working-class women:

...many women replied 'yes' to the question 'do you usually feel fit and well?' In answer to the next question, 'What ailments do you suffer from?', the same women listed a whole series of problems including anaemia, headaches, constipation, rheumatism, prolapse of the womb, bad teeth and varicose veins.

(Spring-Rice, 1939: 69)

As is the case today, certain 'ailments' had to be suffered, but the women were 'well enough to carry on'. Women's domestic and caring roles mean that they cannot be ill because they have to care for their families. Williams (1983) found in Aberdeen that fatigue or weakness did not constitute 'illness', and 'fit' meant being able to work. Jocelyn Cornwell (1984), in her study in Bethnal Green, also found that women regarded themselves as 'not ill' if they could carry on. Pill and Stott (1986) suggest, from their study of 204 women in Cardiff, that working-class women have a low expectation of health and that the women were not accustomed to thinking particularly about their health. Women are also the ones who decide when their husbands and children are ill and may adopt the sick role (Locker, 1981).

It is also important to consider why working-class women are less likely to make use of the health services than middle-class women. There has been a tendency to blame the working-class woman, to suggest that she is less able to perceive the benefit of the services offered, especially preventive ones. However, feminists have suggested that it is necessary to turn the question around and ask what is wrong with the way the services are provided. They argue that often the provision does not meet the needs of the woman, that there are no arrangements to care for the young children they often have to bring with them, that working-class women find it difficult to communicate with middle-class professionals, and that the women are aware that the main causes of their ill health (children, housing, lack of money, and so on) lie outside the province of the medical profession and also outside their own control (Pill and Stott, 1986; Blaxter, 1985; Cornwell, 1984). While working-class and black women experience the greatest control from health professionals – at the extreme, being pressured to have unwanted abortions or prescribed Depo-Provera (a long-term birth control measure with serious side effects, banned in the United States) without informed consent – feminists argue that all women are controlled by medical ideology.

While radical feminists emphasize the ways in which male medical ideology is used to control women, Marxist feminists have been concerned to point to health inequalities between women from different social classes and ethnic groups and the ways in which the state controls the health care system to meet the needs of capitalist society. Doyal (1987) suggests that the NHS was a powerful mechanism of social control, both because it appeared to be a major move to meet the needs of the working class and because it served the interests of the capitalist class by ensuring a healthy work-force. However, despite forty years of the NHS, the inequalities in health between women from different social classes persist, and while the health of all women has improved, the relative inequalities have remained the same – or even increased to some extent (Whitehead, 1987). Indeed, it could be argued that the NHS has failed to meet the specific needs of women because the ways in which services are provided do not enable women to make full use of them. Lack of facilities for caring for young children, the timing of appointments, the centralization of provision, and the attitudes of the profession have all been cited as reasons why services have not been used (Graham, 1984).

Iatrogenic medicine

Some medical intervention, it is suggested, is *iatrogenic* – that is, it causes more harm than good; the treatment actually does more harm than the original illness. A good example of this is the recent use of a particular drug to treat arthritis. Some patients who were prescribed the drug, which relieves the pain of arthritis, have ended up with poor health as a result of the so-called side-effects of the drug – such as an inability to tolerate daylight. However, with women's health there is greater concern because some drugs or treatments that are prescribed on a routine basis, not to treat illness but to prevent unwanted pregnancies, have been found to be iatrogenic. The coil, for example, has been found to cause extensive menstrual bleeding and low back pain in some women. However, the main cause for concern has been the contraceptive pill, the most reliable method of contraception available to most women. The pill was introduced into the USA in 1960 and has subsequently been used by millions of women throughout the world. It was seen as an effective, modern, and scientifically respectable method for controlling fertility and was freely prescribed by doctors to women of child-bearing age. However, by the mid-1960s it began to be suspected that there was a link between the pill and cancer of the cervix and circulatory (heart) diseases. Attempts to assess the validity of this suspicion uncovered serious deficiencies in the testing of contraceptive drugs. It was found that they had not been tested on women for the whole period of the reproductive cycle, so that the possible effects of taking the pill for twenty or thirty years was unknown. A study by the Royal College of General Practitioners (RCGP) in 1974 found that the risk of dying from circulatory disease was five times greater for women taking the oral contraceptive pill than for others. Women who were over 35 years old who had been taking the pill for five or more years and who smoked were found to be at the greatest risk. The pill has also been found to have a number of side effects – depression, a loss of libido (sex drive), headaches, nausea, and excessive weight gain – but there has been little research into these. Furthermore, the subjective experiences and feelings of women have often been dismissed as irrelevant or 'not real' by the medical profession. Furthermore, it has by now, and as a result of availability of such devices as the pill and the coil, become generally accepted that it should be women who take the responsibility for birth control precautions, and it is women who suffer the serious consequences if contraception fails. (This may be changing to some small extent, however, with the AIDS risk and the emphasis on using condoms and barrier cream.)

It seems unlikely that what are often referred to as the 'side effects' of female contraception would be so readily ignored if men were the users. It would be interesting to know how many men would be prepared to use the intrapenile device described by Dr Sophie Merkin:

The newest development in male contraception was unveiled recently at the American Women's Centre. Dr Sophie Merkin of the Merkin Clinic announced the preliminary findings of a study conducted on 763 unsuspecting male undergraduates at a large mid-Western university. In her report, Dr Merkin stated that the new contraceptive – the IPD – was a breakthrough in male contraception. It will be marketed under the trade name *Umbrelly*.

The IPD (intrapenile device) resembles a tightly rolled umbrella which is inserted through the head of the penis and pushed into the scrotum with a plunger-like device. Occasionally there is a perforation of the scrotum, but this is disregarded as the male has few nerve-endings in this area of his body. The underside of the umbrella contains a spermicidal jelly, hence the name *Umbrelly*.

Experiments on 1000 white whales from the continental shelf (whose sexual apparatus is said to be closest to man's) proved the IPD to be 100% effective in preventing the production of sperm and eminently satisfactory to the female whale since it does not interfere with her rutting pleasure.

Dr Merkin declared the *Umbrelly* to be statistically safe for the human male. She reported that of the 763 undergraduates tested with the device only two died of scrotal infection, only twenty developed swelling of the testicles and only 13 were too depressed to have an erection. She stated that common complaints ranged from cramping and bleeding to acute abdominal pains. She emphasised that these symptoms were merely indications that the man's body had not yet adjusted to the device. Hopefully the symptoms would disappear within a year.

One complication caused by the IPD and briefly mentioned by Dr Merkin was the incidence of massive scrotal infection necessitating the surgical removal of the testicles. 'But this is a rare case', said Dr Merkin, 'too rare to be statistically important'. She and other distinguished members of the Women's College of Surgeons agreed that the benefits far outweighed the risk to any individual man. (From *Outcome* magazine, the East Bay Men's Centre newsletter, and *The Periodical Lunch* published by Andrew Rock, Ann Arbor, Michigan, USA.)

This is of course a spoof – no such device has actually been invented. The account was published to illustrate the fact that most men would not be expected to suffer what many women experience with an IUD, such as heavy bleeding, backache, and vaginal infections.

While it may be true that women choose what method of contraception to use, their choice is limited by what is available. Modern methods do enable a woman to have control over her own fertility, rather than relying on her partner or risking having an abortion after conception, but her choice is limited by decisions that have already been made by drug company executives, doctors, researchers, and others, about which methods will be developed and made available. Given that most methods have their own problems, the choice is often a negative one. Women choose the method that affects them least – so one may choose the pill because the IUD caused excessive bleeding, while another may make the reverse decision because the pill resulted in excessive weight gain. Medical control of many of the newer methods of birth control means that women are dependent on their doctors for advice, and doctors are generally inadequately trained in this area. Most women will have to make a judgement based on what their doctors tell them, and doctors often become resentful if female patients question their advice or reveal that they are knowledgeable in the area. Doctors frequently expect patients to accept that they know best. Yet they rarely talk to their female patients about birth control in detail and are inclined to dismiss subjective experience and base their advice on what they regard as sound scientific judgement. Nevertheless, doctors' *non*-medical values do influence the decisions they make about sterilization and abortion, for example. While white middle-class women have been demanding the right to choose to be sterilized or to have an abortion, working-class and black women have pointed out that they have often been pressurized into having an abortion or being sterilized against their inclinations (Bryan *et al.*, 1985).

Gender: power and medicine

Medical images of women

The way in which medical men 'construct' women is a powerful element in their control of their female patients. While in the nineteenth century medical men argued that women were *physically* frail, in the twentieth century they have suggested that they are *mentally* weak and easily dissatisfied with their domestic roles. Medical images of women are, of course, reinforced by the ways in which medical education is carried out and the contents of what is taught. Female medical students (and feminist doctors – see Eisner, 1986) have argued that sexism is rampant in medical training and that women are often treated as sexual objects of ridicule by (male) lecturers. Men are seen as the norm against which women are seen as abnormal.

Analysis of medical textbooks shows that they include 'facts' about women that are little more than prejudices. They stress the superiority of doctors' objective knowledge and clinical experience over women's own subjective perceptions – even when women's own experience is under examination. Little attention is paid in the medical curriculum to problems specifically suffered by women except those relating to pregnancy and childbirth; thus common female problems such as cystitis (bladder infection) or vaginal infections are not taken seriously. Gynaecologists and obstetricians are considered to be experts on women, yet it is a male specialism. They exercise great power *vis-à-vis* women and are in a position to define 'normal femininity' and 'normal sexuality'. Not only are they often given little training on female sexuality, but an analysis by Scully and Bart (1978) of the major gynaecology textbooks suggests that what they are taught is out of date. They found that myths about female sexuality continued to be stated as facts even after major surveys had revealed them as myths.

Doctors tend to see women's medical problems as emotional and mental rather than physical. Penfold and Walker (1984) review a number of cases where women received a psychiatric diagnosis but were subsequently found to have a physiological problem. Furthermore, women's depression is assumed to arise because of their inherent weakness – because they cannot cope with the demands of a family, the isolation of domestic labour, and so on. However, the research of Brown and Harris (1978) has suggested that depression in women relates primarily to their life circumstances, while the American feminist Jessie Bernard (1973) has argued that being a housewife makes women sick because they become depressed and suggested that paid employment protects women from depression. (However, Arber *et al.* (1985) have suggested that married women under the age of forty with children may suffer more physical illness if they have full-time paid employment.) Maggie Eisner (1986) has referred to the attitude of male general practitioners and suggested that it is because women have to cope with their families' problems that they turn to the GP for emotional support:

> A speaker said that women ask their GPs for more emotional support than men do, implying that women, being weaker than men, have greater need for such support. I pointed out that the women spend a lot of their time and energy giving emotional support to many people in their lives and often have no-one but the GP to turn to for their own emotional support.
>
> (Eisner, 1986: 121)

Scully and Bart (1978) suggest that doctors 'blame' women's emotional and hysterical behaviour on the female reproductive tract, and this was certainly the case in the nineteenth century. Nineteenth-century doctors argued that women were controlled by their biology – women, it was argued, were entirely under the control of their reproductive organs, and so doctors could provide a 'scientific' explanation of this truth. A malfunctioning uterus or ovary could result in the spread of disease throughout the body. Some Victorian doctors thought that women did not have sexual feelings, while men had strong sexual urges. Instead of sexual urges, women were said to be endowed with a strong maternal instinct, and their most important duty in life was motherhood.

The upper-class woman in particular was portrayed as frail and sickly – her delicate nervous system was seen as needing protection as much as her sickly body. Middle-class women were encouraged to have long periods of rest – especially at times of menstruation. It was thought especially dangerous for women to engage in intellectual activity. Higher education was seen as a special danger, and women were excluded from the universities on the grounds that they were a risk both to their health and to their femininity. It was claimed that a woman who developed 'masculine' intellectual qualities would necessarily underdevelop her 'female' qualities, endangering both her fertility and her capacity for motherhood. While middle-class and upper-class women were encouraged to be idle, working-class women were expected to work, but the work assigned to them was hard manual labour. Thus the inherent inferiority of women was used to justify the two very different life-styles enjoyed by middle-class and working-class women in Victorian England.

The cult of frailty among upper-class and upper middle-class Victorian women was strengthened by the view that a man should be able to support a leisured life; to be able to afford domestic servants was a status symbol. Some Victorian wives rebelled, but the majority did not because they were totally dependent on their husbands/fathers. The boredom and confinement of upper-class women resulted in a cult of hypochondria, and especially hysteria. Doctors argued that it arose from a morbid condition of the uterus, which began at puberty and ended with the menopause. Medical intervention was said to be necessary to establish personal and social control. 'Cures' included hysterectomies, clitorectomies, ovarectomies and other forms of genital mutilation. While most women were not 'treated' surgically, they did consult medical men and came to define themselves as inherently sick – a view that was reinforced as hysteria was represented as a contagious disease and isolation from other women was considered essential to successful treatment.

The portrayal of women, and especially upper-class and middle-class ones, as inherently sick created more work for medical men, which enhanced the status and income of those who were doctors to wealthy women. It also underpinned doctors' campaigns against midwifery, as they claimed that all women's complaints, including pregnancy, were diseases and demanded the care of a doctor. It was thus in the financial interest of doctors, as well as sustaining their claim to the exclusive right to treat the sick, to maintain the view that women were not only weaker than men but also inherently sick. It also justified the exclusion of women from the public sphere of education, business, and the economy and reinforced the view that woman's role was in the domestic sphere and that women's fulfilment came from motherhood. This view is still evident in the ways in which women are treated during pregnancy and childbirth by the medical profession to this day.

Women, medicine, and reproduction

Medicine is involved in three areas of reproduction:

1 conception – the prevention of unwanted pregnancy;
2 pregnancy and childbirth;
3 reproductive technologies designed to enable women who could not otherwise do so to become pregnant.

While feminists have been critical of medical intervention in these areas, it is nevertheless important to recognize that there have been positive aspects to this intervention. In the nineteenth and early twentieth centuries women did face extreme hazard in childbirth, and many, including upper-class women, had severe complications and long-term ill health as a result of pregnancy and childbirth, including prolapse of the uterus and irreparable pelvic tears. Medical advances have made pregnancy and childbirth a much less hazardous process for both the mother and the child (Himmelweit, 1988; Llewelyn Davies, 1915). Medicine cannot take all the credit – improved diet, hygienic conditions, and a general rise in the standard of living have all played an important role in reducing maternal and infant mortality and morbidity. None the less, credit is due.

However, medical dominance in these areas of women's lives means that women are controlled to a large extent by the medical profession, and they rely on doctors for advice and information. For example, pregnant women are treated 'as if' something is going to go wrong – women are required to make regular ante-natal visits and are virtually forced to have their babies in hospital, where doctors control the management of labour and childbirth. As Ann Oakley (1984a) argues, motherhood has become a medicalized domain.

The key point is not that medical intervention has played no role in making pregnancy and childbirth safer, but that doctors have taken over total control of the management of pregnant women, so that women are unable to make informed decisions about their lives. This came out clearly in the case of Wendy Savage, the consultant obstetrician who was suspended on a charge of incompetence (of which she was eventually cleared) after a campaign by her male colleagues, who objected to the ways in which she practised (see Savage, 1986). During the campaign to clear her and the subsequent inquiry it became evident that the key issues surrounded how pregnancy and childbirth were to be managed. She argued that women should be allowed to make informed choices during pregnancy and childbirth, that ante-natal care should be provided in clinics near women's homes, and that they should be allowed to give birth at home if they wanted to do so. The role of the doctor was to assist women, not to control them and make decisions for them.

Feminists have argued not only that women do not feel in control during pregnancy and childbirth, but also that there is little evidence to support the view that technological intervention in childbirth is beneficial for mother and/or child. Ann Oakley (1982), reporting on research carried out in 1975, found that 69 per cent of first-time mothers did not feel in control of themselves and what was going on in labour. She also quotes research carried out in Wales, finding that the increased use of induction (artificial starting of labour) did not reduce perinatal mortality (death of the baby in the first two months of life), but did increase the number of low birth-weight babies. Induction carries risks to both maternal and foetal health – for example, the tearing of the peritoneum in the mother and an increased likelihood of a forceps-assisted birth with its associated risks. There has also been an increase in the use of Caesarian section without clear evidence that this has improved the health of babies or mothers. Other routine procedures such as foetal heart monitoring and episiotomy (cutting the peritoneum to prevent tearing) are also of doubtful benefit.

Feminists have suggested that women and doctors have very different views about pregnancy and childbirth. During pregnancy, they suggest, the mother is seen by doctors as a life-support system for the foetus, and the emphasis is on the needs and health of the baby rather than those of the mother. Doctors regard themselves as the experts on childbirth and pregnancy. Medical practice is based on the assumption that doctors have access to a scientific body of knowledge about childbirth, but doctors deals mainly with illness and they tend to treat pregnancy as if it were a sickness. This means that they are more interested in the pathological than the normal, in using technology, and in women taking medical advice.

Graham and Oakley (1981) argue that while doctors see pregnancy as a medical problem, women see it as a natural phenomenon. While for the doctor pregnancy and childbirth are medical events starting with diagnosis and ending with discharge from medical supervision, for women they are parts of a process which has to be integrated with other social roles. They are accompanied by a change in status, to mother, with the obligations that this imposes permanently and comprehensively on a woman's life. While for medical men the success of pregnancy and childbirth is measured by low perinatal and maternal mortality rates and low incidence of certain kinds of morbidity, and a 'successful' outcome is a healthy mother and baby in the immediate post-birth period, for the mother success is measured by a healthy baby, a satisfactory personal experience of labour and delivery, the establishment of a satisfactory relationship with the baby, and integrating the demands of motherhood into her life-style. While the doctor sees himself as the expert, possessing superior knowledge and therefore in control, the mother sees herself as knowledgeable about pregnancy, as perceptive about the sensations of her body and its needs. However, mothers felt they were not in control. Pregnant women spoke of problems in communicating with their doctors, of not being able to ask questions, and of being treated as ignorant. They also disliked being seen by different doctors at each visit and complained that they felt like battery hens – as just one unimportant item in a factory production system.

While feminists have argued that doctors have medicalized childbirth and in the process taken away control from women, they have also pointed to medical control in other areas of reproduction. Doctors control the most effective means of birth control – the pill, the coil, the cap, and sterilization. Women have to seek medical advice to be able to use these methods of controlling their fertility. The 1968 Abortion Reform law made abortion on medical grounds legal and more freely available, but the decision as to whether a woman can have an abortion is made by doctors. Doctors also control the new reproductive technologies concerned with helping women to conceive and have children. Doctors often refuse sterilization or abortion to young married women, while single women and women from ethnic minority groups are positively encouraged to have abortions. Doctors also decide which women should have access to reproductive technology, and the decision is often based on moral rather than medical judgement. Also, access to reproductive technology and abortion is mediated by ability to pay; NHS provision is greatly outstripped by demand, so many women are forced to turn to private practitioners. This option, however, is available only to those with money. Scientific and medical advances in the area of reproduction have on the one hand given women the possibility of deciding if, when, and under what conditions they will have children. On the other hand, however, the dominance of so much of reproductive technology by the medical profession and the state has permitted doctors to have even greater control over women's lives.

The development of *in vitro* fertilization in the late 1970s, which was seen as a 'miracle cure', has led feminists more recently to turn their attention to what are commonly described as the 'new' reproductive technologies. These include not only technologies that make it possible to extend parenthood to people who have been unable to realize their wish to have a child, but also techniques that can be used to diagnose genetic or chromosomal abnormalities *in utero* and which at the same time enable the sex of the child to be determined. While some feminists have been concerned about the availability of the services on the NHS and the ways in which access to them is controlled by the medical profession, others have raised questions about the impact that they will have on women's lives. Some have suggested that the new technologies will be used by men to control and exploit women even further. Amniocentesis, it is argued, will be, and has been, used to determine the sex of the unborn foetus and force women to have an abortion if the foetus is not of the desired sex – generally male.

Other feminists (e.g. Michele Stanworth, 1987b) have suggested a more cautious approach. While recognizing the strong desire of some women to have children and the ways in which they will be assisted by the new technologies, Stanworth suggests that insufficient attention has been paid to questions of safety, women's health, and their ability to make informed decisions. Also, it is necessary to recognize that there are a range of reproductive technologies – not just the various 'new' techniques that have been the focus of public attention. While many of these techniques are flawed and their safety questionable, nevertheless they provide an indisputable resource on which women draw according to their priorities. What is necessary is for women to be better informed about these technologies so that they can make better-informed decisions. While science may be seen as helping women, the control over it is not in their hands, but those of doctors. These issues can be illustrated by reference to ultrasound – a method of enabling doctors and patients to see an image of the foetus on the screen. Doctors use it to detect abnormalities and to date conception exactly (women's knowledge of when they became pregnant is regarded as unreliable, and some women cannot give an exact date for the first day of their last period, which is used to date conception). Women gain great benefit from seeing their own baby in this way (Petchesky, 1987), but, as Ann Oakley (1987) has pointed out, it is not entirely certain that the procedure is completely safe – it may cause some risk to the health of the mother and/or the foetus.

Women as providers of health care

Women form the majority of health-care workers, both formal and informal. Over 75 per cent of all employed health-care workers in the UK are women (Orr, 1987). Women are concentrated in the lower-paid, lower-status jobs. While 90 per cent of nurses are female, only 25 per cent of doctors are. Also, the majority of cleaners and kitchen hands are women. Black women tend to be in the lowest-paid, lowest-status jobs (Doyal *et al.*, 1981). Thus, there is horizontal and vertical occupational segregation in the health service (see Chapter six). Within particular types of work there is further vertical segregation; while women constitute 25 per cent of doctors, they form only 9 per cent of consultants and 15 per cent of gynaecologists.

Women are also the major providers of unpaid health care in the home (Graham, 1984). Even excluding those caring for dependent children, about 75 per cent of adults caring for an elderly or disabled relative in the home are women. Much health education is directed at women, who are assumed to care for other relatives in the household. Health visiting was developed in the early part of this century specifically as a way of educating mothers in how to look after their babies and young children. Girls' education at school has been seen as part of the process of training them for motherhood. Mothers have been blamed for the poor health of their husbands and children, and maternal education has been seen as a way of improving the nation's health. Often the poor material and economic circumstances under which women are caring for their families have been ignored and the blame for the poor health of children has been placed on the ignorance of mothers rather than on poverty.

Women as healers, men as professionals

Feminists have rediscovered the historical role of women as healers, showing that until the eighteenth century healing was mainly women's

111

work, but that since then men have come to play a dominant role in medicine. However, long before this men had tried to prevent women practising medicine, and from the eighteenth century they challenged their right to practise midwifery autonomously.

While there is evidence that women practised medicine in medieval Europe (Versluysen, 1980), a law was passed in England in 1421 preventing this practice. Pressure for this law to be passed came from male doctors (Versluysen, 1980), and in this they were supported by the Christian belief that women were inferior and had an evil nature (Daly, 1978). However, health care given by women, as it is today, extended far beyond professional work. Women cared for the sick members of their families and community and played a central role in childbirth, which until the seventeenth century was seen as the exclusive concern of women. Women learned about helping the sick and assisting women in childbirth from other women in the community who had acquired the necessary skills and expertise. Thus, while women were barred from formal institutions of learning, they learned from each other (Ehrenreich and English, 1979). Indeed, the poor had little access to formal medical care until the nineteenth century, with the growth of the voluntary hospitals, and the available evidence suggests that women continued to rely on informal knowledge in areas such as birth control and abortion until well into the twentieth century.

A key question that has concerned feminists is how men came to usurp women's traditional role as healers. It seems unlikely that this happened because men's skills and knowledge were superior, as there is little evidence that qualified doctors had effective treatments to apply before this century, although the claims made by male medical men that they had superior skills may have been believed by some patients. Also, the ability to afford the high fees charged by physicians may have been a way of achieving and maintaining a high status in middle-class society.

Ehrenreich and English (1979) have suggested a link between the campaigns against witches that occurred in Europe between the fourteenth and seventeenth centuries and the suppression of female healing. They argue that women healers were singled out to be executed as witches and that thousands of women peasant healers were seen as part of a subversive social movement threatening the (male) authority of Church, Crown, the aristocracy, and the few university-trained physicians. However, there is no clear evidence that all or even most women healers were regarded as witches during this period, and indeed there is considerable evidence that unqualified women healers continued to practise in England after the witch-hunts had ceased.

Other feminists have argued that the changes that accompanied the Industrial Revolution were a major factor in men achieving control and dominance in medical practice. Alice Clark (1919) argued that the displacement of women healers by qualified medical guilds (the precursors of the Royal Colleges) was part of the process whereby skilled workers in general moved out of the family into the market-place and excluded the unskilled and unqualified from practice. Margaret Versluysen (1981) also points to the development of hospitals. Before the eighteenth century, medical men treated only the wealthy, in their own homes. By the end of the eighteenth century hospitals had begun to be built in the growing towns. These hospitals were built with charitable money donated by the wealthy for the exclusive use of working-class patients. In them, medical men began to treat 'charity' patients who were their 'inferiors'. Doctors were therefore able to develop and test new ideas on these patients. At the same time the growth of the middle class meant that there was an increase in the number of fee-paying patients for doctors to treat at home. The growth in clientele and the claims to new scientific knowledge provided a base from which qualified doctors pressed for the banning of their unqualified female rivals.

Witz (1985) has argued that the ways in which medical men struggled to establish and sustain a sexually segregated division of labour provides an example of social closure and demarcation (and that they were aided in applying this closure by the state) – closure in that women were excluded from practising medicine, and demarcation in that doctors defined what was medical work and therefore the preserve of medical men and what was ancillary and could be carried out by female nurses and midwives. In 1858 the Medical Act established the exclusive male prerogative. The Act defined a person who could practise medicine as one who was a *qualified* medical practitioner by virtue of possessing a British university degree or a licentiate, membership, or fellowship of one of the medical corporations. The Act did not exclude women in itself, but women were not allowed in practice to go to universities or become members of medical corporations.

The exclusion of women from medical practice was challenged by women who conducted a protracted struggle to gain admittance to the medical profession. The first qualified female medical practitioner to practice in Britain was Elizabeth Blackwell, who qualified at an American medical school in 1849. Elizabeth Garrett (Anderson) qualified in 1865 with the Society of Apothecaries, the only medical corporation not explicitly excluding women. However, the society immediately changed its rules so that the same could not happen again.

Women campaigned to be allowed to qualify as doctors on the basis of equal rights claims – a common demand of feminists in the nineteenth century and based on the dominant liberal political philosophy (see Chapter eight). Women also argued that women and children should have the right to be treated by a woman doctor. They had to gain the support of male members of Parliament to introduce legislation. In 1875 an Enabling Bill was passed, permitting universities and medical corporations to admit women, but this did not force them to do so. (In 1899 an Act of Parliament removed all the remaining legal barriers to women training as doctors, so that they had in theory to be admitted to training, but the *de facto* barriers remained.) In the late 1870s Sophia Jex-Blake and other women established the London School of Medicine for Women. However, even when women were admitted to medical training and became qualified medical practitioners, they tended to confine their practice almost exclusively to women and children, working in hospitals or in dispensaries they themselves established, or as medical missionaries.

While women won the right to train as doctors and practise medicine, it continued to be a male-dominated profession. There has been a steady increase in the number of women training as doctors and in the proportion of female to male medical students; nevertheless the high-status jobs continue to go to men. Female general practitioners argue that they are frequently expected to look after women and children, yet they want to deal with the full range of patients and medical complaints dealt with by general practitioners (see also Chapter six).

Nurses, midwives, and medical men

A key feature of health care is the dominance and control that doctors exercise over paramedical workers, including midwives and nurses, a position that is sustained through state support (Johnson, 1972; Larkin, 1983). Nursing was established as a profession supplementary to medicine (Gamarnikow, 1978), and the Midwifery Act of 1903, which required that only registered midwives be permitted to practise, placed them finally under medical control. Hearn (1982) has argued that the process of professionalization is a process of male assumption of control over female tasks. Thus, as male doctors acquire the status of a profession they not only exclude female healers from practising but gain control over other female workers, who take on a subordinate role in the medical division of labour.

Women healers retained control over childbirth for a much longer period than they did over healing generally, but even in midwifery they began from the 1660s to have their dominant role challenged by male midwives (obstetricians). It is possible that the origins of male midwifery relate to the invention of the obstetric forceps, or more simply that it was just another example of males attempting to take over a field previously dominated by females. However, there was opposition to male midwifery – first, from the general public, who thought it indecent, second, from female midwives because of the threat to their livelihood, and third, from established medical men who saw it as degrading women's work and not part of medicine at all.

The invention of the obstetric forceps was certainly an important breakthrough; prior to their invention, an obstetric delay (slow birth) resulted in the death of the mother and/or the child. The use of them was restricted to barber–surgeons and therefore to men, and the number of cases helped was small and the risk of infection and death as a result of their use was enormous. The growth of the laying-in hospitals where male midwives delivered women also played a role in raising the status of male midwifery, especially as women were excluded from the scientific knowledge they claimed to have. Probably more important was the fact that from the seventeenth century a fashion gradually developed for the wealthy to use male midwives, giving support to the male midwives' claim that their knowledge was superior to that of female midwives. This was supported by the argument that only the male midwives could do surgery if complications should arise.

It was in the late nineteenth century that medical doctors accepted that midwifery should be undertaken and controlled by men. During the nineteenth century the Colleges of Physicians and Surgeons both argued against doctors' involvement in midwifery, but by 1850 lectures in midwifery were being given in British medical schools and by 1866 proficiency in it was necessary for qualification as a medical practitioner. The claim by doctors to control childbirth was made on the basis that medical men had superior knowledge: 'By 1880 a great advance had been made in the science and art of midwifery. This was due chiefly to the introduction of male practitioners, many of whom were men of learning and devoted to anatomy, the groundwork of obstetrics' (Spicer, 1927, quoted in Oakley, 1980: 11). This claim was not justified on medical grounds. In the nineteenth century a quarter of women giving birth in hospital died of puerperal fever, and those delivered at home were more likely to be infected if they were attended by a male doctor rather than a female midwife. (Puerperal fever is an infection transmitted by doctors from other areas, and especially from dead bodies, to women in childbirth.) Nevertheless medical men were determined to gain control of midwifery and to determine the role of female midwives – to establish the division of labour between themselves and the female midwives. Thus they set out to demarcate what areas were rightfully theirs at the same time as defending the medical prerogative. The struggle between medical men and female midwives since the seventeenth century had begun to establish a distinction between *assistance* at childbirth and *intervention* in childbirth – one between normal and abnormal childbirth. Only male doctors (qualified medical practitioners) were allowed to use forceps and to intervene surgically.

The Midwifery Registration Act of 1902 resulted in the registration and education of midwives coming under the control of medical men, and a doctor had to be called in if anything went wrong with a delivery. A major reason why doctors did not usurp the role of midwives was that they realized that there was no way in which they could meet the demand – in the late nineteenth century seven out of every nine births were attended by female midwives. Also, many doctors did not want to attend poor women. Doctors thus deskilled midwives, and while female midwives continued to attend poor women in childbirth, doctors attended the wealthy. Medical domination of childbirth continues in the late twentieth century, and indeed it could be argued that it has increased, because the majority of births are in hospital under the (official) control of a consultant, and because of the increased use of medical technology. While most women are actually delivered by a (female) midwife, the ultimate control remains in the hands of the (generally male) obstetrician.

Nurses, too, play a subordinate role in the medical division of labour. Nursing has always been, and continues to be, a predominantly female province. Most nursing is, of course, done by women, as unpaid carers in the domestic sphere. However, nursing in the public sphere is also predominantly a female occupation. While caring for the sick was undertaken in a variety of institutions in the past, it was not until the middle of the nineteenth century that nursing emerged as a separate occupation. Prior to that, nursing in hospitals was seen as a form of domestic work that required little specific training and was usually undertaken by married women, doing little different for their patients than they did for their families at home. The demarcation between nurses and patients was blurred – able-bodied convalescent patients were expected to help the nurses with the domestic work on the wards. Florence Nightingale suggested that in the mid-nineteenth century, nursing was mainly done by those 'who were too old, too weak, too drunken, too dirty, too sordid or too bad to do anything else' (quoted in Abel-Smith, 1960, p. 53). The argument that nurses needed training, and the recognition by doctors that bedside medicine meant that patients needed monitoring, developed before Florence Nightingale's reforms. However, she did attempt to develop nursing as a profession and to recruit middle-class women, who received a training. These reforms took place in the voluntary hospitals, and it was not until late in the nineteenth century that nurses in workhouse hospitals were trained.

While Florence Nightingale recognized the need for trained nurses, she trained them in obedience, so that in the division of labour between nurses and doctors, nurses were seen and saw themselves as the subordinates of doctors and as under medical control. Nor did Nightingale challenge the link between womanhood and nursing. Gamarnikow

(1978) has pointed out that in the Nightingale model nurses were still responsible for the cleaning of the wards as well as the care of the patients. She suggests that the relationship between doctor and nurse paralleled the relationship between the Victorian husband and wife in the family. The nurse looked after the physical and emotional environment, while the doctor decided what the really important work was and how it should be done. Thus the good nurse was the good mother, concerned with caring for her patients (family).

In the twentieth century, while nurses no longer see themselves as handmaidens of doctors, they have remained trapped in their status as subordinate to doctors. In 1918 the Nursing Register was introduced, and the Nurses Act 1943 established state enrolled nurses as well as state registered ones, but neither kind is recognized as independent practitioners. Anne Williams (1987) has argued that the subordinate role of nurses is exemplified in the ways drugs are administered in hospitals:

> ...doctors prescribe drugs and nurses administer drugs. Here is an example of nurses as 'handmaidens' to doctors. They have no say in prescribing drugs. They are not authorised to prescribe what they give. Yet they are accountable for what they give, how much, etc, etc.
>
> (Williams, 1987: 107)

while Ann Oakley (1984b) confessed:

> In a fifteen-year career as a sociologist studying medical services, I confess that I have been particularly blind to the contribution made by nurses to health care. Indeed, over a period of some months spent observing in a large London hospital I hardly noticed nurses at all. I took their presence for granted (much as, I imagine, the doctors and patients did).
>
> (Oakley, 1984b: 24)

Nursing in the late twentieth century is seen predominantly as a lowly paid female occupation, but there are clear ethnic and class divisions in nursing. The three grades of nursing – auxiliaries, state enrolled, and state registered – form a clear hierarchy with little or no possibility of training to move up the qualification hierarchy. Women from ethnic minorities are concentrated in the auxiliary and state enrolled grades, and white middle-class women in the registered grade in the prestigious teaching hospitals. Furthermore, more men are entering nursing, and the new managerial structures introduced in the 1970s have resulted in a disproportionately large number of men appointed to management posts. Although men have been able to become general nurses only since 1943, they have increasingly moved into senior posts in what was once, as far as the nursing of physical illness was concerned, an all-woman and woman-managed occupation (see Chapter six).

Women, motherhood, and 'informal' care

Women are seen as primarily responsible for maintaining the health of their families, and as informal, unpaid carers they play a major role in caring for the sick, the disabled, the elderly, and other dependent groups. Hilary Graham (1985) argues that women are providers of informal health care in the domestic economy and that this role is shaped by the sexual division of labour, such that men are seen as providers and women as carers, and by the spatial division of labour, where the local community is seen as the setting for routine medical care and centrally located institutions of medicine for the application of specialist medical skills. Graham suggests that there are three aspects to women's health work: providing for health, teaching for health, and mediating professional help in times of crisis. Thus she argues that much routine domestic labour and caring is about health maintenance, while women are seen as responsible for the health education of their children and are generally the ones who decide whether it is necessary to consult a doctor and indeed take the children to the consultation.

The welfare state was built on the assumption that the traditional nuclear family was the norm and that women would care and provide for the members of this family. As is pointed out in Chapter six, more recent policies of community care are built on the assumption that women are prepared to care for dependent members of their families (including the wider, extended family). The Health Education Council's 'Look after Yourself' campaign in the early 1980s was also directed at women, assuming that they wanted to care for and look after the health of their men and children.

Women are also blamed when their families are seen as unhealthy. They are seen as responsible for bringing up healthy children and maintaining the health of their men for the nation. Health visitors, social workers, and other professional state employees 'police' the family to ensure that women are adequately carrying out their task. Since the early twentieth century motherhood has been a medical domain not just in terms of ante-natal care and delivery, but in terms of bringing up healthy children. When, in the early twentieth century, considerable concern was expressed about the poor health of the working class, made visible in public by the poor state of men volunteering to enlist in the army at the time of the Boer War, the blame was placed on negligent mothers. It was argued that women should put caring for their families first, should give up paid employment and be trained in domestic skills and child care. The Government advocated the employment by local authorities of trained health visitors under the control of the District Medical Officers, building on the voluntary movement that had developed in the nineteenth century which visited the houses of working-class families with young children. Scant attention was paid to the poverty and the appalling conditions in which working-class women were struggling to bring up their children and the poor health experienced by most of these women. The available evidence suggests that, then, as now, women put the needs and demands of their families first and gave little consideration to their own needs.

While it is rarely given official recognition, and the tendency is to see paid health workers as the primary providers of health care, women provide most health care, within the confines of the family. The unpaid, rarely recognized, health care work of women in the domestic sphere is extensive. The welfare state is built on the assumption that women will perform this work and that women naturally want to care for their partners and their children.

While feminists are correct in arguing that male medical men have usurped women's role as healers in the public sphere, women continue to have the major role in the private sphere. However, women are under medical dominance and control in the medical division of labour, whether they are paid workers in the public sphere or unpaid workers in the domestic one.

Summary

1 Women are some of the main workers in the health services. The medical services are highly segregated by gender, with employment such as nursing associated with feminine roles – caring, nurturing, domestic work, and so on – being associated with female workers while high-status posts associated with specific expertise, such as consultancies, are associated with male professionals.
2 Women are the main consumers of health services because:
   a they are responsible for the health of the family and are likely to see the doctor on the family's behalf;
   b women are themselves more likely to suffer from a variety of ailments;
   c women live longer than men.
3 Western medicine is defined according to masculine models of health and illness. It is not concerned with the well-being of the individual but rather with curing disease.
4 Women are more likely to be the informal carers and the ones responsible for health outside of the formal services – for example, treating the illnesses of family members.

Further reading

Black Report (1978) *A Report of a Royal Commission on Health Inequalities*, London: HMSO.
Roberts, H. (1985) *The Patient Patients: women and their doctors*, London: Pandora.
Whitehead, M. (1987) *The Health Divide*, London: Health Education Council.

Chapter six

Women's work

Sociologists divide people's lives into 'work' (paid employment), 'leisure' (the time when people choose what they want to do), and 'obligation time' (the periods of sleep, eating meals, and other necessary activities). Feminists have pointed out that this model reflects a male view of the world and does not fit the experiences of the majority of women. This is partly because unremunerated domestic labour is not recognized as work, and partly because married women participate in few leisure activities outside the home. Most studies of paid employment have been of men – coal-miners, affluent assembly-line workers, and male clerks – and the findings from these studies have formed the hard data on which general theories about all workers' attitudes and behaviours have been based. Even where women have been included in samples, it is assumed that their attitudes and behaviours differ little from men's, or married women have been seen as working for 'pin money', paid employment being seen as relatively unimportant in their lives as they are assumed to identify primarily with their domestic roles as wives.

A growing body of feminist research both challenges these assumptions and provides more detailed information on women as workers. Feminists have argued that domestic labour is work and should be regarded as such. They have also maintained that the majority of women do not take on paid employment 'for pin money' but from necessity, and that paid work is seen as meeting important emotional and identity needs by many women. This does not mean that women's experiences of paid employment are the same as men's, however, nor that their attitudes and values are identical.

The sexual division of labour

All societies have a division of labour based on sex – work that is seen as women's work and work that is seen as men's work. However, the nature of the work that is done by men or women varies from society to

121

society and has changed historically in our own society. In almost all societies the care of babies and young children is seen as women's work, but in many societies men take on the task of caring for young boys, in others older children generally look after younger ones, and in others again the older women care for the children. Cooking is mainly seen as women's work, except the preparation of feasts and ceremonial meals which is frequently seen as men's work. In many, but not all, societies hunting and fishing is regarded as men's work, but planting and harvesting is frequently undertaken by women either alone or alongside men. Women, in many societies, are responsible for the care of livestock. On the basis of this evidence Ann Oakley (1982) has suggested that the sexual division of labour is socially constructed and not based on natural sex differences. Jobs become identified as men's jobs or as women's jobs.

In Britain, following the Industrial Revolution, work became separated from the home, and work done in the public sphere – paid work – became more highly valued than unpaid work done in the domestic sphere. Women became seen as those who were 'naturally good' at domestic work and caring, and men as the providers – those in paid employment in the public sphere. Male trade unionists, employers, and the state were able to restrict women's paid employment and exclude them from certain occupations. Consequently, men were able to define the conditions and rules of the game, so that for women to succeed in the male world of paid work it is necessary for them to play the same game. In order to have a career, to be seen as promotable, women have to be prepared to work full time and to have no 'career breaks'. Even then, women face problems because they are likely to be excluded from the informal world – drinking in bars, pubs, and clubs – and not to have a 'wife' to entertain for them and look after the home. It is not just the problem of getting promoted, however, that women face. Women are often refused training, and recruited on the assumption or given work experience on the basis that they do not want a career because they will have career breaks – because their main role is as wives and mothers. In manual work, 'skill' is socially constructed, so that jobs that involve tasks associated with masculine expertise – such as driving – are seen as more skilled than jobs that involve feminine dexterity – such as sewing.

Both men and women believe that work is less important for women than for men and that men should have higher wages and more secure employment because of their role of supporting the family. Men are seen as 'bread-winners' whereas women are seen as domestic carers. There is no necessary reason why this should be the case. It would be quite possible for men and women to be seen equally as responsible for the economic support of the household and for the necessary domestic labour and child care. Indeed, there is a gap between the ideology that a woman's place is in the home and the reality for many women who have paid employment. However, the ideology still has real consequences for married women; most assume, as do their husbands, employers, and the state, that even if they have paid employment they are still solely or primarily responsible for child care and domestic labour. This ideology is so pervasive, so much a part of our taken-for-granted common sense, that it is rarely questioned or challenged. It has important consequences for the type of paid employment that most married women seek and are offered. It influences the type of occupations that young women enter on leaving school, not only because of their own aspirations but also what career officers, their parents, school, and employers see as suitable for them (see Chapter three).

Employers clearly have views of what is appropriate work for women, and women generally share these views (Chaney, 1981; Yeandle, 1984; Massey, 1983; Beechey and Perkins, 1982). Many 'female' occupations are clearly regarded as using the 'natural' abilities women require in the domestic sphere – caring for young children, nursing, preparing and serving food, and so on. Much of the growth of part-time work in the recent restructuring of the labour market is dependent on the needs of women with domestic responsibilities to take on paid employment even if the pay is low and the conditions of employment poor (Land, 1982; Beechey and Perkins, 1986). Obviously these assumptions are not only sexist but also frequently untrue. Not all women marry. Many (including some who do marry) have a life-long commitment to the labour market (Dex, 1987; Martin and Roberts, 1984). Many women work out of economic necessity, not for extras (Land, 1978).

A history of women and employment

An analysis of the history of women's work reveals a complex relationship between work in the home and in the labour market. In pre-industrial Britain there was no clear separation between work and the home; economic production was not concentrated in factories, offices, and other places of employment. Most people worked in, or near, the home. Nor was there a gendered separation between productive work and unproductive work. All work was seen as contributing to the maintenance of the household, although some tasks were seen as men's and some as women's. However, with the Industrial Revolution in the nineteenth century, paid employment became separated from the home – in factories, offices, and so on. Men, women, and children (at least in the working class) went out to work. Production and consumption, productive and unproductive (domestic) work became separated, and

123

gradually men became associated with the former and women with the latter. Women were excluded from paid employment, and it became seen as 'natural' that women, or at least married women, should stay at home and care for their children. (Most nineteenth-century and early twentieth-century feminists accepted this and argued for women having a choice – the choice between paid employment and marriage.) What aroused concern in the nineteenth century was not whether or not women should work – women's work in the domestic sphere and the home caused no concern. It was the public appearance of wage-earning working women that produced hostile comments. Working wives and mothers in particular were regarded as unnatural, immoral, and neg-ligent home-makers and parents. They were also accused of taking work from men.

This concern was underpinned by a developing domestic ideology which was formed among the middle class between 1780 and 1830 and gradually spread to all classes and to both sexes. The ideology main-tained that the world was divided into two separate spheres, the public and the domestic. Men should be involved in the public sphere of work and politics, making money and supporting their families (Davidoff *et al.*, 1976). Women should stay at home in the domestic sphere, caring for their children and husbands, and dependent on their husbands for financial support.

Although many single and even married working-class women had to work, by the end of the nineteenth century they would not have expected to be lifelong workers and generally shared the domestic ideal. Married women believed that their primary commitment was to their families and worked only when this was essential for the maintenance of the family; while 25 per cent of married women worked according to the Census of 1851, this had fallen to 10 per cent by 1901. However, poverty did drive many married women to work, and it is estimated that in the period 1890 to 1940, when the Census recorded 10 per cent of married women as working, 40 per cent worked at some time during their married lives. It is also probable that the Census underestimated women's employment, partly because of the nature of it – for example, domestic service, taking in washing – and partly because of the in-creased status of a man who earned enough to support his wife and children, so that men might have been reluctant to record their wives as working on the Census forms. However, female participation in the labour market was quite high because the majority of single women worked and they comprised as many as one in four women at some points in the nineteenth century. In 1871, 31 per cent of women aged over 10 years were in employment, and in 1931, 34 per cent of women over 14 were in employment. (The school leaving age was 10 in 1871 and 14 by 1931).

By the end of the nineteenth century women had become segregated into a small range of lowly paid, low-status occupations. The low pay of women is partly explained by the comparative youth of female workers, as most women gave up employment on marriage. The male trade unions kept women out of higher-paid jobs and fought for a family wage for men – that is, one sufficient for the support of a non-working wife and children. Even when women did the same work as men they did not receive the same pay. Equal pay for male and female teachers, for example, was not fully implemented until 1962. The state also played a role in 'creating' occupational segregation and making men more desirable as employees. Restrictive legislation, supposedly introduced to protect women, also excluded them from certain occupations, restricted the hours they could work, and set the hours between which they could work. The Mines Act 1884 forbade women to work underground, but women were still able to work above ground as pit-brow girls. The protection afforded by legislation did not extend to housework, or to domestic servants, or to preventing women doing dirty and dangerous work in agriculture, for example.

Most men saw working women and especially married working women as a threat to their own paid employment and status as breadwinners. They argued that there was only a limited amount of paid employment, and if women were allowed to work then some families would be left without an income. Women were also thought to lower the level of wages in general because they could work for less than men. Consequently, it was argued that women should be excluded from paid employment or confined to low-status, lowly paid jobs – women's jobs. The trade unions were dominated by men and were concerned to protect men's conditions and wages. Women were prevented or discouraged from joining trade unions, and in any case trade unions were seen as not concerned with representing women's interests. Thus the protective legislation could be said to be designed as much to protect male workers from female competition as to protect women.

Not all women were passive. Women at all levels fought for the right to participate equally with men in paid employment. Women, for example, fought for the right to go to university and qualify as medical doctors. Women formed their own trade unions and fought against the conditions of their employment. A notable example of this is the Match Girl Strike. However, on the whole, men, the trade unions, and the state succeeded in creating a segregated labour market, and the domestic ideology was generally accepted by the end of the nineteenth century by men and women in all social classes. Although women worked in large numbers during the First World War, they accepted that after the war men should have priority in the labour market. Many employers, including banks and the Government, operated a marriage bar, so that women had to give up employment on marriage; the marriage bar on female teachers was not removed until the 1944 Education Act. Since the Second World War increasing numbers of women have taken on paid employment, especially married women. However, despite the Equal Pay and Equal Opportunities legislation, a segregated labour market persists and domestic ideology is pervasive.

Domestic labour

Understanding women's role as unpaid domestic workers is crucial to understanding women's position in modern Britain and their role in the labour market. However, it is only recently that housework has become a topic of serious academic concern. Functionalist sociologists argued that it was necessary for women to undertake the physical and mental servicing of men in complex industrial societies. Marxists argued similarly that this was necessary in capitalist societies; women were responsible for the reproduction of labour power – both for the bearing and rearing of children and the mental and physical refreshing of employees. While both Marxists and functionalists argued that domestic labour was a private 'labour of love', the Marxists pointed out the ways in which it related to the economic system of employees – ensuring that there was a continuing supply of well serviced workers to meet the demands of capitalism.

The view that domestic labour is the responsibility of women is also widely held by the British people. In a national survey in 1984 it was found that a majority of people thought that women have more responsibility for domestic labour than men. Women were also found to be solely responsible for most domestic tasks: 88 per cent for washing and ironing, 77 per cent for providing an evening meal, 72 per cent for house-cleaning and 63 per cent for looking after schoolchildren (*Social Trends* 16, 1986, Table 2.12 on page 36). Despite an increased participation of men in domestic work, women retain the responsibility for most work in the home (see Chapter five).

Feminists have examined empirically what housewives actually do and have developed theories that explain the relationship of housework to the social structure and the economy in general. All feminists have argued that housework is hard, physically demanding work and that the notion of the weak housewife has developed because housework is hidden from public view and done out of affection and duty rather than for payment.

The vast majority of housewives are women. According to Ann Oakley (1974a), 76 per cent of all employed and 93 per cent of non-employed women are housewives. Housework is seen as women's work and it is assumed that women will do it if they live in the household. The general assumption is that women can do domestic tasks naturally and men cannot. Furthermore, Oakley argued that the refusal to acknowledge that housework is *work* is both a reflection and a cause of women's generally low status in society. She argues that housework is largely underrated, unrecognized, unpaid work that is not regarded as 'real' work. However, domestic labour involves long hours of work: in 1971, in Oakley's sample, women did 77 hours a week on average. The lowest was 48 hours, done by a woman who also had a full-time job, and the highest was 105 hours (Oakley, 1974a).

Oakley (1974a, 1974b) studied housework within the framework of the sociology of work. She spoke in depth to forty mothers in London aged between 20 and 30. The majority of them were full-time housewives, and half had husbands in working-class occupations and half in middle-class ones. The women described housework in terms similar to the way in which male assembly-line workers have described their work, reporting even more monotony, fragmentation of tasks and excessive speed of work than the assembly-line workers in Luton (Goldthorpe *et al*, 1969). However, unlike male manual work, domestic labour is not closely supervised and is performed largely on the basis of personal rather than contractual relationships. It is unpaid, with no fixed remuneration linked to the hours put in or the quantity or quality of the goods or services produced. Women got little pleasure from housework as work, although working-class women invested more in the role and searched for satisfaction in it. Overall the nature of the tasks included in domestic labour were rated negatively even among women who claimed to be satisfied as housewives. Seventy per cent were dissatisfied with the role, the commonest complaint being loneliness. Autonomy was the most valued aspect – the control over one's own pace of work – and the women set themselves routines and standards of work to which they forced themselves to adhere. Oakley suggests three explanations for this task-setting strategy:

1 it was one way of gaining a reward from housework tasks – a woman gained satisfaction if she reached her own 'high' standards;
2 self-imposed standards were a way of emphasising the housewife's autonomy;
3 it was a method of overcoming the fragmentary nature of housework and imposing a unity on it.

However, Oakley argues that these self-imposed rules come to take on an objectivity, become seen as external and actually diminish the autonomy and control that women have, by enslaving them to what were originally their own standards.

127

Domestic labour, then, is seen by feminists as real work. They also argue that the demands of housework, and the economic and personal conditions under which it is performed, mitigate against the formation of a sense of solidarity among women. Domestic labour is a solitary activity, and women are bound to housework by ties of love and identification. Women like to feel reasonably good about their domestic work; in the absence of clear standards or the praise of employers, women tend to use other women as the standard against which to measure their own performance in a competitive way. Housework consequently tends to divide women rather than to unite them.

Explaining the division of labour in the domestic sphere

Radical feminists argue that all men derive benefit from the expectation that women will perform domestic labour. Men work to earn a living and expect not only an income from their employment but personal service from a wife at a cost to themselves of less than the market value of the goods and services provided. Delphy (1977) argues that gender inequalities derive from the ways in which husbands appropriate their wives' labour. The wife does not receive an equitable return for the domestic labour and child care she does for her husband. Delphy argues not only that domestic labour is work just as much as factory labour is work, but also that it is provided in a distinct 'mode of production' – the domestic mode. In the domestic mode of production the husband appropriates the labour power of his wife; in return for the economic support provided by husbands, women are expected to provide domestic services. The marriage contract is a labour contract the terms of which only become fully apparent when it is alleged that the wife has failed to fulfil her side of the bargain. According to the radical feminists, men benefit from the unpaid labour of women in the domestic sphere, and therefore they have a vital interest in maintaining the sexual division of labour. Consequently men resist equal opportunities legislation, support policies that protect men's privileged position in the labour market and 'allow' their wives to work – but still expect them to do the housework (see Chapter nine).

Marxist feminists argue that it is the capitalist system that benefits from the unpaid domestic labour of women. (Socialist feminists argue that the benefit goes both to men as individuals and to the system as a whole.) Not only does women's domestic labour reproduce the relations of production, but it also contributes to the maintenance of tolerable living standards for men and may reduce political pressure for radical change. Women expend considerable effort and energy stretching the household income and maintaining the household's standard of living.

In the 1970s a number of attempts were made to specify the place of household/domestic labour within the capitalist system. The primary focus was on the relationship between domestic labour and capital. This work has become known as 'the domestic labour debate'. Marxists have tried to develop theory to account for domestic labour. Wally Secombe (1974) argued that domestic labour is work, and although it is 'invisible' because it is not paid work, it should be counted as part of the capitalist system of production, because it enables capitalists to increase their exploitation of male labour and hence surplus value. Without it the capitalist system would collapse, because domestic labour constitutes a free service which if it were provided at market rates would be an additional expense. The exploiter of women, then, is the capitalist who extracts surplus value from their unremunerated labour. Other Marxists have suggested that domestic labour produces only 'use-value' for immediate consumption, but in doing so enables capitalists to pay workers lower wages.

There are a number of problems with this perspective, since domestic work is not fully equivalent to work outside the home in that it is not subject to measurement, control, or rates of payment in the same way. Rather, it is done out of a sense of love, obligation, and duty, so the relationships are different. The major problem with Marxist theories is that they fail to take account of men's interest in perpetuating women's role as domestic labourer. Also, they tend to derive women's oppression from capitalism, whereas women's oppression predates capitalism. The radical feminists, on the other hand, tend to ignore the benefits that capitalists derive from women's domestic labour and their accounts tend to be descriptive rather than explanatory. Also, they assume that it is men who benefit from the unpaid labour of women, but employers also benefit, as well as other dependent groups.

Women's unpaid 'caring' work

Women's unpaid labour extends beyond what is generally seen as housework. Women are expected to care not only for their husbands and children, but also for other dependents, and in a voluntary capacity for people generally in the community. Women are also frequently seen as necessary to their husbands' work role. As Janet Finch (1983a) has demonstrated, this extends beyond the wives of managers and business-men who are expected to entertain for their husbands. Men in many occupations 'need' a wife, and the employer benefits from this labour. Finch refers to the village policeman's wife who not only manages a police home but substitutes for him, to the doctor's wife, the clergy-man's wife, and so on. Goffee and Scase (1985) have suggested that wives play a vital role in helping self-employed husbands, who are often heavily dependent on the (unpaid) clerical and administrative duties undertaken by their wives. Wives are often forced to abandon their own careers to underwrite the efforts of the 'self-made' man. Furthermore, given the long hours self-employed men work, wives are left to cope single-handed with the children and the domestic chores. Sallie Westwood and Parminder Bhachu (1988b) have pointed to the importance of the labour (unpaid) of female relations in the ethnic business community – although they also point out that setting up a business may be a joint strategy of husband and wife.

Women are also expected to care for relations who cannot look after themselves. Policies of community care that have been advocated by successive governments since the 1950s have a hidden agenda for women. Such policies, which involve closing down or not providing large-scale residential care for the mentally handicapped, the mentally ill, physically handicapped people, and the elderly, have frequently assumed that women are prepared to take on the care of dependent relatives. While it is generally suggested that 'the family' should care where possible, in practice it is women who perform the care. It is generally assumed that it is part of a woman's role and that women are natural carers; that carers should be women is an unquestioned assumption.

While it is probably true that many women take on the caring role relatively willingly, it none the less radically alters their lives. Michael Bayley (1973), in a study of the family care of mentally handicapped children in Sheffield, argued that community care means in reality care by mothers. In a study of 44 married couples caring for an elderly dependent relative, Nissel and Bonnerjea (1982), found that wives spent on average two to three hours a day doing essential care for the relative, whether or not they were in employment. (Husbands spent on average eight minutes a day.) Abbott and Sapsford (1987b) found that in families with a mentally handicapped child the mother took on most of the responsibility for the child, with, if anything, *less* help from the community than received by mothers of other children. Abbott (1982) has suggested that 'normalizing' life for mentally handicapped people de-normalizes it for 'Mum'. Married women who have to care for a relative can no longer look forward to the time when the children are older, when they can have more freedom to develop their own lives, return to paid employment and enjoy a measure of economic freedom. The physical and mental demands of the caring role combine with the expectation that, where necessary, the carer will cover 24 hours per day, seven days a week. Even when day care or schooling is provided the carer is not freed; she has to be there to see the child/elderly person on the transport and be at home when the dependant is returned.

What is at stake is not just the loss of potential earnings estimated at an average of £8700 a year (Nissel and Bonnerjea, 1982) or the amount of labour involved – worth £47.50 a week in 1980 terms – but the fact that women are trapped in the domestic sphere. Janet Finch and Dulcie Groves (1980) have argued that in the context of public expenditure cuts, policies of community care are incompatible with equal opportunities for women, because community care means care by the family, which in practice means care by women. Processes of labour market segmentation mean that most women cannot earn as much as their husbands, making it economically non-viable for the men to give up their jobs even if they were prepared to take on the caring role. Nor would the provision of additional services radically alter the situation; more provision of day care, respite care, home nursing and the like would ease the immense burden on a woman caring for a dependent relative, but it would not liberate her from the domestic sphere nor from her responsibilities for taking on the main burden of caring.

Summary

1 Women do substantial amounts of unpaid work in the home, and this is concealed by the fact that it is assumed to be part of their 'natural' function.

2 The work women do in the home as housewives – partly in maintaining the domestic dwelling and partly in caring for the other family members (husbands, children, other dependants) – is different from that done in the paid economy. Although all the same services could be bought outside the home, within the home they are provided out of 'love' and 'duty' rather than for a wage.

3 There is some debate as to who benefits from this unpaid and hidden work. Marxist feminists argue that capitalism benefits economically from housework in terms of improved profits. Radical feminists argue that men are the main beneficiaries.

Women and paid employment

There has been a steady increase in women's rate of participation in the labour market in Britain during the twentieth century, especially in their part-time employment. The most dramatic rise has occurred in the participation rates of married women, since the Second World War. Familial ideology may see a woman's primary role as that of wife and mother, but the majority of women (including married women) have paid employment for the majority of the years during which they are employable. According to the 1981 Census women formed 40 per cent

131

of the labour force, though with substantial regional and ethnic variations (Stone, 1983; Massey, 1983).

In 1986 in Great Britain there was a civilian labour force of 26.7 million people, of whom 11.2 millions (41.9 per cent) were women. In the same year 49.2 per cent of women over the age of 16 were economically active (that is, in employment or registered as unemployed). However, there were marked variations in economic activity rate by age, with about 70 per cent of women aged 16 to 54 economically active but only 51.7 per cent of those aged 55 to 60 and 6.5 per cent of those older than 60, the effective retirement age for women in 1986 (see Table 6.1). These figures may be an underestimate, because women who have casual employment or are homeworkers may not be recorded, and women who are unemployed and seeking work may not be registered as unemployed.

Table 6.1 Proportions of men and women in employment in 1986, by age

Age:	16–19	20–24	25–44	45–54/59	55/60–59/64	60/65+
Men	73.7	84.5	94.0	88.0	53.4	7.5
Women	71.1	69.2	67.2	70.2	51.7	6.5

Source: Social Trends 18.

Married women are less likely to be in employment than those who are not married. In 1985, of married women aged 16 to 59 with husbands aged 16 to 64, 63 per cent were economically active, with 32 per cent working part time. There are also variations between women from different ethnic backgrounds, both in participation in the labour market and in whether they engage in full-time or part-time work (see Table 6.2). Afro–Caribbean women and non-Muslim Asians are more likely to be in the labour market than white women. Muslim women are less likely to work, but the figures do not take account of the homeworking in which they may engage. Also, Afro–Caribbean and Asian Muslim women are more likely to work full time than white women if they do work. Of white women in employment, 44 per cent are in part-time work, compared to 29 per cent of West Indian women and 16 per cent of Asian women – the figures are derived from the Labour Force Survey for 1984 (*Employment Gazette*, December 1985). It also seems likely that women of West Indian origin are more likely to work while they have young children than are other women. Of women aged 25 to 44, 66 per cent of indigenous white women are economically active, compared with 77 per cent of women of West Indian origin, but only 62 per cent of women of Indian origin (non-Muslim) and 17 per cent of Bangladeshi and Pakistani origin (Muslim).

132

Table 6.2 Economic status of the female population of working age in 1984–6, by ethnic group

Ethnic group		Employed FT	PT	Self-employed	Un-employed	House-wife	Full-time student	Other
White	%	31	24	1	7	22	4	11
West Indian/ Guyanese	%	41	14	–	13	14	9	9
Indian/Pakistani/ Bangladeshi	%	22	7	–	9	41	7	14
Other	%	27	14	–	10	24	12	13

Source: Social Trends 18.

Women are more likely than men to be in non-manual occupations. Sixty-five per cent of women are in non-manual jobs, compared with 46 per cent of men. However, men are more likely than women to be in professional or managerial occupations; 34 per cent of men are in such occupations, compared with 25 per cent of women. Women are more likely to be in routine non-manual (clerical and related) occupations – 80 per cent of employed women are in this type of job, but only 5 per cent of employed men. Within the manual category, men are much more likely than women to be categorized as skilled (craft and similar) workers, 26 per cent of employed men compared with 4 per cent of employed women (*Social Trends* 18, Table 4.13). West Indian and Asian women are more likely than white women to be in unskilled manual work, and West Indian women are less likely than white or Asian women to be in the highest social class (see Table 6.3)

Table 6.3 Job levels of white, West Indian, and Asian women in 1982

Social class (RG)	Ethnic group White	West Indian	Asian
	%	%	%
I	9	1	7
II/IIIN	52	53	35
IIIM	9	3	14
IV	19	36	42
V	11	6	3

Source: Brown (1984) Table 120.

Women's labour-market participation is clearly affected by their domestic responsibilities. It is not so much marriage as having dependent children that conditions participation. Women with young children tend to withdraw from the labour market, to return to part-time work when the children reach school age and to full-time work when the children are older. Not only do a high proportion of women return to paid employment after having children, but many return between births, and the time that women are taking out of the labour market for childbirth and child-rearing is decreasing. Women are spending an increasing proportion of their lives in employment, though very few have continuous full-time careers because of their domestic responsibilities (Martin and Roberts, 1984). Dex (1987) points out that a high proportion of women are permanently attached to the labour force, with a recognizable occupational profile even if they take breaks from employment. She suggests that female teachers, nurses, clerical workers, and skilled, semi-skilled, and unskilled manual workers in factories have lifelong occupational profiles. Women often take on other jobs temporarily, but they generally return eventually to the type of work they did prior to having children.

This does not mean that women's experience of work is the same as men's. The type of work, the hours that women work, and the return that they receive for their labour all differ from men's. Even where women are employed in the same occupation as men and have equal pay, their experiences may differ greatly from men's. Crompton and Sanderson (1986) argue that many married women have semi-professional jobs while their husbands have careers. In many occupations women are found predominantly on the lower rungs while men hold a disproportionate percentage of senior posts – this is most notably the case in teaching, nursing, and social work. However, women and men are frequently concentrated in different jobs, often with men supervising or controlling women. Women often work part time, while the vast majority of men work full time. Women, as a result, often do not enjoy the same conditions of employment as men, or even (if they work less than 16 hours per week) the protection of employment legislation. The most exploited of women are not only without fringe benefits; they also lack seniority and are unlikely to be promoted, and this is the case for part-time professional and managerial employees as well as those further down the occupational scale (Martin and Roberts, 1984). In addition women are more likely than men to be doing homework – producing industrial goods at home – on piece-rates that may work out at as little as £0.40 per hour (Allen and Walkowitz, 1987). It is estimated that there are anything up to half a million homeworkers in Britain, though it is impossible to estimate the exact numbers because much of this work is subcontracted or concealed.

In explaining the patterns of women's labour-market participation, supply factors are obviously important. Women's participation is obviously affected by family responsibilities and especially the existence of dependent children. Studies such as those carried out by Susan Yeandle (1984), Judith Chaney (1981), and Beechey and Perkins (1982) show that women have a clear view of what kinds of job are appropriate and available and that they search for work accordingly. These studies also show that demand-side factors are also important. Employers also have a clear view about what is appropriate work for women, and they work to 'activate' a supply of female labour. Many jobs, especially part-time, lowly paid ones, are created as women's jobs, often with hours to suit women with domestic commitments.

Women's orientation to work

Martin and Roberts (1984) provide some information on women's attitudes to work. They found that social and domestic circumstances had a considerable influence on the way women thought about it. Some, for example, find it difficult to cope with paid work and domestic responsibilities. However, type of job and the employment situation also affected women's orientation to work. Contrary to popular opinion, they found that the majority of women, including married women, were highly dependent financially on their wages from work, and that the majority of women were fully committed to work, but this varied over the life cycle, the most highly committed being childless women older than thirty.

Irrespective of whether they worked full or part time, women thought that the most important aspect of employment was doing 'work you like'. Part-time employees thought 'convenient hours' was equally important but were less likely than full-timers to see pay and job security as important. Part-time employees also stressed having friendly people to work with as important. Both full- and part-time employees gave low priority to the career aspects of the job or the opportunity to use one's abilities, although these were seen as important by younger women and women in full-time work. Women who were forced to work out of economic necessity, who tended to be in low-status, lowly paid jobs, reported a general sense of dissatisfaction with their jobs. Women who worked because they enjoyed working, and were often in more highly paid jobs, reported a higher level of satisfaction.

Feminist studies of women factory workers (e.g. Anna Pollert, 1981; Sallie Westwood, 1984; Ruth Cavendish, 1982) suggest that women's orientation to work is primarily as housewife. Women on the shop floor have a shared culture of romance, marriage, and family. However, studies such as the one by Martin and Roberts (1984), and Oakley's study (1974a, 1974b), demonstrate that paid employment is central to the lives of women employees. Women are expected, however, to cope with the double shift, and this influences their ability to demonstrate total loyalty to the job in the way in which many men can. They have to juggle their responsibilities to their families and to their employers in ways that men rarely have to do.

Women's pay

As we have seen, remuneration from paid employment is important for women, and especially for single women, women who are heads of household, and women in poor families. Women's earnings also give them more economic power in the household and money that is their own. Sallie Westwood and Parminder Bhachu (1988b) argue that female migrants who have not had paid employment prior to coming to Britain gain some power when they make an economic contribution to the household. Presumably this is true for all women, who become less dependent on their husbands when they have an income of their own.

However, women earn less for their labour than men; women's full-time earnings are substantially lower than men's – in 1966 an average of 66.2 per cent of men's (see Table 6.4). The earnings of single women are lower than those of single men; the median take-home pay of single men in 1986 was £127.78, while that of single women was £89.53 (*Social Trends* 18, Table 5.12). The differences in pay between men and women are partly explained by differences in hours worked; men work longer hours and do more overtime. In 1986 men employed in manual work earned on average £25.10 per week for 5.4 hours of overtime, while women on average earned £5.10 for 1.4 hours. (*Social Trends* 18, Table 5.4). However, the major difference lies in occupational segregation, that men and women are concentrated in different occupations, and when in the same job women are in lower-grade posts. In teaching, for example, a third of the discrepancy between the earnings of men and women is explained by the concentration of women in the lower-paying primary sector, and two thirds by the concentration of women in the lower-scale posts (Department of Employment, 1976). In the 1970s, with the implementation of the Equal Pay Act, women's wages did rise as a percentage of men's, but not to equality. Between 1970 and 1977 women's hourly average earnings increased from 63.1 per cent to 75.5 per cent of men's and have subsequently remained at about three quarters of men's.

The differences in pay between men and women are justified on the basis that men do more skilled work than women. However, feminists (e.g. Phillips and Taylor, 1980; Coyle, 1984) have suggested that 'skill' is a socially constructed category.

Table 6.4 Gross weekly earnings of full-time employees in 1986, in pounds

	Male £	Female £	Female as per cent of male
Manual employees	174.4	107.5	61.6
Non-manual	244.9	145.7	59.5
All employees	207.5	137.5	66.2

Source: Social Trends 18, Table 5.3.

Occupational segmentation

Catherine Hakim (1979) has argued that the labour market is segmented horizontally and vertically by gender; women are concentrated in a narrow range of occupations and in lower-status jobs within occupations. Martin and Roberts (1984) found that 63 per cent of women were in jobs done only by women, and 81 per cent of men were in jobs done only by men. Women are also concentrated in a narrow range of occupations. Of the eighteen occupations listed in the New Earnings Survey for 1985 (Part E, Table 135 on pp. 100-5), over 70 per cent of full-time female workers and an even higher proportion of part-time ones are concentrated into just three occupational groupings: clerical work; professional and similar occupations in education, welfare, and health; and personal services. Within these three occupations female employees are even further concentrated into jobs that are generally defined as 'women's work'. In the 'professional and similar occupations in education, welfare, and health', the largest occupation for women is nursing. Women 'personal services' workers are mainly domestic staff and school helpers (98 per cent of whom are women), counter hands and kitchen assistants (92.5 per cent) or cleaners, road sweepers, and caretakers (74.4 per cent). (The figures come from the 1981 Census, *Economic Activity – Great Britain* Table A, pp. xviii-xx.) In 1981, women made up 70 per cent of clerical workers and over three quarters of typists, maids, laundry workers, waitresses, kitchen hands, nurses, canteen workers, charwomen, office cleaners, sewing machinists, and hairdressers. These occupations provided jobs for over 50 per cent of employed women (Equal Opportunities Commission, 1984) – see Table 6.5.

Table 6.5 Sexual divisions within the superstore labour force[1] (numbers)

	Male	Female	Full time	Part time
Managers	16	3	19	–
Supervisors	4	14	14	4
Professonal and technical	–	1	1	–
Sales	38	168	49	152
Clerical	–	8	5	3
Trainees	1	–	1	–
Ancillary	21	9	19	11

Note 1: based on 175 superstores.

Source: Dawson, Findlay, and Sparks (1987) 'Opportunities in superstore retailing' *Equal Opportunities International* 116 :1, 1–5.

Women are more likely than men to be in lowly paid, lower-status jobs within occupational categories as well as in general. Although women are more likely than men to be in non-manual occupation, few are in professional or managerial ones. Those women who are in professional occupations are mainly in the lower-status semi-professional areas like school-teaching, librarianship, nursing, and social work, while men predominate in the higher-status professions of dentistry, accounting, medicine, architecture, and the law. In 1980, for example, 90 per cent of nurses were female (although women held only 70 per cent of senior administrative posts in nursing), while only 17 per cent of medical general practitioners and 0.7 per cent of medical consultants were female (Elston and Doyal, 1983, p. 411). In the Civil Service in 1984, 76 per cent of clerical assistants, 68 per cent of clerical officers, 5 per cent of under secretaries and no permanent secretaries were women (Equal Opportunities Commission, 1985, Figure 4 on p. 281). A similar situation can be found in shop work (see Table 6.6).

Occupations are segmented not only by gender but also by ethnicity. While it seems that the differences in job levels between men and women are more striking than the differences between women from different ethnic origins, nevertheless differences do exist. Annie Phizacklea (1983b) suggests that employment status – that is, working full or part time – rather than race is the crucial variable in determining occupational position. The earnings of men from different ethnic groups are broadly similar. However, white women are over-represented in shop and office work, while women of West Indian origin are over-represented in the Health Service, where they are concentrated in the lowly paid, low-status jobs, and are more likely, if nurses, to be State

Enrolled than State Registered (Doyal *et al*, 1981). Asian women are more likely to work at home or to be shop assistants, secretaries, or factory workers and are often employed within the ethnic economy working for relatives. It is important to recognize that migrant women and their descendants experience racism as well as sexism in the labour market. Black women came to Britain as cheap workers, to work in jobs that native workers did not want to do. Like male migrant workers, they were seen as a source of cheap labour.

Table 6.6 Occupations in which 90 per cent of the employees are of one gender

Predominantly female occupations	Predominantly male occupations
Hand- and machine-sewers and embroiderers	Miners and quarrymen
	Furnace, forge, and foundry workers
Nurses	Electrical and electronics workers (excluding assembly)
Maids, valets, etc.	
Canteen assistants	Engineering trades (excluding assembly)
Typists, secretaries, and shorthand writers	Woodworkers
	Construction workers
	Painters and decorators
	Drivers: stationary engines and cranes
	Drivers: road passenger and goods
	Postmen and mail-sorters
	Butchers and meat-cutters
	Building contractors and labourers
	Groundsmen and gardeners
	Commercial travellers etc.
	Police
	Administrators and managers
	Engineers
	Technical and related workers
	Armed forces

Source: Reid and Wormald (1982), Table 6.10.

Occupational segmentation is even more pronounced in part-time work than in full-time work, and part-time work is generally conducted in lower levels of occupations. Fifty per cent of part-time jobs are in Registrar General's classes IV and V, and part-time workers are more likely than full-time ones to work only with women. Veronica Beechey and Tessa Perkins (1986) have suggested that certain jobs are created as part-time ones because they are seen as women's jobs. Even when women are in part-time occupations that are also done by full-time employees, and in higher-status occupations, they lack opportunities for promotion and training, are less likely than full-time employees to be entitled to holiday or sick pay or to join an occupational pension scheme, and their work is seldom seen as central to the organization or production process (Martin and Roberts, 1984; Beechey and Perkins, 1986).

Women in employment

As with malestream studies of male workers, feminist sociologists have tended to study female *factory* workers, and there is a growing number of ethnographic studies of women in factories. There has also been some attention paid to female office workers and women in the professions. However, there are large gaps and much research still needs to be carried out to fill in our knowledge about women in paid employment.

Women factory workers

A number of studies of factory workers (e.g. Cavendish, 1982; Pollert, 1981; Coyle, 1984; Westwood, 1984) show a similar pattern: women and men working in separate occupations, with men working in jobs classified as skilled and women doing work classified as semi-skilled or unskilled and earning substantially less than men. They all agree that 'skill' is constructed in such a way that it is seen as a characteristic of men's work and not of women's work. Ruth Cavendish (1982), describing a London factory, notes that the complex skills expected of women on the assembly line actually took longer to acquire than those of the male skilled workers. She provides a graphic account of what it is like to do unskilled factory work. The factory in which she worked employed about 1,800 people, of whom 800 worked on the factory floor. Virtually all the women were immigrants – 70 per cent Irish, 20 per cent West Indian, and 10 per cent Asian, mostly from Gujarat in India. She notes that the men enjoyed significantly better working conditions than the women – their jobs enabled them to stop for an occasional cigarette, to move around and to slow down without financial penalty, while the women were tied to the line. Male-dominated trade unions and management worked together to protect the interests of male workers. Women were also frequently supervised by men, so that the women were controlled by men at the workplace.

All the women were semi-skilled assemblers with very few exceptions. Men, on the other hand, were spread throughout the grades and were divided from each other by differences of skill and pay. Even in the machine shop, where men and women worked together on the same job, the men were paid at a higher rate than the women on the grounds that they could lift the heavy coils of metal and the women could not. While young men were trained as chargehands, the young women were not; the latter lacked the possibilities for promotion that were open to the former.

The women were controlled by the assembly line and the bonus system. The views of the women workers were not sought when new designs and new machinery were introduced. The women had no chance to move or think while they were working and no time for a quick break, and if they could not keep up with the line then they were dismissed. At work the women were controlled and patronized by the men, but other women were generally supportive and friendly. The most important things in the women's lives appeared to be their family and home; the single women looked forward to marriage and domesticity. All the women shared a general interest in a cult of domesticity.

Anna Pollert, in her study of a tobacco factory in Bristol, found, similarly, that the women worked for money, but the men thought that they worked for 'pin money' and that women's work in the factory was routine, repetitive, fiddly, low-grade work that would not be done by men. They thought that women should be paid less than men because they had babies, were inferior, and did not have to support a family. If women were paid the same as men they would price themselves out of paid work, they argued.

The women accepted the low pay, because they compared it with the wages of other female jobs. While they rejected the idea that their place was in the home, they thought of themselves as dependent on men and conceived of their pay as marginal to a man's – even though two thirds of the work-force were young, single women. They saw marriage and a family as their 'career' and conceived of themselves as at the bottom of the labour market in class and gender terms. The unmarried girls looked to marriage as an escape from low-status, monotonous work (even though they worked alongside married women for whom this had proved not to be the case).

Val, one of Anna Pollert's informants, expressed this well:

> Get married [laugh] Anything's better than working here. Well, most women get married, don't they? Not all of them works all their lives like a man. Put it this way, I don't want to work when I'm married. I don't really believe in married women working. Well. 'cos there's not much work anyway, and they ought to make room for people what have got to lead their own lives.
>
> (Pollert, 1981: 101)

Romance permeated the talk of the women on the shop floor. Appearance, courting, and marriage dominate the conversation and work was seen as temporary. Among the married women, who all did the double shift (as both housewives and paid workers), their main identity was as housewives.

Women and clerical work

In clerical work, one of the major types of work done by women, women are found in lowly paid dead-end jobs, seen as 'female jobs'. Women are often recruited on the basis that they will not be promoted, while men are recruited on the assumption that they will. Once in employment, women are less likely than men to be offered structured work experiences and the opportunity to study that would enable them to seek promotion and to be seen as promotable. As clerical work has declined in status and the tasks it involves become standardized, fragmented, and rationalized, so increasingly women have been recruited to office work. The de-skilling of office work is mediated for men by the possibility of promotion. While women are recruited to the lowest grades, paid at lower rates and replaced by other young women when they leave to have children, men, it is assumed, will be mobile out of clerical work.

One of the major debates in malestream sociology since the Second World War has been whether or not clerical workers have been proletarianized – that is, whether the pay, conditions of employment, and nature of work of clerical workers are comparable to those of manual workers. British sociologists, following a Weberian analysis, have looked at the market situation, work situation, and status situation of male clerical workers and argued that they are middle class because they enjoy superior conditions of work, are accepted as middle-class and do not identify themselves as working class (see Lockwood, 1958; Goldthorpe *et al.*, 1969). Braverman (1974) argues that clerical workers *have* been proletarianized and that the feminization of clerical work is part of this process. Reviving the debate, Crompton and Jones (1984) argue that while women's clerical work is proletarian, men's is not – primarily, they suggest, because male clerical workers have the possibility of upward mobility out of clerical work. They suggest that this situation may change as more women seek and are seen as potential candidates for promotion. However, the view that female clerical workers are proletarian holds only if they are compared with male manual workers. Martin and Roberts (1984) and Heath and Britten (1984) argue that female clerical workers enjoy pay and conditions of work more comparable to women in professional and managerial work than to women employed in manual work, where few are in work defined as skilled.

Women in the professions and as managers

Women tend to be concentrated in the 'female' semi-professional occupations rather than in the male-dominated professions. Semi-professional occupations have less autonomy than professional ones, lower status and less pay. Women are often seen as 'naturally' suited to the 'caring' work involved, for example, in nursing, primary-school teaching, and social work. However, even in these occupations the women tend to be concentrated in lower grades and to be controlled by men.

In management a similar position emerges, with women concentrated in more junior positions. In 1979, 18.8 per cent of salaried and administrative workers were women, but women were most likely to be managers in traditional occupations such as retailing, catering, and personnel. There are an increasing number of women entering management and taking university management courses; the proportion of women on such courses rose from 12 per cent in 1973 to 27 per cent in 1977. Whether this will result in a higher proportion of women in top management is difficult to determine, but Cooper and Davidson (1982) suggest that while it is relatively easy for women to gain employment on the lower rungs it is difficult for them to gain promotion. They also suggest that, as for men, management is a high-stress occupation for women, but unlike men, home life, rather than supporting their careers, actually obstructs them.

In the established professions there has been an increase in recent years in the number of women. Medicine is the profession that has the largest proportion of women. In 1976, 23 per cent of all doctors on the General Medical Council Register were women, and the proportion of women entering medical school has increased from between 22 and 25 per cent in the years from the Second World War to 1968, to 37.8 per cent in 1978 (Elston, 1980). However, despite being 25 per cent of medical graduates in the 1960s, women are under-represented in top posts in the 1980s; only 13 per cent of hospital consultants are women, and 20 per cent of principals in general practice (Allen, 1988). Women are also unevenly distributed across the medical specialities, and this is not solely the outcome of chance and personal preference. Women are heavily represented in community medicine and the school health service, in general practice, and in certain hospital specialisms such as anaesthesiology, radiology, mental illness, and children's mental illness (Mackie and Pattullo, 1977). These tend to be the specialisms where women's real or potential conflict between home and work can be reduced as well as being the areas that are less 'popular' with men – women tend to be concentrated in the same specialisms as immigrant doctors. It is also sometimes argued that women have the 'innate characteristics' necessary for such specialisms, but women's assumed 'married' destiny and assumed specialist knowledge do not lead to many women specializing in plastic or neuro-surgery, nor in obstetrics, gynaecology, or paediatrics (Young, 1981).

It is often argued that the reason for women's lack of career prospects is their domestic commitments, because they take time out to have children, seek part-time work, and are not 'really' committed to their work. It could, however, be argued that women are disadvantaged because the training and promotion is based on assumptions about continuous, full-time work, that part-time training is not provided in many medical specialisms, and that candidates for promotion are expected to have had certain experiences by a certain age – difficult for a woman who has had a career-break or worked part-time for a period.

Isobel Allen (1988) found that from the point of entry to medical school through to hospital consultant posts, women doctors face sexist attitudes, have to compete within an 'old boy network' of patronage, are asked discriminating questions at interviews – for example, questions about child care arrangements were asked of women, some of whom did not even have children – and that they were frequently treated in less favourable ways just because they were women. Barbara Lawrence (1987), in a study of single-handed female general practitioners, found that they had decided to set up on their own to avoid being dominated by male partners. They had found that in mixed-group practices they were paid less than their male colleagues and expected to see the women and children. Young (1981) has suggested that sexism is built into the medical curriculum and that women are portrayed as inferior.

In contrast to the male-dominated professions, women form the majority in the 'female' semi-professions. Jobs such as nursing and teaching are seen as 'good jobs for women' because of the hours worked, the demands on interpersonal skills and the relatively steady employment prospects. However, these occupations lack the autonomy enjoyed by professionals and women in them are often dominated by men – nurses by (male) doctors and teachers by (male) headmasters. While the pay is relatively high in these occupations, compared with the pay of women in general, it is poor in comparison with the salaries enjoyed by those employed in the 'male' professions. In both nursing and teaching women are under-represented in the top grades when account is taken of the ratio of men to women in the occupation as a whole. In 1976 women made up 60 per cent of the full-time teaching force, but only 43 per cent of teachers in secondary schools. In secondary schools women held just over 30 per cent of senior posts, but only 18 per cent of headships. Thirty-four per cent of deputy headships and 65 per cent of senior mistress/master posts were held by women; however, these posts often involve pastoral responsibilities which are assumed to be a 'feminine' skill (Kelsall, 1980). In 1976 only 10 per cent of nurses were men, but men held 29 per cent of regional and district managerial posts. In hospital nursing, 10.7 per cent of the nursing force were men, but 25 per cent of nurses above the professional grade (staff nurse), and 72 per cent of male Registered General nurses were in grades above staff nurse, compared with 47 per cent of female Registered nurses. Community nurses, who appear to enjoy more autonomy and are predominantly female, are likely, however, to be under the control of the general practitioner to whom they are attached (McGuire, 1980). (See Chapter five for further discussion of doctor/nurse relationships.)

Women are marginalized, then, in professional and managerial work as well as in skilled manual work. They occupy the lower-status, less well remunerated levels within all sectors of the labour market.

Women and unemployment

Traditionally, in sociology, unemployment has not been thought to pose a problem for women, or at least for the majority of married women. This is because it is argued that women's wages are marginal, not essential to the family, that women's main identity and status is derived from their role as wives and mothers, and that women can 'return' to their primary domestic role. Women's unemployment is also hidden – a high proportion of women seeking employment are not registered as unemployed – in the Martin and Roberts survey (1984), 50 per cent.

However, feminist research has challenged this view and has argued that work and work identities are central to many women's lives, and that the money women earn is essential. Angela Coyle (1984), in a study of 76 redundant women, found that only three, two of whom were pregnant and one near retirement age, took the opportunity to stop work. All the others sought alternative employment – and found work that was less skilled, had poor working conditions, and was less well paid than their previous posts. The women said that they worked because a male wage was inadequate for the needs of the household and because they valued the independence they gained from paid employment and having their own income. She concludes that paid work was seen as central to the lives of these women and that redundancy was viewed as an unwelcome interruption to their working lives.

Explanations of women's position in the labour market

Women's dual role

In the 1950s, with increasing numbers of women going out to work, sociologists began to try to explain women's labour market participation. The pioneering study, which was followed by a number of others, was *Women's Two Roles* by Myrdal and Klein (1956). Such studies assumed that there was something problematic about married women having paid employment, because in the accepted sexual division of labour women were consigned to the domestic sphere. They unquestioningly accepted the natural connection of women with the role of housewife and mother, and married women were seen as the economic dependants of men. In explaining the increased labour market participation of women they focused on the question of labour supply. Married women were said to be able to 'go out to work' because of smaller family size and labour-saving devices. However, these studies paid no attention to occupational segregation or to the structural basis of women's employment.

The dual labour market

Dual labour market theory distinguishes between two labour markets, the primary (made up of jobs offering training and promotion) and the secondary (comprising insecure and lowly paid unskilled jobs). Workers in the secondary sector are easily dispensed with in times of recession, are poorly remunerated and have poor conditions of employment.

Barron and Norris (1976) developed this theory to explain the position of women in the British labour market. They argue that women form the secondary-sector work-force in Britain and men the primary. Women are in the secondary sector because:

1 sex was an obvious way of segregating the work-force which would raise little opposition from male employees;
2 women would work for less money than men, being not so committed to employment on account of their domestic roles;
3 women frequently left work of their own accord and would be easier to lay off at short notice;
4 women were less likely to join trade unions.

This analysis drew attention to occupational segregation as a major problem to be explained and to the concentration of women in poorly paid jobs classified as semi-skilled or unskilled. It also shifted the focus of analysis away from the question of the supply of labour to an analysis of the demand for labour. However, to divide the market into two sectors is too simple; there are a plethora of sectors based on age, class, ethnicity, and locality. Dex (1985), for example, has argued that some women are employed in the male primary sector and that there is a female primary sector and a female secondary sector. In addition, Barron and Norris rely upon a number of stereotypes of women workers which have since been challenged. For example, women are not necessarily happier to work for lower wages; they just seldom have any choice.The theory ignores the role of the male trade unions in creating and maintaining the segmented labour market and takes an objectivist view of 'skill', ignoring the fact that skill is at least in part a social construct and that what is seen as 'skilled' work is generally associated with work that men do.

Marxist feminist explanations

Marxist feminists argue that the sexual division of labour within the family and familial ideology explain why women enter the labour market on disadvantageous terms and are used by capitalists in distinctive ways. They suggest that there is a congruence between the sexual division of labour in the domestic sphere, which consigns women to domestic labour, and the 'needs' of capitalism for a distinctive kind of labour force – part time, lowly paid, and flexible. This explains the job segments that are occupied by women in the labour market (Beechey, 1976, 1977).

The recent explanations put forward by Marxist feminists have differed to some extent. Some have argued that women are an industrial 'reserve army of labour' that is pulled into productive work in periods of economic expansion, when there is a shortage of labour, and disposed of in periods of recession. An alternative view is that women were drawn into the labour force as work became de-skilled – as work was broken down into smaller units and was seen as less skilled. Cheap female labour was used to replace expensive male labour. However, some Marxist feminists have argued that occupational segregation is so established that women are unlikely to substitute for men – that the labour market is divided into men's and women's jobs. Milkman (1976), for example, has suggested that occupational segregation by sex creates an inflexibility in the labour market which prevents women's expulsion during periods of declining demand for labour. She suggests that it is necessary to investigate under what conditions women do and do not act as a reserve army of labour. Bruegel (1979) argues that women acted as a reserve army of labour in the 1970s in the manufacturing sector but not in the service sector, which is the major site of women's employment.

The advantage of the Marxist feminist approach is that it attempts to theorize the relationship between women's oppression and other forms of exploitation and oppression. It explains women's position in the labour market by reference to the 'needs' of the capitalist system. However, like the dual labour market explanation, it takes an objectivist view of skill and the view that changes brought about by new technology result in de-skilling. Coyle (1984), looking at changes in the clothing industry brought about by new technology, argues that what was classified as 'skilled' work was generally work done by men and that unions negotiated higher rates for their members by claiming that the men's work was more skilled than the women's work. The Marxist feminist perspective also adopts a manufacturing model of work and tends to exaggerate the extent of de-skilling. Marxist feminists tend also to fall into a kind of functionalism, reading off an analysis of women's employment from an analysis of the needs of capitalism – which is a circular argument. Finally, Marxist feminists have been overly economistic and have paid insufficient attention to the role of familial ideology in determining women's position in the labour force.

Radical feminist explanations

Radical feminists argue that patriarchy, a system in which men dominate and exploit women, is the first and fundamental form of domination and subordination. Men exploit and dominate women in the domestic mode of production, and it is to the advantage of men to keep women in the home serving their needs. Men have attempted to keep women out of the labour market and, when women are in paid employment, to control them.

The advantage of the radical feminist position is that it points to the ways in which men benefit from the domestic labour of women and the ways in which the male-dominated trade unions and the male employers have worked to keep women out of paid employment, or to the extent that they are in employment to control them. However, the explanation tends to be descriptive and fails to explain the ways in which women have entered the labour market, which according to the theory is to the disadvantage of men.

Socialist feminist explanations

Socialist feminists argue that capitalism and patriarchy interact at every level within society. Heidi Hartmann (1978), for example, argues that job segregation by sex and the introduction of the family wage can only be understood in terms of the ways capitalism and patriarchy articulate together. She suggests that men have organized to exclude women from much paid work, to ensure that they receive low wages in the jobs that remain open to them and that they are forced to remain dependent on men within the family. She argues that both men and capitalism benefit from this arrangement. With the concept of the family wage, she argues, capitalism and patriarchy find a mutual accommodation.

However, while Hartmann sees the interests of patriarchy and capitalism as identical, Sylvia Walby (1986) argues that they are not always in harmony and, indeed, frequently in conflict. She suggests that the social relations of domestic work are conducted in a patriarchal mode of production and that this determines gender relations. When patriarchy is in articulation with the capitalist mode of production, then patriarchal relations at work are of central importance in maintaining the capitalist system and the patriarchal mode of production. It is important to realize, then, that the exploitation of women by men is independent of the capitalist exploitation of workers. In the capitalist mode of production women still get married and serve their husbands because they are excluded from paid work on the same basis as their husbands. Patriarchal relations at work are central in preventing women from entering work as freely as men. The state is also patriarchal and historically has played a role, both by preventing women from selling their labour on the same terms as men and by supporting a particular form of household (the nuclear family) in which women provide unpaid domestic services. She concludes by arguing that women continue to put up with the conditions of work in the domestic mode of production because the type of paid work available for most women offers no better conditions. Housework is as good as anything else women get.

The advantage of the socialist feminist position is that it recognizes the role that both men and capitalism play in the subordination and exploitation of women. It offers an explanation for women's participation in the labour market, and Walby points to ways in which what men want and what capitalism wants may be in conflict, and also to the ways in which men dominate and control women in both the domestic and the public sphere. However, like the other theories it tends to underplay the ways in which women fight their subordinate position. It also tends to 'have it all ways' – if something is wanted by men or is in the interests of men and they do not get it, it is because capitalism won on that occasion, and vice versa.

Conclusions

Thus, although Victorian feminists fought for the right for middle-class women to work, on the assumption that work would lead to liberation, and many latter-day Marxists – including those in the Soviet Union – have done the same, we can see that work is not necessarily a source of liberation for women. The work that women do merely reinforces their traditional roles within the family. We can also see how important it is for sociology to be aware of women's work as well as men's; some of what has been described here is very much at variance with the traditional 'sociology of work'.

Summary

1 When women are in paid work they do different jobs from men.
2 Jobs that women do receive less pay and are of lower status than men's jobs.
3 'Skill' is used as a way of justifying differences between men's and women's jobs. However, feminists argue that skill is an idea constructed by male workers.
4 Women experience work in different ways from men because of their different relationship to the labour market.
5 Feminists argue that malestream sociology has 'naturalized' the real work that women do in the domestic sphere – that it has made it seem the exercise of a natural function rather than the performance of real work.

Further reading

Dex, S. (1985) *The Sexual Division of Work*, Brighton: Wheatsheaf.
Walby, S. (1986) *Patriarchy at Work*, Cambridge: Polity.
Westwood, S. (1984) *All Day Every Day: factory and family in the making of women's lives*, London: Pluto Press.

Chapter seven

Women, crime, and deviance

Explaining crime – women as criminals

We are all concerned to explain or make sense of criminal behaviour – to make sense of actions that appear to us as unnatural or strange. Of course, some behaviours may seem more problematic than others: for example, we may find it relatively easy to understand why a single-parent mother on supplementary benefit stole food from the local supermarket, but much more difficult to understand why our next-door neighbour beat his wife. When we try to explain the criminal behaviour, we tend none the less to use a few single-factor motivational or trait categories – sickness, jealousy, hate, greed, overpermissiveness, and lack of social (especially parental) control. We tend to assume that the behaviour can be explained by characteristics of the individual or her life experiences. Sociologists and other criminologists tend to argue that lay explanations or common-sense theories are simplistic and inadequate. Despite this, there are close parallels between common--sense and social-science explanations.

Much crime seems to us inexplicable; we cannot understand how any human being could have committed it. We hear the details of the behaviour with incredulity and see the perpetrator as less than human, as an animal. Theories of crime that see criminal behaviour as innate (genetic/biological) were developed at the end of the nineteenth century by the Italian criminologist Lombroso and other degeneration theorists. Criminal conduct was seen as caused by biological or physiological characteristics of the individual. The biological factors were said to project the individual into a life of crime. Lombroso argued that criminals were atavistic – that is, genetic throwbacks to an earlier form of man (*sic*). While Lombrosian theories of crime are no longer given wide credence, biological theories continue to have some influence. The psychologist Hans Eysenck (1970), for example, argues that extraverts are more likely to commit crime than other types for ultimately biological reasons – differences in neural organization with behavioural consequences – and Katerina Dalton (1961) has suggested that some female crime can be explained by hormonal changes during the menstrual cycle (pre-menstrual tension).

Another way in which we try to account for what appears to be totally incomprehensible behaviour is by seeing the perpetrator as mentally sick and suggesting that he or she is mad and therefore not responsible for his or her actions. Some criminological theories have suggested that criminal behaviour is caused by serious mental pathology or at least is the result of some emotional disturbance. These types of explanation have been especially prevalent in explaining female criminality, and we discuss them more fully below. Here we shall note only that while it must be acknowledged that some law-breakers may suffer from mental disturbance, the same can be said of many non-offenders.

A further way in which criminal behaviour is explained is by suggesting that it is a result of the social conditions in which the offender lives or of life experiences of individuals. Two sets of explanations are frequently encountered: those that 'blame' the socialization of the individual and the family, and those that see the immediate 'bad' social environment as the cause. Thus, wife-beating is frequently explained by reference to the socialization of the offender in a home in which he either saw his mother beaten or was beaten himself. Child abuse is sometimes explained in the same way, or sometimes by reference to the current living conditions of the family – for example living in poverty in one room.

In the 1960s some sociologists began to challenge the idea that it was possible to establish the causes of social behaviour in the same way as it was possible to establish causes in the natural sciences, as the theories described above have done. The positivistic mode of analysis had argued that it was possible to discover the causes of criminal behaviour in the same way as it is possible to establish laws in physics, and that it was possible to be value-free and objective about the social world (see Chapter nine). The new criminologists, as they became known, argued that, in the guise of value freedom, sociologists had studied things from the perspective of those with power in society and had ignored the perspectives of the powerless. Furthermore, they pointed out that by paying attention to violations of law, criminology had ignored the legal system and devalued the place of human consciousness and the meaning that criminal activities had for those engaged in them.

The new criminologists were concerned to examine the relationship between law and crime, the purpose and function of the legal system and the relatively autonomous role of individual meaning, choice, and volition. Labelling theorists suggested that if criminals do differ from non-criminals in social characteristics, this is not the cause of their law-breaking but because these very characteristics are used by society to label some people as criminal and ignore others. Maureen Cain (1973) and Steven Box (1971), for example, suggest that the police are more likely to suspect and arrest a working-class man than a middle-class one. Furthermore, it was suggested that the only way that criminals differed from non-criminals was that the former had been involved in the criminal justice system. Sociologists, then, became concerned to identify the key mechanisms by which crime is socially constructed through law creation, law enforcement, and societal reaction.

More recently, some sociologists, from what is called a left realist position (see, for example, Matthews and Young, 1986), have argued that the new criminology was idealistic and romanticized the criminal. They point out that the people who suffer most from criminal acts are working-class people. We can also add that the new criminology, like most of the old, neglected women and crime. Women are relatively powerless, yet these sociologists rarely considered them. Furthermore, women frequently are the victims of abuse from men, both in the domestic sphere and in public. While the new deviancy theorists were challenging the view that it is possible to establish the causes of men's law-breaking, their failure to include women in their analysis meant that biological and pathological explanations continued to be accepted as explaining female law-breaking.

Women and crime – the evidence

One of the reasons that 'women and crime' has been a neglected area in sociology is that women appear to be remarkably non-criminal. With the possible exceptions of shop-lifters and prostitutes, women convicted of crime are seen as exceptions and extreme deviants both from the law and from femininity – that is, acceptable female behaviour. This is probably, at least in part, because so few women compared with men are convicted of crimes, but it also relates to what is seen as acceptable behaviour from women as compared with men. Much male deviance is associated with what it means to be 'a man' – theft using force, fighting in gangs, football violence, and so on.

The Home Office's annual statistics on crime provide information on convictions for criminal offences. These are broken down by age, sex, and type of offence, but *not* by social class or ethnicity. We can ask three questions of the statistics which will enable us to begin to determine whether women are less criminal than men and how female criminality differs from male:

1 are there differences in the amount of crime committed by men and women?

153

2 are there differences in the kinds of crime committed by men and women?
3 are there any recent changes in the amount or kind of crime committed by men and women?

The crime statistics for England and Wales for 1986 (Home Office, 1987) suggest that women are considerably less criminal than men, and this appears to be as true for the more serious (indictable) offences as for the less serious (summary) ones. (Indictable offences are those for which an offender has the right to have, or must have, a trial before a jury in a Crown Court; summary offences are triable only in a Magistrate's Court.) Table 7.1 shows that in 1986 86.9 per cent of those convicted of indictable offences were men, and 13.1 per cent women. There are some age differences: boys and young men are even more likely to have been convicted of an indictable offence than girls and young women. Similarly, men are much more likely to have been convicted of a summary offence than women.

Table 7.1 Persons sentenced for indictable offences in 1986, by sex and age, in England and Wales

Age	Males		Females		Total
	No. (000)	%	No. (000)	%	No. (000)
10 and under 14	6.1	92.4	0.5	7.6	6.6
14 and under 17	37.7	91.1	3.7	8.9	41.4
17 and under 21	99.0	88.6	12.7	11.4	111.7
21+ years	189.7	85.1	33.1	4.9	222.8
Total	332.5	86.9	50.0	13.1	382.5

Source: Home Office (1987), Tables 7.8, 7.10, 7.12 and 7.14.

Women are convicted for all categories of crime, but men commit a far higher number of crimes in all categories (Table 7.2). There are only two categories of crime, 'theft and handling stolen goods' and 'fraud and forgery', where less than 90 per cent of those convicted were men. Theft and handling stolen goods is the offence for which both men and women had the highest conviction rates. However, the category accounted for 69.7 per cent of all females convicted and only 44.4 per cent of all men convicted; 81 per cent of the people convicted in this category were men and 19 per cent women. Furthermore, Table 7.3 shows that women are mainly convicted of shop-lifting in this category

– 64 per cent of all women convicted of theft or handling stolen goods were convicted of shop-lifting, compared with 26 per cent of men. Even in this category far more men are convicted of shoplifting than women, however – 46,018 men compared with 29,189 women.

Table 7.2 Offenders found guilty of indictable offences at all courts in England and Wales in 1986, by sex and type of offence – percentages by gender

Offence	Males		Females	
	No. (000)	*%*	*No.* (000)	*%*
Violence against the person	39.8	92.3	3.3	7.7
Sexual offences	5.4	98.2	0.1	1.8
Burglary	54.8	97.0	1.7	3.0
Robbery	4.0	95.2	0.2	4.8
Theft and handling stolen goods	148.6	81.0	34.9	19.0
Fraud and forgery	18.1	78.7	4.9	21.3
Criminal damage	9.3	93.0	0.7	7.0
Drug offences	14.7	87.0	2.2	13.0
Other (excluding motoring)	13.4	91.8	1.2	8.2
Motoring offences	26.8	96.8	0.9	3.2
Total	334.9	87.0	50.1	13.0

Source: Home Office (1987), Table 7.2.

The statistics on sentencing also suggest that there are differences in the types of crime committed by men and women. Women are more likely to be given a conditional discharge than men – 24 per cent of women compared with 10 per cent of men among those convicted of an indictable offence in 1986 – or a probation order – 19 per cent of women compared with 7 per cent of men. Men were about as likely to be fined as women – 41 per cent compared with 38 per cent – but more likely to receive a community service order – 7 per cent compared with 3 per cent – or a prison sentence, immediate or suspended – 33 per cent compared with 15 per cent (Home Office, 1987, Table 7.15). Men were also likely to receive longer prison sentences than women. Of all those over the age of 21 sentenced to an immediate term of imprisonment at Crown Courts, 41 per cent of women received a sentence of six months or less, but only 29 per cent of men (Home Office, 1987, Table 7.29). However, the difference in sentence length was much less clear in the Magistrates'

Courts, where the maximum sentence usually given is six months. Men did seem more likely to receive a sentence of over three months and less than six months (27 per cent, compared with 20 per cent of women), and less likely to receive 14 days or less (8 per cent, compared with 14 per cent – Home Office, 1987, Table 7.28).

Table 7.3 Offenders found guilty of theft offences in all courts in England and Wales in 1986, by sex and type of offence

Offence type	Males		Females	
	No. (000)	%	No. (000)	%
Theft from the person	1.9	1	0.4	1
Theft in a dwelling	2.5	1	0.7	2
Theft by an employee	5.8	3	1.5	3
Theft from mail	0.2	0.1	< 0.1	0.1
Abstracting electricity	2.6	2	1.0	2
Theft of pedal cycle	3.3	2	0.1	0.2
Theft from vehicle	11.6	7	0.2	0.4
Theft from shops	46.0	26	29.2	64
Theft from meter etc	5.2	3	1.3	3
Theft of motor vehicle	28.8	16	0.7	2
Other theft	48.5	27	6.5	14
Handling stolen goods	22.9	13	3.9	9

Source: Home Office (1987), Table 5.1.

The official statistics on convictions suggest that women are far less criminal than men and that while women do commit all crimes, the majority of women convicted of a crime are found in the one category – theft and handling stolen goods. It also seems that women, on the whole, commit less serious crimes than men.

The final question concerns changes in women's behaviour – has the number of women convicted of criminal offences changed in recent years, and how does this compare with men? Numbers convicted fluctuate from year to year, and trends are therefore difficult to determine. However, between 1977 and 1986 the number of women found guilty of crime in England and Wales has increased steadily from 207,000 in 1977 to 277,000 in 1986. During the same period there has been a decline in the number of men convicted – from 1,744,000 in 1977 to 1,617,000 in 1986 (with a high point of 1,842,000 in 1982). However, if we look just at indictable offences (a rough indication of the incidence of more serious offending) a different pattern emerges. Here the number of women convicted has declined from 68,000 in 1977 to 50,000 in 1986; the major increases have been in summary offences (excluding motoring offences) – from 50,000 in 1977 to 114,000 in 1986. Conversely, for men we find that from 1977 to 1986 there was an increase in the number convicted of indictable offences from 358,000 to 385,000 in 1985 (there was a decline in 1986), while there was a decrease in the number of men convicted of summary offences (see Table 7.4). The official statistics on conviction rates do not suggest that there has been a large increase in female criminality in recent years. They do suggest that to the extent that there has been an increase, it has been in the more trivial offences.

Table 7.4 Offenders found guilty at all courts in England and Wales, by sex and type of offence, 1977–86

Males	1977	1978	1979	1980	1981	1982	1983	1984	1985	1986
	(Figures are nos. of offences, in tens of thousands)									
Violence	3.9	4.1	4.5	4.8	4.7	4.8	4.7	4.4	4.4	4.0
Sexual offences	0.7	0.8	0.7	0.8	0.7	0.7	0.6	0.6	0.6	0.5
Burglary	6.8	6.6	5.7	6.5	7.4	7.4	7.0	7.0	6.7	5.5
Robbery	0.3	0.3	0.3	0.3	0.4	0.4	0.4	0.4	0.4	0.4
Theft and handling	18.0	17.5	17.3	18.4	18.4	19.0	18.0	17.6	17.4	14.8
Fraud and forgery	1.6	1.6	1.6	1.9	2.0	2.0	2.0	2.0	2.0	1.8
Criminal damage	0.8	0.9	0.8	1.1	1.1	1.1	1.1	1.1	1.1	0.9
Drugs	–	–	1.0	1.3	1.3	1.5	1.7	1.6	1.7	1.5
Other (excl. motoring)	1.4	1.4	0.9	1.2	1.2	1.3	1.3	1.4	1.4	1.3
Motoring	2.3	2.0	2.1	2.5	2.7	2.9	3.0	2.8	2.8	2.7
Total indictable	35.8	35.1	35.0	38.8	39.9	40.9	39.8	39.0	38.5	33.4
Total summary	138.6	131.8	134.0	157.5	146.4	138.7	144.4	133.1	127.8	128.3
All offences	174.4	167.0	169.0	196.3	186.4	179.6	184.2	172.0	166.2	161.7

Source: Home Office (1987) Table 5.8.

Table 7.4 contd.

Females	1977	1978	1979	1980	1981	1982	1983	1984	1985	1986
	(Figures are nos. of offences, in thousands)									
Violence	3.5	3.5	3.9	4.2	4.0	4.1	4.0	3.6	3.6	3.3
Sexual offences	< 0.1	0.1	0.1	0.1	0.1	0.1	0.1	0.1	0.1	0.1
Burglary	2.4	2.6	2.2	2.7	2.6	2.6	2.4	2.2	2.1	1.7
Robbery	0.2	0.2	0.2	0.2	0.2	0.2	0.2	0.2	0.2	0.2
Theft and handling	54.0	51.7	48.0	50.1	48.2	49.0	45.3	43.0	42.2	34.9
Fraud and forgery	4.5	4.4	4.6	5.5	5.5	5.2	5.5	5.6	5.4	4.8
Criminal damage	0.6	0.7	0.6	0.8	0.8	0.8	0.8	0.8	0.8	0.7
Drugs	–	–	1.5	2.0	1.9	2.0	2.1	2.3	2.4	2.2
Other (excl. motoring)	1.7	1.7	0.9	1.2	1.3	1.2	1.3	1.1	1.2	1.2
Motoring	0.8	0.7	0.7	0.9	0.9	1.0	1.0	0.9	0.9	0.9
Total indictable	67.7	65.5	62.7	67.8	65.5	66.1	62.7	59.9	59.0	50.0
Total summary	139.7	144.0	145.9	181.0	175.6	169.4	190.4	183.0	189.3	227.4
All offences	207.4	209.5	208.6	248.8	241.0	235.5	253.1	242.8	248.4	277.4

Source: Home Office (1987) Table 5.8.

A major problem with the official statistics on convictions is that they tell us only the numbers arrested and convicted for crimes. There is a large amount of unsolved crime, and we know nothing about those who perpetrate it. In 1986, for example, 3,847,000 crimes were recorded by the police, while there were only 1,895,000 convictions. Much of the crime recorded by the police is never 'cleared up' – that is, no one is ever convicted of it. Furthermore, self-report and victim surveys suggest that there is a large amount of crime that is never reported to the police. The problem is that we do not know the size or distribution of this hidden crime. Known crime is like the top of an iceberg, that which is visible; research suggests that some crimes, visible ones, are more likely to be reported to and recorded by the police than hidden crimes, those that take place in private. A mugging is much more likely to be reported than an assault by a husband on a wife, for example. The police and public

are more likely to suspect some people of crimes than others –
working-class men and ethnic minority men are more likely to be
suspected and arrested than middle-class white men (Box, 1971;
Chapman, 1968). The crime statistics do not, then, represent the 'real'
amount of crime, nor are those convicted of crime necessarily
representative of all law-breakers.

We can ask, then, if the differences between the conviction rates of
men and women represent a 'real' difference in the law-breaking of men
and women, or just reflect the fact that women are better at hiding their
crimes and less likely to be suspected of crimes – that is, that they do not
fit the stereotype of the criminal. Pollack (1950) argued that women
were *not* less criminal than men. He argued that women were naturally
good at concealing their actions and naturally secretive because they
had to hide the fact of menstruation. Women commit large amounts of
crime that remain hidden, he argued, especially child abuse and murder
of spouses. However, even if this were the case it seems unlikely that the
amount would be sufficient to increase women's incidence of law-
breaking to that of men, especially as there is also hidden male crime,
for example male middle-class crime, wife abuse, and other domestic
crimes. Self-report studies suggest that women are indeed less criminal
than men. Mawby (1980), for instance, found that both young men and
young women in Sheffield admitted to more crime than would seem to
be indicated by the official statistics, but that the ratio of male to female
crime seemed about right. Feminists conclude that on balance the
available evidence does indicate that women commit less, and less
serious, crime than men. Also, while it is true that more women have
become involved in crime in recent years, this seems to have been
mainly petty crime, and male crime has also increased during the same
period (Box and Hale, 1983). Thus there is no evidence to support the
claim that as women become more liberated they increasingly develop
the same patterns of criminality as men.

The need for feminist theory

Feminists have suggested that to understand the issues surrounding
women and crime two key questions need to be considered:

1 why do so few women commit crimes?;
2 why do those women who commit the crimes do so?

They suggest that malestream theories have either failed to tackle these
questions or provided inadequate answers.

Thus psycho-positivistic (biological/psychological) theories of
female criminality have stereotyped women and do not provide an

adequate explanation. However, they continue to hold a dominant place in the explanation of female crime long after they have been seriously challenged as adequate explanations for male criminality. Thus Hilary Allen (1987) has argued that women accused of serious violent crimes are much more likely than men charged with comparable crimes to be portrayed in court reports as suffering from psychological problems that suggest they are not responsible for their actions. Furthermore, women are more likely to be found insane or of diminished responsibility and, if convicted, more likely to be given psychiatric treatment in place of a penal sentence than is a man. Another example is pre-menstrual tension (PMT): women have successfully defended themselves against criminal charges by pleading diminished responsibility on the grounds that they were suffering from PMT at the time they were convicted of the crime. The success of these pleas, feminists argue, depends not only on the evidence of expert witnesses, but also on the courts' preparedness to believe this evidence because it fits their stereotype of female criminals. This stereotype has itself been informed, at least in part, by psycho-positivistic theories of crime, theories which argue that female law-breakers are either biologically different from those who do not break the law or that they are out of their minds – mentally ill – and therefore not responsible for their actions.

Sociological theories, on the other hand, have with few exceptions ignored women. They have not seen gender as an important explanatory variable and have assumed that theories based on male samples and a male view of the world can be generalized to women. In some cases they have implicitly or explicitly accepted biological theories, as, for example, Durkheim (1952) did in his study of suicide, when he agreed that women were less likely to commit suicide than men because they were biologically at a lower stage of development than men and therefore less influenced by the social forces that resulted in people committing suicide. Even major critics of conventional criminology have failed to raise the issue of women and crime (e.g. Taylor, Walton, and Young, 1973).

Feminist theories of crime

Feminists have argued that a paradigm shift is essential so that gender can be seen as an important explanatory variable in explaining why some women are law-breakers; women have their experiences mediated by gender and class relationships. Feminists are also agreed that patriarchal relationships, ideologies of femininity, and women's assigned role in the family all play key roles (see Chapter four). While the individual must be seen as free to shape her own actions, destiny, and consciousness, this happens in an economic, ideological, and political environment which she does not control (see Chapters one and eight). Furthermore, it is recognized that empirical studies of women who have engaged in law-breaking are essential so that it is possible to determine under what circumstances women do break the law. An analysis which makes connections between women's law-breaking and how they are handled in the criminal justice system is also essential. Finally, while the double control of women in the class and gender system may explain why most women do not break the law, theories need to be developed that explain why some women do break it.

The ideology of femininity constructs girls and women in a particular way. The natural role for a woman is seen as that of a wife and mother. Girls and women are seen as needing protection and care. Consequently, young girls tend to be controlled more than their brothers and given less freedom. Of especial concern is the protection of girls' virginity. While boys are expected to 'sow wild oats', girls are expected to remain virgin until they marry – or at least to have a 'steady' relationship. While young men who come before the courts and are handled in the juvenile justice system have generally committed criminal offences, girls are more likely to come before the courts for being in need of care and protection, including from their own promiscuity – what are referred to as 'status offences', coming within the ambit of the law only because of the age of the 'offender'. This seems to remain true even when the girls have in fact committed criminal offences (Shaklady Smith, 1978).

This alerts us to the important fact that the boundary between normality and abnormality is elastic – that is, what is seen as normal for men may be seen as abnormal for women, not to mention class and ethnic variations as well. Crime and deviance are not immutable, but historically and culturally variable. Whether or not behaviour is seen as criminal/deviant depends both on the context and on the individual doing the behaviour. The stereotype of the criminal as male, and of female criminals as being psychologically inadequate, influences not only sociological theories, but also the people involved in the administration of the criminal justice system on the one hand and our common-sense view of the nature of women on the other.

However, studies of women who have been convicted of criminal offences and who have been imprisoned (e.g. Dobash *et al.*, 1986; Carlen, 1983; Carlen *et al.*, 1985, Mandaraka-Sheppard, 1986) have confirmed the main feminist criticisms of traditional criminology. Four major characteristics of female offenders have been highlighted:

1 that women who engage in property crime are motivated by economic factors – that is, they steal because they need or want the goods they steal;
2 that women commit all types of offences;

161

3 that women do fear and feel the impact of the stigma of the 'criminal' label;

4 that women are seen as doubly deviant – deviant for breaking social rules, and also 'unfeminine' and 'unnatural' because they have offended against rules of feminine behaviour.

Feminists argue that what is necessary is eventually to develop theories that are adequate for explaining and understanding the law-breaking of both men and women. This does not mean that feminists are looking for a universal theory that will explain all criminal behaviour in all circumstances. There is no reason to assume that all criminal behaviour can be explained in the same way. What are necessary are theories of crime that take account of gender, ethnic, and class divisions and studies that are situated in the wider moral, political, economic, and sexual spheres which influence women's and men's status and position in society. However, as Carol Smart (1976) argues, initially it will be necessary to carry out research on women, in order to make women visible and to find alternative ways of conceptualizing the social world so that the interests and concerns of women are adduced and included rather than subsumed or ignored.

However, some feminists have argued that existing theories of crime can be developed to the point where they account adequately for women. There is no reason, they suggest, why explanations for female crime should be different from those for male crime. Morris (1987), for example, argues that disorganization theory and differential association can both be extended to account for female crime. Leonard (1978) has suggested that a reformulated labelling theory with elements of critical theory can be developed, and Shaklady Smith (1978) has used labelling theory to explain female juvenile delinquency.

Disorganization theory

Cloward and Ohlin (1961) argued that crime occurs because not everyone is able to achieve the accepted goal of society (economic success) by the legitimate means (hard work), especially via the gaining of educational qualifications. Cloward and Ohlin suggested that crime happens because, just when working-class adolescents have been encouraged to adopt a set of economic and material aspirations of which the larger society approves, the means of achieving these goals is locked off from them – that is, they do not gain the necessary qualifications to embark on a career that will enable them to achieve economic success by legitimate means. In reaction to this, adolescents most at risk of becoming criminals develop an alternative authority to that of the state – the delinquent gang.

Given that women experience unequal opportunities even more than men, then this would seem to be a possible explanation for female crime. Indeed, given that opportunities are more restricted for women than for men, we might expect women to exhibit a higher rate of crime than men. The fact that they do not can be explained, however, by their limited access to illegitimate opportunities. Alison Morris (1987) cites studies by Figueira-McDonough which suggest that if boys and girls are equally frustrated, then they will commit the same amount of crime, provided they have equal knowledge of, and equal access to, illegitimate means. However, another study, by Datesman *et al.*, found that both black and white female delinquents regarded the opportunities open to them less positively than non-delinquent girls, and that this perception was more strongly related to girls' involvement in delinquency than that of boys.

There are major problems with this theory, however. It assumes that there is universal agreement on societal goals and accepted means of achieving them, and that crime is committed mainly by working-class men and women. While it recognizes that there may be differential access to the goals, based on gender as well as class, it fails to recognize differential access to the means. More important, however, it fails to take account of the key fact that social goals are different for men and women. Girls are socialized into a world that sees marriage, child care, and domesticity as the main goals. Indeed, girls who reject the societal view of appropriate feminine behaviour and who consequently endanger their chances of achieving these goals are seen as deviant (Lees, 1986).

Differential association

Sutherland (see Sutherland and Cressey, 1966) developed differential association as a theory of crime as a result of his criticisms of socio-logical theories of crime which regarded crime as a male working-class phenomenon. He argued that the official statistics under-represented middle-class criminals because their crimes were often dealt with by the civil rather than the criminal courts – or out of court altogether, by the 'private justice' of employers, clubs, and private institutions. Sutherland argued that criminal behaviour was a result not of poverty or inadequate socialization, but of the people with whom one associates. Behaviours, values, and justifications were picked up by association with others. Sutherland argued that people who commit crime have more contact with those who condone criminal behaviour than with those who oppose it. He also suggested that this approach applied equally to women and men. However, his theory fails to explain why brothers and not sisters become criminals, why the wives of criminal men do not become criminals, and so on.

Critical (Marxist) criminology

Critical criminology has sought to understand the basis of social inequality and power relationships within capitalist societies. It has explored the class dimension of crime and has illustrated the ways in which the criminal law is selectively enforced against the powerless. However, women are not easily accommodated within these accounts, as women are relatively powerless in capitalist societies and also rarely commit crime. Thus, despite the relatively subordinate social and economic position of women and their exploitation and domination by men, women appear in the crime statistics much less frequently than men.

Leonard (1978) and Gregory (1986) have argued that Marxist theory needs to be reformulated so that the considerable impact of gender, as well as class position, on crime is taken into account. What is needed, they suggest, is a socialist feminist theory (see Chapter nine) that can understand women and crime adequately. A theory is needed that enables us to understand why women are relatively uninvolved in crime and what structural factors influence the particular pattern of the crimes in which women do participate. It is necessary to understand the way that legitimate and illegitimate means to socially valued goals are different for women than for men and how women's associates affect them as compared with men's. It is necessary to take into account the ways in which the distribution of wealth and power affect women in capitalist societies and how this influences their criminality. It is necessary to consider why women who are relatively powerless are none the less infrequently labelled criminal. Finally, it is necessary to consider what role women play in a class society, the difference in the oppression of working-class women and working-class men, and the way in which women are controlled and handled in the legal system and in society generally.

Using a socialist feminist perspective, Dee Cook (1987) has studied women who committed fraud against the supplementary benefit system. She argues that the majority of women claiming supplementary benefit are single-parent mothers. They are seen as deviant because they are not living in families that conform to ideas of a normal family in capitalist societies (see Chapter five). The major reason for these women fiddling supplementary benefit, she argues, is economic necessity. When they are caught for fiddling they provoke a negative reaction because of their deviant personal status as well as because of their criminal acts. Social security fiddling for women is seen within a framework that takes into account their class situation and patriarchal ideology.

Labelling theory

Leonard (1978) has argued that labelling theory is potentially valuable for understanding female crime. Using labelling theory it is possible to look at the inherent bias in the law, its relativity, and the different ways in which it is enforced. Within such a framework it would also be possible to examine social reaction to female criminals and how this influenced their self definitions.

Labelling theory developed in the 1960s as one response to positivistic criminology. It was argued that crime was caused by a number of factors, that it was impossible to obtain a representative sample of people who commit crimes from which to generalize, and that deviancy theorists should concentrate on studying societal reaction to crimes and criminals and how labelling as an outsider resulted in changes in self identity. Labelling theorists also argued that crime and deviance were relative and not universal categories. Finally, they rejected the view that value-free research was possible in the social sciences and argued that it was important to look at things from the perspective of the underdog.

Labelling theorists have been criticized for ignoring female deviance and crime. Milkman (1976) has suggested that while labelling theorists presented sympathetic accounts of male deviants, they failed to do so for female ones. She points out that labelling theorists portrayed prostitutes, for example, in a stereotypical way and through the eyes of ponces and pimps rather than through their own self-perceptions.

However, labelling theory has been used by feminists carrying out research on young people. Sue Lees (1986), in her study of teenage girls, has argued that the ways in which young men and young women label young women act as a powerful mechanism of social control (see Chapter three).

Shaklady Smith (1978), in a small ethnographic study of teenage girls, has argued that labelling theory can be used to understand the pattern of female delinquent activities. Using open-ended interviews she studied three groups of young women in the Bristol area in 1970 – thirty girls on probation orders, fifteen girl members of gangs, and thirty girls who had never been referred to any agency dealing with juvenile delinquency, as similar as possible to the first group. She found that girls committed all the kinds of offences with which young men but not girls are usually associated; for example, 63 per cent of the probation group and 73 per cent of the gang sample had deliberately damaged property (see Table 7.5). An analysis of the responses of the gang and probation samples demonstrated that many of them had committed most of the offences for which male juveniles are usually taken to the courts.

Women, crime, and deviance

However, an analysis of court records suggests that girls are much more likely to be brought before the court as in need of care and protection than as charged with offences, but if charged are more likely to be given a custodial sentence.

Table 7.5 Self-report of delinquent acts and offences committed by girls in research by Shaklady Smith

Type of offence	Control sample	Probation sample	Gang sample
Total numbers	30	30	15
	%	%	%
Skipped school	63.3	90.0	93.3
Shoplifting	36.7	90.0	80.0
Breaking and entering	10.0	33.3	26.7
In car without owner's permission	16.7	60.0	60.0
Deliberate property damage	26.7	66.7	73.3
Running away from home	3.3	76.0	53.3
Sex under age of consent	13.3	70.0	73.3
Taken drugs	3.3	10.0	33.2
Taken part in a fight	23.3	63.3	73.3

Source: Shaklady Smith (1978).

Her data also suggests that girls tend either to be conformist or very delinquent. Girl delinquents were labelled, she argues, by parents, teachers, and non-delinquent girls alike, as unfeminine and to be disapproved. However, the labelling of them by others as unfeminine did not result in further status loss, nor did they become promiscuous. Rather, they responded with aggressive behaviour and remained popular among their peers. None the less, they did suffer a double rejection; they were rejected both on account of their violation of the law and because they rejected femininity. The girls saw themselves as tough, dominant, and tomgirlish.

Once labelled, these girls became isolated from their normal peers; parents of non-delinquent girls forbade their daughters to mix with the girl juvenile delinquents. The girls became more and more dependent on the delinquent group.

...social definitions of female delinquency lead not so much to a total rejection of femininity in that a male role is aspired to, as a rejection of certain elements of culturally stereotyped female role which is perceived by the girls as too constraining.

(Shaklady Smith, 1978: 84)

Labelling propelled them into more extreme forms of delinquency. Shaklady Smith suggested that the protective attitudes of probation officers, social workers, and other agencies paradoxically resulted in the same labelling of behaviour as 'common' or 'sluttish'. Long before they reached court, girl juvenile delinquents had 'experienced a continued defining process which classified them as unfeminine'.

Carlen *et al.* (1985) have also shown the ways in which labelling influences the patterns of female crime and the ways in which female criminals are labelled unfeminine. However, labelling theory does not explain why people become criminal in the first place, nor does it take full account of power (class and patriarchal relations) in advanced capitalist societies.

Social control theory

Heidensohn (1986) has suggested that the question we should be asking is not why some women commit crime, but why women are so non-criminal. In other words, we should be explaining why women do *not* become criminal. She suggests that the reason is because of the ways in which women are controlled. She argues that women are controlled within the family and within society generally. She suggests that there are two types of theory of social control. Some theories emphasize the ways in which societies are cemented together by a shared value system. These values or ideologies are transmitted via the media, the educational system, the family, courts, police, and so on. A second type of theory emphasizes bonding in relationship to the family, the peer group, and the school, whereby people are bound into society's norms and values. Thus women are controlled by ideologies of appropriate behaviour for women and by their role in the family.

However, Carlen (in Carlen and Worrall, 1987) has suggested that the problem with control theory is that it does not explain why some women do become criminal. She attempts to develop feminist control theory so that it can do this. She suggests that:

1 Women generally conform while they perceive it to be worth while to do so. Such calculation takes into account the costs and benefits of criminal behaviour.
2 Working-class women are controlled within two areas, the workplace and the family – that is, they are doubly controlled. They thus have to make a 'class deal' – to accept a wage for work – and a 'gender deal' – to take on feminine behaviour.
3 Most working-class women make the class deal and the gender deal because the exploitative nature of these two deals is obscured by the ideology of familialism and community

working together in women to engender an attraction to the (imaginary) norm of respectable working-class womanhood.

4 A commitment to the norms of respectable working-class womanhood is most likely to happen where girls are brought up in families where there is a male bread-winner and a female carer – although girls can learn appropriate behaviour from the mass media, especially women's magazines and pop songs which report marriage coupled with a wage-earning job as a deal to which young women should aspire. Thus the woman most likely to become criminal is one brought up in care or taken into care in adolescence.

5 The majority of women are not criminalized even when caught breaking the law. While they remain in the family as a daughter or wife they are seen as having made the gender deal. It is unassimilated women, women who have been in care or rejected 'normal' family life, who are likely to be seen as recidivist law-breakers.

6 Women who see themselves as marginalized and consequently have nothing to lose may turn to law-breaking and see it as preferable to poverty and social isolation.

Social control theory emphasizes the ways in which girls and women are controlled within both the public and the private spheres and how they are therefore likely to be more conformist than men. The stereotype of women and women's roles plays an important part in explaining the ways in which the control of women is achieved. These assumptions underlie the law governing sexual behaviour, the social benefit system, the interventions of health visitors, and the ways in which the criminal justice system handles and disposes of female offenders. The normal woman is seen as a wife and mother who is in need of protection, while the deviant woman is seen as needing to be trained to perform domestic tasks and child care. However, it is evident that more research needs to be carried out before we can answer the key questions that have been raised concerning women and crime: explanations for the patterning of crime; explanations for why women's crime differs so much from men's; and assessment of how far and in what ways gender differences in crime are linked to class, age, and race.

However, it is clear that explanations which see female crime as a result of a failure of individual women to adapt themselves to their supposedly natural biological role are inadequate and misleading. Women's behaviour, criminal and non-criminal, needs to be explained by reference to a social formation which imposes restrictive and exploitative roles on women. Furthermore, it must be recognized that, in certain economic and ideological circumstances, crime may be a rational and coherent response to women's awareness of the social disabilities imposed on them by class and gender roles.

Radical feminists

Radical feminists have paid more attention to analysing crimes of which women are victims rather than looking at female criminality – that is, to manifestations of male power, and especially to domestic violence, rape, and pornography. However, a radical feminist account would emphasise patriarchal power relationships and women's exploitation and subordinate position in examining female crime.

Sue Edwards (1987) has carried out research into women and prostitution. She argues that explanations for why women become prostitutes are an extension of explanations of the oppression and exploitation of women in patriarchal society: she suggests that because of women's low earning potential, a decline in job opportunities for women, and the erosion of welfare benefits, more girls and young women drift into prostitution. Prostitutes, she argues, are harassed by the police if they walk the streets and controlled by pimps if they work off-street. While women prostitutes face high risks of prosecution or exploitation, the pimps, ponces, and others benefiting from prostitution remain relatively free to exploit prostitute women, as they are placed in an increasingly valuable position in both the law and the economy.

Summary

1 Most theories of deviance have been developed to account for *male* crime and deviance.
2 Women appear less often in official statistics of crime, and the evidence suggests that they do in fact commit fewer crimes. The pattern and nature of their crimes is likewise different from men's.
3 Feminists have tried to extend malestream theories of deviance – such as the labelling perspective – to fit female crime. However, they also have highlighted the importance of taking other factors into account, such as the economic position of women and their role in the family, in understanding women's crimes.

Crimes against women

Women are likely to be victims of all forms of crime, but they are especially vulnerable to violent attacks by men, both sexual and physical and by the men with whom they live as well as men not previously known to them. It is not just that women are the victims of violent men, but that fear of violent crime is a powerful control over women's lives.

Feminists have not only been interested in explaining why men are violent towards women, but in exposing the ways in which women who have been attacked by men are treated in the criminal justice system and by welfare agencies. Frequently, it is argued, women who have been assaulted, whether physically or sexually, end up feeling that they themselves are to blame. Indeed, attacks on women are frequently explained by saying that 'she deserved it' – for example, rape victims are blamed because they went out late at night alone, or wives who have been beaten by their husbands are blamed because they failed in their wifely duties, or daughters who are the victims of incest are said to have tempted their fathers with their flirtatious behaviour.

Sue Lees (1989) has analysed cases in which men have pleaded provocation as a mitigating circumstance when they are being tried for killing a wife, lover, or former lover. (A successful plea of provocation means that the jury returns a verdict of manslaughter rather than murder. The former carries a mandatory life sentence, but in the case of the latter a judge can give any sentence from a conditional (or even in theory an absolute) discharge to life imprisonment.) Lees quotes a number of cases in which male killers who have used the plea of provocation have been given relatively light prison sentences on being found guilty of manslaughter. She argues that the evidence for provocation is often based on the uncorroborated assertion of the accused and his friends, and that verdicts of manslaughter (unpremeditated killing) are often brought in even when there is evidence of premeditation. She points out that if a man kills his wife on finding her in bed with another man he can successfully plead provocation and be found guilty of manslaughter.

She suggests that

> The concept of provocation is based on three very questionable assumptions. Firstly, that a reasonable man can be provoked into murder by insubordinate behaviour – infidelity, bad housekeeping, withdrawal of sexual services and even nagging....The law provides for a legitimation for men to behave violently in the face of insubordination or marriage breakdown....If it can be successfully alleged that the victim was unrespectable, negligent in her wifely duties, then provocation is usually accepted. Secondly, the idea that women can be similarly provoked even when they have been beaten up or raped is seldom entertained. This would be a 'licence to kill' rapists or wife batterers. Thirdly, although the main distinction between murder and manslaughter revolves around whether the killing is premeditated or not ('malice aforethought', or intention to

kill, is murder, but if someone kills by accident or through negligence, or is provoked, it is manslaughter) a defence of provocation on the basis of 'loss of self-control' in practice...often over-rides evidence of premeditation.

(Lees, 1989: 2–3)

Three major forms of explanation of violence towards women have been developed, the first two within malestream theory, and the third (by feminists) as a critique of the malestream theories and an alternative account:

1 *The traditionalist.* In this perspective crimes such as rape and assault on wives are seen as infrequent. While not all women are seen as the cause of the violent behaviour, many are. Thus, rape victims are said to have enticed the rapist and 'caused' him to have uncontrollable sexual urges. This can be either because of their behaviour in public places or by 'leading on' the man with whom they have been out, encouraging him to expect that he will be given sex. It is accepted that some victims are innocent, but they are expected to demonstrate this by resisting the attack and showing considerable evidence of physical injury.

   Assaults on wives are also seen as being deserved by the wife for failing in her duties, and men are assumed to have responsibility for controlling their wives. Indeed, until the nineteenth century in England the debate concerned not whether a man could beat his wife but how much he could beat her. The saying 'a rule of thumb' comes from one legal judgment that a man could legally beat his wife with a stick provided it was no thicker than his thumb. It was not until the end of the nineteenth century that assaults on wives of this nature became illegal. In the traditionalist perspective, as with rape, it is accepted that some men beat their wives without just cause, but this is thought to be a relatively small proportion.

2 *Liberal/psychiatric* This perspective accepts that violence towards women is a social problem, but it sees it again as a relatively minor problem. In this view either the male perpetrator is seen as sick or disturbed or the female victim is seen as seeking out violence. Thus for rape the rapist is seen as mentally ill or socially inadequate, or female victims are said to be masochistic. Similarly, men who beat their wives are said either to have been brought up in a home where they were battered as children or to beat their wives as a result of being drunk, or the wives are said to want to be beaten.

In this perspective men who are violent to women are seen as sick and as needing treatment, or to be the 'victims' of women who invite violence.

3 *Feminist perspectives* There is no single feminist perspective, but all feminist approaches locate violence to women by men within the broader context of women's position as subordinate to men. In the 1970s, feminists tended to try to explain rape and assaults on wives as serious indications of men's violence towards women. However, more recently feminists have challenged this view and suggest that anything that frightens or intimidates women must be seen in the context of men's control of women's behaviour. Thus women's fear of violence acts to control their behaviour, so that they restrict and limit their activities, and if they do go out at night they place themselves in the protection of a man. Furthermore, the advice to women is always not to go out when another woman has been raped in an area; it is never suggested that men should stay in so that it is safe for women to go out. Feminists have also become more concerned with doing research that explores how women experience male violence and power and how fear of rape and attacks from men restrict their behaviour, rather than in developing explanations for male violence. Feminist research has also demonstrated the limited value of legal reforms aimed at helping women who are the victims of male violence and the failure of the police and the courts to deal adequately with such men.

Until the 1970s the victimization of women by men remained hidden. However, with the rise of second wave feminism the extent of assaults on wives, of rape, and of child sexual abuse has become more evident. Women have become more prepared to report men who commit violence against them and, more importantly, welfare agencies, the police, and the courts have become more prepared to believe women and children. However, feminists argue that the extent of these crimes is still grossly underestimated and that the criminal justice system is still reluctant to accept how widespread violence against women and children is and to deal with the offenders. Feminists argue that rape and assaults on wives are serious crimes and should be treated as such. The perpetrators of these crimes should be charged and punished in the same way as they would be for any other serious violent crime.

Rape

Feminists argue that: 'the fear of rape affects all women. It inhibits their actions and limits their freedom, influencing the way they dress, the hours they keep, the routes they walk. The fear is well founded, because no woman is immune from rape' (Lorrine Clarke and Debra Lewis, 1977, p. 23).

In Britain rape is legally defined as unlawful sexual intercourse (which in turn means that the penis must penetrate the vagina). The Sexual Offences (Amendment) Act 1976 says that a man commits rape if:

1 he has sexual intercourse with a woman who at the time of intercourse does not consent to it;
2 at the time knows that she does not consent to the intercourse or is reckless as to whether she consents to it.

A man cannot rape his wife, as the law assumes that the marriage contract gives him the right to have sexual intercourse with her. Feminists have been concerned to examine three issues: first, to ask why rape occurs and what attitudes and beliefs support it, second, to examine the social and legal constraints which prevent women obtaining their legal rights, and third, to understand the experience of rape victims.

Rape is commonly viewed as the outcome of the male sex drive – that men have uncontrollable sexual urges. However, Barbara Toner (1977) suggests that anthropological evidence shows that the strength of the male sex drive depends on cultural attitudes and values. She points out that amongst the Arapesh of New Guinea rape is virtually unknown, while amongst the Gusii of Kenya it is a major form of social control.

Feminists argue that rape is an act of violence and domination which devalues and dehumanizes the victim. Susan Brownmiller (1976), a radical feminist, argues that men are natural predators and women their natural prey. Men have the ability to rape women but women cannot retaliate in kind. Rape, she argues, is used by men to generate fear in all women, and this is a conscious process of intimidation. Women, she argues, continue to be subordinated by men through the threat of rape. Women will be able to overcome their subordination only when they are fully integrated into the state apparatus for legislating against rape and for enforcing that legislation. The state will then be able to protect women from rape.

Most feminists, however, reject biological explanations for rape and argue that rape is sustained and justified by patriarchal ideology and patriarchal relations. Radical feminists argue that patriarchal ideology defines women as either mothers who are respected or sexual objects for men's pleasure. Men want to gain sexual possession of women, and men control women's sexuality for their own purposes. They argue that while patriarchal ideology overtly condemns rape, it covertly legitimates it by viewing it as normal. In courts of law rapists often use the excuse, successfully, that the victim 'asked for it'. Furthermore, feminists argue that the rape law is concerned to protect the interests of men as much as the honour of women. Rape is viewed as a crime against property – daughters and wives; the father's/husband's property is damaged.

Feminists argue that rape is a political act that takes away a woman's autonomy to decide what to do with her own body. It is an act of aggression which carries with it the threat of death. Rape victims are chosen indiscriminately, in that no woman is immune from rape. Rape teaches all women that they are subordinate to men and it keeps women in a state of fear. It is thus an effective way of controlling women and restricting their freedom.

Feminists argue that the victims of rape are frequently 'put on trial' by the court procedures and blamed for the crime themselves. This is especially the case if the woman leads a sexually active life or her behaviour is seen as having 'caused' the rape by, for example, hitching a lift at night. Recent changes in the law so that a woman's sex life could not automatically be examined in court have not protected women from this, as most judges have in practice given permission for the woman to be questioned about her sexual history (Edwards, 1984).

Also, in rape trials the rules of corroboration play a key role. Juries are warned by the judge that it is dangerous to convict on the uncorroborated evidence of the complainant, but that they may do so if they are satisfied that it is true. The dangers of convicting on the basis of uncorroborated evidence are present in all trials, but the law requires the jury to be warned of this only in rape trials, treason trials, and when the evidence has been given by children or accomplices. In rape trials the implied insult, that rape victims are no more reliable as witnesses than children or accomplices, is compounded by the jury being told that the experience of the courts is that women accuse men of rape for totally malicious reasons and innocent men must be protected from such allegations. Given that there are rarely witnesses to rape, and often the victim's and accused's accounts differ only as to whether she consented to sexual intercourse, rape convictions are difficult to obtain unless there is corroborative evidence – for example, if the victim received injuries.

Indeed, long before the crime comes to trial women are degraded and disbelieved. Women are reluctant to report rape in the first place because of the ways in which rape victims are questioned by the police and the ways in which medical examinations are carried out. The police are less likely to believe the rape allegation of some women than others. For example, Ann Burgess and Linda Holmstrom (1979) studied the cases of 146 women and girls who reported to a hospital emergency room (casualty reception) in the United States as having been raped. They suggest that the responses of the police and the decision as to whether to prosecute or not was based on stereotypes of rape. The woman was believed and the police carried out an investigation if the woman was previously a virgin, if she was judged emotionally stable, if the rapist was a stranger and if the rapist used, or threatened to use, a weapon. The case was dropped if the victim had gone willingly, if she was unmarried and sexually experienced, if she had emotional problems, if she was calm when she was making the report, and if the rapist was known to her. Barbara Toner (1977) found that the police in Britain held similar stereotypes of rape. Women reporting rape are more likely to be taken seriously if they report the offence immediately, are upset, did not know the rapist, and show signs of having put up a struggle. (However, feminists have suggested that women do not want to be beaten, and victims of rape have often said that they were too frightened to resist and that they were afraid they would be killed if they did.) Toner found that women who reported rape often felt they were treated unsympathetically by the police and found the medical inspection conducted in an insultingly matter-of-fact way.

Feminists have challenged a number of myths about rape:

1 Rape is widely believed to be impossible. It is argued that women can always avoid being raped by running away or resisting and fighting back. This ignores the aspect of fear, that women are too frightened to run away and are scared of the consequences if they resist.

2 It is believed that women enjoy rape. However, studies of women who have been raped suggest that they felt humiliated and frightened. Also, men benefit from the belief that women want intercourse.

3 It is believed that rape is a rare act. However, victim studies and the experience of rape crisis centres suggests that only a small number of rapes are reported to the police. Ruth Hall (1985), in the only published UK incidence report, found prevalence figures of 17 per cent for rape and 20 per cent for attempted rape.

4 It is believed that rape is committed by strangers. Statistics show that the rapist is as likely to be known to the victim as to be a stranger. Also, rapes are as likely to happen indoors as in the open. For example, Amir (1971) found that 57 per cent of rapists were known to their victims.

5 It is believed that rape is committed only by psychopaths. However, studies suggest that few convicted rapists are mentally abnormal. Carol and Barry Smart (1978) point out that rapists are not treated differently from other offenders by the legal system and generally receive short sentences, and that few are dealt with under the Mental Health legislation.

Furthermore, the criminal records of convicted rapists often include non-sexual as well as sexual crimes.

6 It is believed that rape is an impulsive act, the result of uncontrollable sexual urges, and is unplanned. Women are said to 'cause' the urges which men cannot control. However, research has demonstrated that most rapes are planned. For example, Amir (1971) found that 70 per cent were planned, 11 per cent partially planned, and only 16 per cent what he called 'explosive'.

7 It is believed that rape is a problem of the lower classes. However, men of all ages and all social classes attack women.

Assaults on wives

The extent to which wives are violently assaulted became evident in the early 1970s when women's liberation groups began to respond to the obvious need for refuges for women who wanted to leave violent men. The women who came to refuges had often been living with men who had beaten them violently for years. Many had tried unsuccessfully to leave their husbands or partners on a number of occasions, but the problem of finding accommodation and supporting themselves and their children had frequently driven them back to the violent home. Welfare agencies, the police, and the courts were reported to be at best unhelpful and at worst likely to advise them to 'make the best of it'.

This comes about at least in part because violence in the family is seen as a private affair, something to be sorted out by the husband and wife themselves, rather than something needing intervention by welfare agencies, the police and the courts. The police frequently refer to such incidents as 'domestic' rather than regarding them as serious cases of assault. Furthermore, calling them domestic shifts the blame for the violence from the husband to the husband and wife and normalizes it as part of family life. Police reluctance to take assaults on wives seriously is also evidenced by their reluctance to charge husbands with assault and take them to court. They argue that this is because wives usually refuse to testify and forgive their husbands. However, evidence from states in the USA where police are required to charge husbands who assault wives does not support this contention, and nor does research in Britain that has examined this 'attrition rate'.

Most research into assaults on wives has been carried out by interviewing women in refuges. In the main the research has been carried out by academics. Indeed, the Department of Health and Social Security has been criticized for commissioning research on wife-assault from academics rather than involving the women in the refuge movement, it being suggested that the DHSS spent large sums of money on research that could better have been spent helping the victims of abuse (Hanmer and Leonard, 1984). The findings of research, they suggest, have added little that the women in the refuge women did not know already.

The largest single feminist study of wife-beating was carried out by Rebecca and Russell Dobash (1980) in Scotland. They argue that the problem of violence against women is a deep-rooted societal one arising out of the patriarchal family system, a system in which the husband's authority over the wife creates a particular marriage power relationship and a subordinate position for wives and mothers. They argue that men are more powerful than women and exploit the labour of women in marriage – that is, women are expected to service their husbands by providing domestic services for them. They argue that one of the major factors precipitating male violence to their wives is husbands' perceptions that a wife is not performing her wifely duties satisfactorily; for example, a house seen as not cleaned properly, a meal not prepared promptly, or a wife suspected of not being sexually faithful. Jan Pahl (1985), in her research, also found that men who beat their wives had frequently tried to control their behaviour and expected them to stay at home and not go out alone.

Feminist researchers have also explored why women find it so difficult to leave violent men. They argue that there are economic, social, ideological and legal factors which all interact to make it difficult for women to leave violent men. In economic terms it is difficult for a woman to support herself and her children, but more urgent is the problem of finding housing. Indeed, Jan Pahl found that the women she interviewed were frequently surprised to discover that they were financially better off on supplementary benefit than they had been when living with their husbands (Pahl, 1985). Housing was a major problem; in the past the women had left home but had been forced back because of their inability to find suitable accommodation. The refuge provided a warm and friendly environment that battered wives could turn to, but it was not suitable for the long term.

In social terms wives who have been assaulted often feel that they cannot admit that their marriage has failed. They blame themselves and see it as an individual problem. Also, a woman's relatives and friends may well tell her that she has herself to blame for being in the situation and that she must put up with it (Homer *et al.*, 1984).

Patriarchal and familial ideology also influence the response of welfare agencies to wives who have been assaulted. Johnson (1985) argues that social workers have not been trained to deal with assaults on wives, that they lack the resources to help women victims and at best they can refer the women to a hostel. A large proportion of assaulted women seek medical help – for example, 80 per cent of the Dobash and Dobash (1980) sample had been to the doctor, and 64 per cent of the women Jan Pahl (1985) interviewed – although they rarely mentioned that they were beaten by their husbands. Doctors do not see marital problems as part of their concern; this is not the kind of problem that 'real' medicine is concerned with. In a number of studies women have been critical of the response of doctors to their attempt to seek help, and especially of the medical practice of prescribing tranquillizers (Dobash and Dobash, 1980; Pahl, 1985). Non-medical advice, when it was offered, was generally to leave the man, but no account was taken of practical problems. The police were also frequently criticized in these studies and by the women who had been assaulted. Police, it is argued, are reluctant to intervene in what they regard as domestic disputes and will rarely take the men to court.

In the 1970s the one major response of the Government to the problem of assaults on wives was a set of legal reforms designed to give women greater protection from violent men and to make it easier for women to leave them. An analysis of how the legal reforms have worked in practice demonstrates, feminists argue, both the limitations of reform and the ways in which patriarchal ideology influences judicial decisions.

Three Acts were passed in the late 1970s, all designed to assist women assaulted by their husbands: the Domestic Violence and Matrimonial Proceedings Act 1976, the Domestic Proceedings and Magistrates' Courts Act 1978 and the Housing (Homeless Persons) Act 1977. The 1977 Housing Act made it the responsibility of local authorities to rehouse certain categories of people – mainly families – providing they had not intentionally made themselves homeless. The Act explicitly stated that women who had left a violent man should not be seen as having intentionally made themselves homeless and should be rehoused if they had dependent children. However, many local authorities have not rehoused women and their children. Furthermore, even if they are prepared to accept the woman as homeless the problem is not solved. The woman and her children will have to live in accommodation designated for homeless persons for some time and then to accept the first offer of permanent accommodation, however unsatisfactory the woman may find it. Also, while she is in temporary accommodation the husband may be able to gain custody of the children; still living in the matrimonial home, he may be able to convince the court that he can better provide for his children than can his wife. If the wife no longer has custody of the children, she is no longer entitled to be rehoused by the local authority.

The Domestic Violence and Matrimonial Proceedings Act (DVMPA) and the Domestic Proceedings and Magistrates Act (DPMA) were both designed to give battered women greater protection. The DVMPA applied in the County Courts and permitted courts to issue non-molestation and exclusion injunctions independently of any other proceedings before the court. Injunctions were to be available in an emergency, could have powers of arrest attached, and men could be sent to prison for breach of an injunction. Relief was available to married and cohabiting women equally. The DPMA extends similar powers to Magistrates' Courts. This meant that women had a local, inexpensive, simple, and quick access to relief if they were assaulted. However, the provisions applied only to married women, magistrates had no powers to exclude men from certain localities, and husbands could be arrested only if they inflicted actual physical injury on their wives.

In practice these Acts have not extended much greater protection to wives. Case law has established legal precedents which demonstrate judges' and magistrates' reluctance to prevent a man entering his property. It has been made evident that the courts see the protection of children as the most important factor. There has been a reluctance to use the emergency powers, and injunctions are frequently issued without powers of arrest attached, which means the police argue that they cannot enforce the injunction. Over and above this, the police have been reluctant to intervene even when powers of arrest have been attached.

We can conclude, then, that the current state of English law on domestic violence is one of a legal system which provides all the necessary remedies, but which in its operation fails to protect women as fully as it should and leaves them vulnerable.

Women, violence, and male power

Some feminists have argued that by concentrating on rape and assaults on wives the real extent of male violence against women is obscured. They argue that all women are affected by male violence and that the crime statistics and official victim and self-report studies seriously underestimate the extent of violence towards women by men. Violence is a powerful mechanism of social control; women's movements are severely restricted by the actual violence they experience and by fear of male violence. Violence, it is argued, encompasses more than actual physical assault and includes all behaviour designed to control and intimidate women carried out by men. The extent to which men control and intimidate women only becomes evident when we include sexual harassment, obscene telephone calls, flashing, and other behaviour by men designed to control women. Liz Kelly (1988) has offered the following definition of sexual violence:

> [Sexual violence] includes any physical, visual, verbal or sexual act that is experienced by the woman or girl, at the time or later, as a

threat, menace or assault, that has the effect of hurting her or degrading her and/or takes away her ability to control intimate contact.

(Kelly, 1988: 41)

Research by Jalna Hanmer and Susan Saunders (1984) and by Jill Radford (1987) has found that women's behaviour is very much restricted by their fear of men – both in the domestic sphere and in the public. Women do not go out at night, or to certain places, not only because they fear attack, but also because the men with whom they live try to prevent them going out alone. They also found that women experience considerable amounts of violent behaviour from men, but that much of this is hidden – it is not reported to the police, nor do women reveal their experience of violence in response to surveys such as the British Crime Survey. They suggest that this is because women are reluctant to reveal the extent to which men are violent and there is no reason to suppose that the women who have not reported the violence to the police are more likely to reveal it to a survey. In their research they acknowledged the reasons why they were doing the research in advance and left the women to define violence themselves. They argue, therefore, that their findings reflect more accurately the experiences of the women and their perceptions of violence.

Jacqui Halson (1989) argues that her research among 14-year-old girls in a co-educational school confirms that sexual harassment is a form of sexual violence commonly experienced by young women both in school and outside. The young women experienced sexual harassment from both male teachers and male pupils, and she argues that the school sanctioned it by not intervening and therefore reproduced the existing imbalances of power between women and men. The girls felt uncomfortable and threatened by the behaviour of one male teacher, who was referred to as 'a right Casanova'. The boys leered at the girls, verbally harassed them and physically assaulted them, although the behaviour usually stopped short of rape. Often one girl was sexually harassed by a gang of boys, and this increased a sense of powerlessness and meant that the girls policed their own behaviour so that they were not likely to meet a group of boys when on their own. The girls did not find the boys' behaviour flattering, but offensive and humiliating, and in no way could it be said to be experienced as 'friendly', 'inoffensive', or 'just teasing'. Nor was it mutual, and it could not be dismissed as banter or mutual flattery. The girls were not empowered to challenge the boys because the school's attitude was that such behaviour was harmless, not a serious problem, and there were no school rules forbidding it.

Halson suggests that one incident reveals the lack of understanding by the school authorities of how seriously the girls viewed sexual harassment. Some graffiti were put up in the school – 'Mary is a slag'. The young woman concerned was extremely upset, and her mother came to the school and threatened to take action. However, a senior member of the staff suggested that the mother was making a lot of fuss over nothing and that 'slag' was a common term of abuse used to refer to girls – precisely missing the key point, that terms like 'slag' are used to diminish women, to humiliate them, and to enable men to control them.

Liz Stanley (1984) has argued that the type of research that seeks to reveal how women make sense of their experiences when confronted by violent behaviour is essential. In analysing her own experience of receiving obscene telephone calls she argues that the police response of advising women to hang up is inadequate, not only because the police fail to understand how women actually feel when they receive such calls, but also because it does nothing to deal with the problem. She found that it was frequently some time into the conversation before it became evident that the call was obscene, and that hanging up does not cut the line; consequently when the telephone was picked up some time later the caller was still there. Her strategy for dealing with such calls was to challenge male power by pretending that she could not hear the caller and asking him to speak up. The usual response of the caller was to hang up after a few minutes.

However, not all male violence is as easy to challenge as that of obscene telephone callers. Carol Ramazanoglu (1987) has pointed out how difficult it is for female academics to challenge sexual harassment from male colleagues, and in other situations women do not have the physical strength to fight men. Other researchers have argued that the response of women to other forms of violence is eminently rational when seen from their perspective. Women who are raped or flashed at say that they are scared of being killed and this conditions their response. Women do not report incidents of violence to the police because they are aware of the patriarchal response that they will elicit. Women who are the victims of male violence are likely to see themselves as blamed for it. Feminists are aware that neither changes in legislation nor asking men to change their behaviour are likely to make much difference, although both are important. They therefore argue that women should organize to help themselves, for more refuges run and controlled by women, for rape crisis centres, and for women to be taught self-defence techniques.

What is also vital is to challenge the view that assaults on wives and rape are in some sense different from other violent crimes. They are, of course, in that they are examples of the ways in which men use violence to maintain or reassert their power over women and control women, but they are *not* less serious. Indeed, it could be argued that they are more

181

serious. What must be challenged is the common-sense view that crimes in the domestic sphere are a private matter and not the concern of the police and the criminal justice system, and that rape is a sexual crime, the result of men's innate sexual urges.

Feminists are challenged by those that argue that women can be violent to men, and that this is also hidden. Rebecca and Russell Dobash (1980) say that they have frequently been asked about assaults on husbands when they give lectures on wife-battering. They argue that there is no evidence to suggest that this is a serious problem. Mildred Pagelow (1985) in her research in the US found no evidence to suggest that assaults on husbands were common. Perhaps, however, the most telling thing is that there are no refuges for battered husbands and no apparent demand. It has been suggested that this is because men are unwilling to confess that they are beaten by their wives. However, men can much more easily leave a violent home than can a woman. Men are not expected to care for the children and they have the economic means of supporting themselves that women lack.

Summary

1 Feminists have highlighted aspects of crime hitherto ignored or considered 'normal' – for example, rape, assault on wives, and sexual harassment.
2 Feminists have argued that these need to be explained in the context of male power and the fact that sexual and physical violence is, in some sense, considered normal behaviour for men in our society, but not for women.

Conclusions

In this chapter we have dealt with two aspects of feminist work on crime. In the first half we discussed feminist work on women and crime, and in the second half work on male violence towards women. The two halves reflect very different feminist approaches. The work on women and crime is heavily academic in orientation and is concerned with either incorporating women into existing theories of crime or arguing the need to reformulate sociological approaches to crime in order that they can adequately explain both why women are so non-criminal and the behaviour of the women who do break the law. The work on women and violence has to a large extent been carried out by radical feminists (see Chapter one for more details) who are concerned not only with researching the problem of men's violence to women but also in developing strategies for dealing with it. They argue that male violence affects all women, irrespective of age or social class, and that it is one of the major ways in which men control women in patriarchal societies. We have included such material in this chapter on women and crime because we want to demonstrate not only the ways in which malestream sociology has ignored or marginalized the crimes that are committed by men against women, but also the ways in which the legal system marginalizes, trivializes, and belies women's victimization, and how it blames it on the victim. Men who are attacked on the street are not told that they should not have been out there; women are. Men who are beaten up are not told it was because of the way they behaved; women are. Men are not advised not to go out at night alone or not to visit certain places; women are. Women's behaviour is controlled by men and this control is reinforced not only by the media, the police and the courts but by other women. Control of women is a key aspect of understanding women's behaviour; why women break the law and why they do not, and why they are attacked, beaten, and abused by men.

Further reading

Hanmer, J. and Saunders, S. (1984) *Well-Founded Fear*, London: Hutchinson.
Heidensohn, F. (1986) *Women and Crime*, London: Macmillan.
Kelly, E. (1988) *Surviving Sexual Violence*, Cambridge: Polity.

Chapter eight

Women and politics

Women are notably absent from what is conventionally seen as 'politics' in Britain. Despite the fact that the Conservative Party leader, Mrs Thatcher, is prime minister and has been since 1979, there are few other women in key positions of political power in contemporary Britain; few women trade union leaders, members of Parliament, or local government councillors. Women are assumed to be less able at carrying out political tasks than men and less interested in politics. Political sociology has tended in the past to accept this common-sense view of women's relationship to politics and to give it scientific authority.

Sylvia Walby (1988a) has argued that there have been four kinds of approach to gender issues in political sociology:

1 women have been seen as irrelevant to politics, or when mentioned have been seen as behaving in less authentically political ways than men;
2 criticisms have been raised of the ways in which women have been distorted in political sociology and especially in voting studies;
3 there have been feminist studies of women's political activity;
4 analyses have been made of gendered politics, examining not only women's political activity but also patriarchal resistance – that is, the power struggle between feminism and patriarchy.

To this we would add a fifth: an analysis of the role of the state in creating and maintaining the nuclear family and the role of women as wives and mothers.

In this chapter we shall examine the feminist criticisms of malestream political sociology and feminist research on women's political activity.

Women and voting studies

Siltanen and Stanworth (1984) have suggested that women's political capacity has been underrated in the malestream literature. Malestream research has suggested that women's participation in politics is less than men's and that women's concerns and demands are a reflection of moral or familial commitments rather than an authentic political stance. For example, men are said to be concerned about pay and hours of work while women are more concerned with working conditions. However, they suggest that this literature has exaggerated the differences between men and women in political behaviour, and while suggesting that women's political behaviour is influenced by the private sphere it has discounted the influence of the private sphere on the political behaviour of men. In terms of voting behaviour, malestream researchers have claimed that women vote less than men, that women are more conservative than men, that women are more fickle than men, and that women are more influenced by personalities. However, a re-examination of the literature and research findings by feminists suggests that the evidence on which these conclusions are based is very flimsy indeed.

Susan Bourque and Jean Grosshaltz (1974) have argued that malestream researchers have often interpreted data and made assumptions that 'fit in' with their preconceived ideas of women's political behaviour. First, Bourque and Grossholtz point to the 'fudging of the footnotes' which enables statements to be made about women's political orientations which are either unsupported by the references or misleading simplifications of the original. Second, they argue there is a tendency to assume that men (especially husbands) influence women's political opinions and behaviour, but not vice versa – especially in terms of voting. Third, there is the unquestioned assumption that the political attitudes, preferences, and style of participation characteristic of men defines mature political behaviour. Women's behaviour is seen as immature by definition, if it differs from this. Fourth, it is assumed that women's political concerns are located in their role as mothers, and this results in a constrained view of women's political potential. Similarly, Dowse and Hughes (1971) have shown that references to the fact that women are more conservative than men are often supported by data which in fact show, at most, very small differences.

Goot and Reid (1975) challenge the view that women's political participation demonstrates that women are less politically aware than men, or less interested. They argue that the evidence indicates the degree to which political parties, trade unions, and the norms of political participation do not resonate with the concerns, needs, and opportunities of many women. The timing of trade unions and political party meetings often makes it difficult for women with domestic commitments to attend and participate. Women often find it difficult to participate in after-meeting drink sessions at the pub, where important business is discussed. Men often argue that issues of central concern to women are less important or somehow 'less political' than the issues which concern men. Indeed, some issues of critical concern to women are seen as tied in with their natural role and not something that should be on the political agenda at all. Local matters which have been interpreted in this light include workplace issues such as paid maternity leave, demands for the provision of workplace nurseries, school holiday play schemes, and paid time off from work to care for sick children. At a national level, 'the endowment of motherhood' – the idea that women should be paid to bring up children on behalf of the nation – has been viewed similarly, and it took a ruling by the European Commission for married women caring for a sick or disabled husband to be allowed to claim the Care Allowance (an allowance of £23 paid to someone who cares for a person receiving attendance allowance). Women have had to fight to get issues such as abortion rights, contraception, equal pay, and so on seen as important political issues. Given this, plus the fact that so few women are candidates in national or union elections, it is perhaps not surprising that women's political participation is not identical to men's.

However, careful research has suggested that gender differences are not a major factor in voting behaviour and that social class is a more important predictor. For example, it has been suggested that women are less likely to cast their vote than men, and this has been used to argue that women are less interested in politics. However, older people are less likely, statistically, to vote than younger people, and there are more old women than old men; when allowance is made for age, the apparent difference virtually disappears (Crewe *et al.*, 1979; Rose, R., 1976). It is often argued that women are influenced in how they vote by the preferences of their husbands (see, for example, Lazarsfeld *et al.*, 1968). However, the best conclusion from the evidence is that the influence is mutual (Maccoby *et al.*, 1954; Jennings and Niemi, 1974; Weiner, 1978; Prandy, 1986). Women are said to be more Conservative than men – that is, more likely to vote for the Conservative Party. Goot and Reid (1975) have pointed out that gender differences in voting behaviour since 1945 have always been small. Indeed, in some general elections women have tended to prefer the Labour to the Conservative Party – in 1945, for instance (Durant, 1966), and in 1964 (Butler and King, 1965). Furthermore, in both the 1979 and the 1983 general elections more men than women voted Conservative.

Political scientists have not in general been much concerned with women's political behaviour, and it has generally been assumed that women are less interested in political issues because their main interest lies in the domestic sphere. However, this division between a public and a private or domestic sphere is itself a political issue, and to say that a concern with working conditions, the education of children, the availability of abortion, and so on is the mark of a moral rather than a political concern is to make a definite and, in many ways, contemptuous value judgement (see Siltanen and Stanworth, 1984). It is indeed possible – likely, even – that women's experiences differ from men's and therefore determine their voting behaviour differently. Women may well be more affected than men by cuts in public expenditure in education, health, and the implementation of community care, or, at least, more aware of the results of such policies. As Dorothy Smith (1979) has argued, women's lives are cast by their circumstances less in the 'abstract mode' of conceptual argument and more in the concrete reality in which such arguments are grounded; men may have theories on education or health care, but it is the women who take the children to school and to the doctor. Issues such as working hours, the provision of nurseries, antenatal provision, and the like may therefore loom larger for women than for men. They are *political* issues, however, and to ignore them or relegate them to domestic-sphere morality is to ignore the basis on which many women make their political choices. Finally, one may argue that if women *were* less interested in public politics than men – a proposition for which the empirical evidence is not strong – it would be because they felt, realistically, that they had little chance of influencing events because the political agenda and the processes of politics are dominated by men.

Thus, some feminists have concluded that an emphasis on gender differences in political sociology is inappropriate. Such an emphasis would have a number of consequences:

1 By emphasizing the characteristics that are seen as 'male' or 'female', studies treat men and women as if they were homogeneous social groups, and the variations *within* each gender are played down. Thus, for example, the 'job model' – the view that a man's political attitudes and behaviour are determined by work experiences – is applied to men, and a 'gender model' to women.

2 Roles in the domestic sphere are seen as shaping women's, and only women's, voting behaviour. It is suggested that women vote for candidates because of their personal qualities, though it has not been suggested that men voted for Mrs Thatcher because of her charms or wifely qualities.

3 The assumption that political parties, trade unions, etc. are gender-fair and that women's lack of active participation is due to their lack of interest, ignores the male domination and

control of such organizations. For example, Siltanen and Stanworth (1984) quote research that shows that many women are committed to the trade union movement but do not join, or leave having joined, because of disenchantment with the union's failure to deal with women's issues.

Feminists have, however, been concerned *not* to argue that women's political action is identical to men's. They have argued that malestream research and male-dominated trade unions and political parties have a taken-for-granted definition of what is to count as political. However, this definition excludes much of women's expertise and political concerns. Feminists offer an alternative interpretation of women's relationship to public life. They demonstrate the extent to which the 'male as the norm' principle operates in political and social analysis – the way in which a demarcation between the 'political' and the 'social' or 'moral' is based on arbitrary but sex-linked criteria. For example, Greenstein (1965) found that girls scored higher than boys on measures of 'citizen duty' and 'political efficacy' but relabels these attributes as moral rather than political. Feminists suggest that it is necessary to attribute new meanings to women's political activities. For example, refraining from voting may actually be a reflection of the low efficacy of voting. Given that women's political concerns are not reflected in politics, the question should be why women should vote rather than why they should not. Finally, it is argued that what are seen as women's skills need to be revalued and seen as of relevance to political life. It is suggested that the priorities, skills, and issues that women bring with them from the domestic sphere are valuable additions to politics. Women's struggle to stay human in the workplace, by arguing for better conditions, might act as an example of this.

Defining feminist politics

Feminists have argued that women do engage in political activities as conventionally defined. As we have seen above, women's voting behaviour is very similar to men's. Women do belong to trade unions. There are women who are active members of trade unions and political parties, women local councillors, women members of Parliament, women general secretaries of trade unions, and so on. Women are active in politics, even if the number of women so engaged is much smaller than the number of men. Feminists have also suggested that women are often alienated from politics and excluded by the control and domination of organizations by men. However, feminists have also argued that women's political activities and concerns have been marginalized and 'hidden from history', as well as that politics, and what is seen as political, need to be redefined. Thus, they have maintained that feminism is itself political and is concerned with the struggle for women's liberation and emancipation. Feminists, for example, have had to rediscover the political activities of First Wave feminists, a movement often portrayed as just a group of middle-class women fighting for the vote. The other activities they engaged in and the writings of nineteenth century feminists are ignored or reinterpreted as concerned with moral/personal issues. However, the major argument of feminists has been that 'the personal is the political' – that is, that politics is concerned with the dynamics of power relationships in society and must therefore be concerned with the power relationships between men and women. Thus, in the public sphere, the power that men exercise over women is often ignored while their domination in the domestic sphere is even less often considered.

Kate Millett, in *Sexual Politics*, defines politics as 'power-structured relationships, arrangements whereby one group of persons is controlled by another' (1977, p. 23). The feminist definition of politics puts on the agenda not only power relationships between men and women at the personal level, but also the importance of patriarchal ideology in controlling women's lives. Thus, the orthodox idea, for example, that women have a free choice in deciding whether to do housework, is challenged (see Chapter four). Furthermore, feminists argue that the very division between public and private is a patriarchal idea used to exclude women and women's concerns from politics. They argue that women have been excluded from participation in politics and public life and that the state has construed the family as private – as an institution outside of state intervention. In this way, in the name of personal freedom and privacy, the arena in which women are most exploited and subordinated, in families, is exempted from political intervention. The separation between the public and the private has made possible the legislation of female equality in the former while ignoring the real differences that exist in the latter. Furthermore, the public/private split makes it possible to keep women's values out of the public sphere. Some feminists, especially radical ones (see Chapter nine), argue that because of their roles as mothers women have a deeper sense of humility, caring and community, of belonging and selflessness, than men. Also, women are prevented from participating on equal terms with men in the public sphere because of the responsibilities they have, or are attributed, in the domestic sphere, and men are often prevented from taking on caring roles in the home.

Feminists have pointed out that this conceptual split between the public and the private does not even necessarily accord with the facts of social and political life. Indeed, it has been argued that the state has actually 'created' and sustained the family as an institution, and women's subordination within it (see Chapters four and five). Legislation on matters such as social security has assumed that women do and should live with a man on whom they are financially dependent. On the other hand, matters arising in the public sphere are said to be private: for example, sexual harassment, legislation on contraception, and abortion have all been said to be private/moral issues rather than political ones.

Feminist politics

The rediscovery of women's history has been a major achievement of feminist scholarship in recent years. As part of the reclaiming of 'herstory', First Wave feminism as a political movement has been uncovered. However, contemporary feminists suggest that nineteenth-century (First Wave) feminists fought for equal rights for women in the public sphere; late twentieth-century feminists have sought to free women from subordination to men.

Women, and especially married women, had few rights in the nineteenth century, and throughout the century women struggled to achieve the same rights as men. Many of these women were middle-class and sought to have the same rights to education, to voting, to work, etc. as middle-class men, but few were concerned about the plight of working-class women, who were often forced to work long hours and had even fewer rights that their middle-class sisters. Nevertheless, working-class women were politically active, especially towards the end of the century, when women founded their own trade unions and participated in the suffrage movement.

The situation of Caroline Norton (Forster, 1984) provides a graphic illustration of the lack of rights which married women experienced. She was married to a man who assaulted her physically and lived off her earnings as a writer. When she eventually decided she could take no more and left him, she found she had no right of access to her own children, no right to control her own property, including even her jewellery and clothing, and no right to her own earnings. It would have been impossible for her to remain separated from her husband if she had not had relatives who were prepared to keep her. In the nineteenth century women were a legally inferior caste; they were not regarded as persons under the law. Women did not gain the right to custody of infant children until 1839, nor to control their own property until 1882, nor to vote until 1918, nor to get a divorce on the same grounds as men until 1934.

Juliet Mitchell (in Mitchell and Oakley, 1986) traces the origins of the feminist movement to the concept of equality and equal rights that was first introduced during the English Revolution in the seventeenth

century and was further developed in the eighteenth-century enlightenment and the French Revolution. The first expressions of feminism were
based on the concept of equality – that men and women should be
treated equally. This was demanded by women who saw themselves as
a social group completely excluded from the tenets and principles of the
'new' society that had developed after the English Revolution.
Eighteenth-century feminists were middle-class women who argued
their case in relation to the economic changes that were taking place.
The emerging bourgeois class was seeking freedom and equality in
society, and the feminists argued that these new freedoms and equalities
should be extended to middle-class women as well as men. Writing on
marriage in 1700, Mary Astell asked: 'If all men are born free, how is it
that all women are born slaves? As they must be if their being subjected
to the inconsistent, uncertain, unknown, arbitrary will of men be the
perfect condition of slavery' (quoted in Mitchell, 1986: 71).

Eighteenth-century feminists rejected the view that women were
naturally different from men. They argued against the social power of
men and the ways in which men used that power to exclude women and
prevent their being equal.

Arguably the main influence on First Wave feminism, however, was
Mary Wollstonecraft, who published *A Vindication of the Rights of
Women* in 1792. She maintained that inequalities between men and
women were not the outcome of natural (biological) differences but due
to the influence of the environment, and especially the fact that women
were excluded from education. She argued that both women and society
in general were damaged by conditioning women into an inferior social
status. What was necessary was both to educate women and to change
society so that men and women were seen and treated as equal. Another
major influence on the First Wave feminist movement was *The
Subjection of Women*, published in 1869 by John Stuart Mill and Harriet
Taylor Mill. This was written at the height of the Victorian repression of
women and put forward a coherent equal-rights argument – that men and
women should have the same rights under the law.

Nineteenth-century feminism was mainly concerned with women
having the same legal rights as men. While women did not achieve
equality with men in the nineteenth century, or even the early twentieth
century, most of the rights have been won with the passage of the equal
opportunity and equal pay legislation implemented in 1975 (see Chapter
seven). However, contemporary feminists have argued that the
provision of formally equal rights is insufficient; while women are
subordinated by men, while they remain dominated by the masculine
ethic, they cannot be equal. Formally equal rights do not enable women
to be equal with men. The demands of Second Wave feminists have
gone beyond those of the nineteenth century.

The contemporary feminist movement has been concerned to make women aware of the shared female condition that controls and constrains all women regardless of individual circumstances. A major element of the movement has been consciousness-raising – women meeting together in small groups to share their common experiences as women. The movement has rejected conventional political organization and has sought to establish itself as a movement with no leaders, no spokespersons, or privileged analysis – a key concept has been sisterhood. While the movement has been accused of being comprised predominantly of middle-class, young, educated, white women, it has nevertheless campaigned successfully and worked on a number of important issues, notably in relation to sexuality. The Women's Movement was primarily responsible for bringing to light the large number of women who are physically assaulted by their husbands, and the inadequacies of state services for these women. Women's groups have established hostels for abused women and their children around the country. Rape has been another issue about which women have campaigned. Not only has there been pressure for changes in attitudes and in the law, but also research that suggests that most women who are raped do not go to the police. Women's groups have also established confidential rape crisis lines to help women who have been raped or sexually abused. The Women's Movement has campaigned actively against sexual harassment at the workplace and raised awareness in trade unions and political organizations about the problems that women experience in relation to men. Women have also campaigned actively around contraception issues and abortion. Initially the movement argued for free access to abortion on demand, but more recently it has argued for the woman's right to choose whether or not to have an abortion. The change came about as middle-class white women were made aware that some others, especially black and working-class women, were pressured into having abortions. Also, feminists are concerned that the choice should be made a realistic one – that is, women who choose to have the baby should have the financial and other necessary support to be able to provide for it adequately. Initially the fight was for abortion law reform, but more recently the fight has been to prevent the law being reformed so that women's access to abortions becomes very limited.

Women have been politically active, fighting for women and challenging laws and institutions that keep women in a subordinate role. The modern movement has recognized that legislation is necessary but not sufficient for women's emancipation. The law has limited power to change attitudes and to transform an essentially masculine social order. As we shall see in Chapter nine, feminists differ in their aims, but all feminists want to emancipate women from the power of men, whether this is seen as the power of individual men over individual women or structural power that maintains the dominance of patriarchal relations.

Gender politics

Sylvia Walby (1988a) has argued that we need to go beyond studies of women's political action and examine gender politics. She suggests that studies of women's political activity tend to portray it as exceptional rather than normal. Also, they focus on women rather than on the goal of gender politics, which is that women's activity is designed to change gender relations in the interests of women whereas men's is to resist changes. Finally, they ask why so few women have participated in political activities rather than asking how men have managed so successfully to exclude women.

Thus, in much feminist research, men as actors have been omitted, but Walby argues that patriarchal political practices are of vital significance in understanding gender politics. Women are not deviants in being concerned about gender politics, for men are equally concerned. In relation to women's struggle for the vote, she points out:

> Women (and a very few men) did not struggle for the vote against a vague non-gendered object. Rather, men (and a very few women) struggled against these feminist demands. Those opposing the demand for the vote for women were not passive, but rather active participants in a battle which raged for decades. They barred women from attending political meetings (for fear they would ask the male politicians whether they would give votes to women), and they forcibly ejected women from these meetings. (Male) police arrested protesters; (male) magistrates convicted protesters; (male) members of Parliament passed Acts which regulated the imprisonment and temporary release of women suffragettes so that suffragettes would not have martyrs from the death of hunger strikers in prison; male by-standers beat up women attempting to present petitions to the Prime Minister.
>
> (Walby, 1988a: 223)

She concludes by suggesting that: 'We cannot understand the suffrage struggle unless we understand the nature and extent of the opposition to feminist demands by patriarchal forces'. (p. 223)

Walby also argues that most feminists have seriously underrated the radicalism of First Wave feminism. She suggests that it was a large, many-faceted, long-lived and highly effective political movement. First Wave feminism existed as an active political movement from about 1850 to 1930 and was involved in a variety of campaigns: examples would be access to training, education, and employment for women, reform of the legal status of married women, equal right with men to divorce and legal separation, the vote for women, and issues surrounding sexuality.

A serious question, though, is why feminist political activity declined after the 1920s. To ask this question, however, Walby suggests, is to see feminism as normal, not exceptional. A number of answers to the question are probable: that women were successful in achieving what they wanted, that they were suppressed, that they had become incorporated in the trade unions and political parties; or that feminism merely *appeared* to disappear. Clearly more research is needed to make sense of what happened.

Walby concludes from her analysis that:

1 women are not as passive as is often assumed by both the malestream and some feminist literature;
2 that men resist women's political demands;
3 that the malestream view that politics is about class conflict may be challenged by the demonstration that it is also about gender conflict.

In the past, Walby suggests, gender politics has been marginalized and hidden; feminists need to uncover it.

Walby concludes her arguments by suggesting a number of key points that need to be taken into account in developing an analysis of gender politics:

1 Gender politics is an integral part of politics. Structural power relations between the interests of men and women are debated and fought over in political institutions.
2 Class politics and gender politics are both affected by gender politics.
3 Most political issues have a gender dimension; that is, they affect men and women differently even where this is not immediately obvious.
4 Gender politics is about the contestation between men and women, not just about women's political actions. Men resist women's demands. It is about the fight between feminists (generally women) and anti-feminists (generally men).
5 Not all women support feminist demands and not all men oppose them, but there is a high correlation between gender and political position.
6 Differences exist between feminists over the political demands to be made. There is not one feminist position. In this book we

have made a distinction between reformist/liberal, radical/revolutionary, Marxist and socialist feminists. These categories do not exhaust the different political positions adopted by feminists.

7 In the same way, there are varieties of patriarchal political position.

8 It is as important to ask why feminist politics appears to decline when it does as to ask why it arises when it does.

Walby is arguing, then, that if politics is about power struggles and contestation it is essential to analyse both parties to the struggle, both feminist and patriarchal political forces. We cannot understand women's political actions, nor women's participation in mainstream politics, unless we also examine the ways in which patriarchal forces resist women's demands and exclude women. So, for example, rather then asking why more women do not join political parties, stand for selection as candidates for parliamentary elections, and so on, we need to ask why they were prevented from doing so.

Marxist feminists and socialist feminists would argue that it is necessary to articulate the analysis of gender politics with class politics, while many radical feminists would want to place more emphasis on the behaviour of individual men and on the politics of interpersonal relationships. Nevertheless, most feminists, we feel, would accept the main thrust of Sylvia Walby's arguments. If we are to understand women's political activities, we must analyse those with whom the women are in contestation. However, some Marxist feminists would argue that this does not take account of the ways in which working-class men and women fight together on class issues, and black feminists would argue that this does not recognize the ways in which black men and women fight as one to resist racism. (However, it is necessary to recognize that all women, black and working class as well as white and middle class, are subordinated by patriarchal relations.) Nor does Walby's argument take sufficient account of the ways in which the political activities of some women may be concerned with issues of relevance to them as, for example, middle-class women totally ignore the problems confronting working-class or black women. This comes up clearly in the campaigns for access to abortion and contraception in the 1960s and early 1970s, and a similar point can be made about nineteenth-century middle-class women's demand to be allowed to take on paid employment while working-class women were forced to work long hours in the factories or mines. That is, while all women have in common their place in the sex/gender system, women's perceived interests and everyday experiences of patriarchal and class relations vary according to their own class and ethnic situation.

Women and the welfare state

Some feminists, especially Marxist feminists, have argued that the state has played an important role in constructing and maintaining the bourgeois nuclear family and the ideologies that suggest that this type of family is normal and natural. They identify the 'welfare' aspect of the state as particularly instrumental in this respect. Here we are using 'the state' to refer to the Government and all the other institutions involved in regulating society: the civil service, local government, the courts, the police and so on. The state is not just a set of institutions, but rather institutions that all exercise power and control in society and have the backing of physical force if necessary. In theory the power of the state is limitless, but in practice it is limited by ideas of non-intervention in civil society and in the domestic sphere. What we are arguing in this section is that the state does in fact play an important role in constructing and maintaining the private/domestic spheres and consequently the continuing subordination and exploitation of women. It is important to remember that women's role in the domestic sphere limits the role they can, and are assumed to be able to, play in the public sphere. As we suggested in Chapter six, feminists have demonstrated the ways in which jobs are 'created' for married women and that women's employment opportunities are limited by assumptions about their future role as wives and mothers.

Women, family, and caring

In Chapter four we saw that feminists have shown how an alliance between the male craft trade unions and the state resulted in the acceptance of the idea that a man should earn 'a family wage' – a wage sufficient to maintain a non-employed wife and children. This ideology was reinforced by protective legislation that limited the hours and types of work that women and children would be employed to do. This effectively resulted in wives becoming excluded from paid employment and the acceptance of the idea that women should care for their husbands and children in the domestic sphere. Similarly, compulsory schooling assumes that a parent (the mother) is available to take children to school and collect them: school hours are not compatible with full-time employment for both parents. Similarly again, the lack of state provision of adequate nurseries, holiday child care provision, and the like makes it difficult for mothers to take on employment.

However, it is the interaction of ideologies about motherhood and the role of women, reinforced by state policies, that confines women to their domestic sphere, or at least makes it difficult for women, and especially married women, to compete with men in the labour market and in political organizations. This is why legislation for equal opportunities has failed to result in women actually being able to compete on equal terms with men in the public sphere and why it has been equally difficult for men to take on responsibilities in the domestic sphere. The general assumption is that it is women's responsibility to care for their husbands and children, and men's to provide economic support for the family. Welfare state policies have been developed on the assumption that this is how people do and should live.

Abbott and Sapsford (1988) have examined how ideologies of the role of women as mothers, especially working-class women, developed in the late nineteenth century. The debates surrounding concern about the health of the working class at the time of the Boer War were used to reinforce the idea that women with children should not work but should care for their children full time in the home, that women (but not men) should be taught domestic skills, and that state intervention in the family was legitimate to ensure that mothers were adequately performing their role.

Elizabeth Wilson (1977) draws attention to the way in which welfare as provided exercises control over its recipients and the way in which welfare provision is underpinned by ideologies that a particular family form is not just how people do live but how they should live – thus privileging one way of life and disadvantaging alternative patterns of social relationship. The welfare state legislation introduced in the 1940s clearly and explicitly made these assumptions in terms of providing, for example, for income maintenance during unemployment, sickness, and old age with the assumption that women would be dependent on men and therefore did not need to pay full contributions in order to be entitled to these benefits.

In the 1970s and 1980s, partly as a result of pressure from the European Court of Human Rights, there have been some changes in welfare and taxation policies that remove the more gross aspects of discrimination. Most women, including married women, now pay full National Insurance contributions when in employment and can have contributions credited for periods when they are caring for dependent children or relatives. Married women are now entitled to claim the Care Allowance, and the chancellor announced in his 1988 budget that he intends to tax married women separately from their husbands. However, few social policy measures have been implemented that would make it easier for married women to take paid employment – indeed, state provision for pre-school children has actually been reduced. Also, the ideological proposition that a woman's place is in the home caring for her children and husband continues to be a widely accepted and unquestioned one.

Women and politics

Abbott and Wallace (1989) have argued that the New Right Conservative Government of Mrs Thatcher has attempted in speeches in publications to reinforce the familial ideology that assumes the economic dependency of married women in the family. Policies such as community care which assume that women are ready, able, and willing to care for dependent and elderly relatives are an important aspect of this, assuming as they do that women are available to take on this burden and are naturally able to provide care. While the Government has not repealed legislation passed in the 1970s that improved the position of women, nevertheless they have been concerned to argue that negligent mothers and mothers who work are a major cause of many contemporary social problems.

Women and poverty

State welfare policies and familial ideology also mean that women are more likely to be in poverty than men. An analysis of the groups most likely to be in poverty in modern Britain and of income distribution within households enables us to see that women are much more likely to be poor than men. Analysis by household also conceals the ways in which women's low-paid employment can keep households out of poverty (Land, 1987) or mitigate against the full impact of poverty being felt by other members of a household (Graham, 1987). The assumption that most women can depend on a man's wages to keep them out of poverty conceals the low pay among women workers and the low resources over which women have command, because some women are seen as financially dependent.

The main groups in poverty in modern Britain are:

1 those on low wages;
2 the unemployed;
3 the long-term sick or disabled;
4 single parents;
5 those over retirement age.

However, none of these factors is a *cause* of poverty. Most of these groups are dependent on state benefits; poverty ensues because state benefits are too low to lift the dependant above the poverty threshold. Governments have been explicit that benefits are designed as income maintenance, to provide a basic subsistence level.

Women are over-represented in all the groups listed above. There are in addition two further reasons why women are likely to be in poverty:

6 as unpaid carers of sick, disabled, or elderly relatives;

7 as dependants of a male wage-earner – either because the wage
   is at the poverty level or because the man does not share his
   resources equitably within the household.

Miller and Glendinning (1987), in an analysis of the 1983 Family
Expenditure Survey, found that two household types are the most likely
to be poor (i.e. living on 140 per cent or less of the supplementary
benefit level) – elderly women living alone (of whom 60 per cent were
in poverty) and lone mothers (of whom 61 per cent were in poverty).
Together the two types account for 32 per cent of households in poverty
but constitute only 15 per cent of all households.

Feminists have argued that women's poverty has to be seen in the
context of women's marginal position in the labour market and the
assumed dependency of women on men for financial support. This latter
assumption is employed both in the income support system (despite
minor changes in recent years) and in the ideology of the 'family wage'.
The assumption is not only that there is a sexual division of labour such
that men are the economic providers and women the carers, but the
ideology also carries over and influences the economic position of
women who do not live with a man, whether because single, divorced,
or widowed. Women's position in the labour market means that they are
less likely than men to earn a living wage and are concentrated in
low-paid jobs (see Chapter six). It is this assumed dependence of women
on men that has been used, historically, to justify the higher pay of men
(the 'family wage') and is reflected in welfare state legislation. The
disadvantages that women in the labour market experience also
contribute to the poverty of single-parent mothers. Even when a woman
bringing up children on her own feels that she can manage to take on
paid employment as well, she may find that there is no economic
advantage in doing so. The kind of low-paid work she is likely to be able
to find, coupled with the expenses of work and child-minding fees, mean
that most lone mothers will not be better off than when drawing benefit.

Finally, women are expected to be primarily responsible for children,
the elderly, and other dependants, although if they take on these roles
they will be in danger of falling into poverty. For many married women
with children or other caring responsibilities, poverty will be the major
problem.

Women's low pay, interrupted labour-market participation, and
tendency to take on part-time employment for a period of time also
affects their entitlement to income maintenance when they are not
economically active. Women are assumed to be dependent on the men
with whom they live, whether married or not, and it is assumed that
these men will make provision for income maintenance for themselves
and their wives in old age. This assumption has been reflected in

legislation, and while there have been some changes in social security legislation in recent years this has not markedly changed the situation. Under Social Security regulations current at the time of writing, a woman whose male friend stays more than three nights per week is deemed to be supported by him, and her benefit is cut. The case for this is particularly strong if she also does his washing or cooks him meals. It is clear that in Social Security regulations economic support should be provided in return for sexual and domestic services. While the 'co-habitation rule', as it is known, can also be applied to female visitors of men, this is very rare.

Women who are caring for children receive no income maintenance, although those caring for a dependant receiving an attendance allowance are entitled to a care allowance. However, this does not compensate for loss of wages, as it is paid at a lower rate than contributory benefits such as unemployment or sick pay. Women who become unemployed are entitled to unemployment pay only if they have made sufficient contributions and can fulfil the criteria for registering as unemployed (i.e. available for work). Women may *not* be entitled to unemployment pay for a number of reasons: because they have not been working for long enough; because they were working too few hours to pay contributions; or because they elected to pay the 'married woman's rate' of contribution (before 1976). They may not be able to register because they cannot demonstrate satisfactorily their availability for full-time work (because they have young children) or because they will not state that they are prepared to travel anywhere in the country. Similarly, many married women are not entitled to claim contributory invalidity benefits, and the 'housework test' of the non-contributory benefit is extremely difficult to satisfy. Income support (the replacement for supplementary benefit) is paid to a household, and the principle of assessment is household need. While the female partner can claim it if she and her partner agree and she can demonstrate a commitment to the labour market, the assessment is based on household income. Feminists have also pointed out that household income is often not equally shared and that women can be in poverty even within a relatively affluent household if benefits and wages all go to the man.

Feminists have therefore concluded that women's poverty can be understood only in the context of gender inequalities that persist throughout life. Ideologies of women's 'natural' abilities and 'natural' roles structure women's opportunities to take on paid work and the type of jobs that are offered to them. The realities of women's lives, structured by these ideologies and state policies, also limit their opportunities to take on employment and the range of types of employment they can take on. Furthermore, the assumption that men support their wives means that much female poverty is hidden. Women are expected to manage on the money, to be wise spenders, and to make the money stretch. They are also likely to be the ones to have to refuse their children the treats, clothes, outings, and activities that many children take for granted and to have continually to disappoint their children. Women also have to suffer the stress, the lack of opportunities for fulfilment, and the feelings of insecurity that go with being poor. Also, women's health as well as their general well-being suffers as a result of being poor, especially if they lack an adequate diet because they put the needs of other family members before their own.

Conclusions

Thus, the ideas of the public and private and the exclusion of women from the public sphere have been created by political processes – Government legislation and state policies. Familial ideologies that place women in the domestic sphere as wives and mothers are reinforced both by legislation and by the speeches and manifestos of political parties.

Summary

1 Women have been stereotyped in conventional accounts of political behaviour as being uninterested in politics, politically conservative, and influenced by their husbands. All of these stereotypes have been shown not to hold.
2 Conventional politics reflects male concerns and has effectively excluded women. Hence women are under-represented in public political life.
3 The welfare state and welfare policies have constructed and reinforced women's traditional position as wives and mothers.
4 Feminists have struggled over issues affecting women – specifically their rights to property and custody of their children in the nineteenth century, and their rights to abortion, equal pay, and nursery provision in the twentieth century. Furthermore, feminists have redefined the notion of politics around personal struggle as well as public campaign.

Further reading

Banks, O. (1981) *Faces of Feminism*, Oxford: Martin Robertson.
Siltanen, J. and Stanworth, M. (1984) *Women and the Public Sphere: a critique of sociology and politics*, London: Hutchinson.
Wilson, E. (1977) *Women and the Welfare State*, London: Tavistock.

Chapter nine

The production of feminist knowledge

A central argument of this book has been that sociology has ignored, distorted, or marginalized women. We have also suggested that this is a result of the systematic biases and inadequacies in malestream theories, not just an omission of women from samples. Malestream theories do not ask questions or do research in areas of concern to women, and frequently women are excluded from the samples; when they *are* included they are viewed from a position that sees males as the norm. As we pointed out in Chapter one, sociological theories have often taken for granted, rather than challenged, the view that the biological differences between men and women are sufficient to explain and justify the sexual division of labour. Feminist sociologists have argued that it is necessary to develop feminist theories: theories that explain the world from the position of women, theories that enable us to rethink the sexual division of labour and to conceptualize reality in a way that reflects women's interests and values, drawing on women's own interpretations of their own experiences.

Thus, feminist theories criticize the abstraction and over-inclusiveness of male-generated categories that conceal women's oppression. They should enable us to make sense of our lives, to understand the ways in which we are oppressed and exploited by men, and to explain how and why men oppress women. Furthermore, they should enable us to relate our experiences to the ways in which the society in which we live is structured. Individual men may be the agents of oppression, but patriarchal relationships also exist in the institutions and social practices of society. Feminist theory must also enable us to understand how we come to see ourselves as individuals – how we come to accept that a woman's role is in the home, that women are capable only of certain jobs, that women are worse at mathematics and sciences than boys, that only women who have had and cared for children are fully developed women, and so on. It must enable us to understand both how we become subjects (housewives, nurses, secretaries) and subject to the idea that it is natural that women should take on these roles and therefore accept our subordinate position in society.

However, it is important to recognize that different women have different experiences of reality; the way in which they are subordinated is different. Feminist theory has tended to be developed by white, middle-class women who work in institutions of higher education. While all women share a subordinate position in our society, not all women experience it in the same way; theories developed by white middle-class women have been correctly criticized for marginalizing the experiences of working-class and black women. To represent reality adequately from the standpoint of women, feminist theory must draw on a variety of women's experiences. To do this it is necessary to find ways in which all groups of women can participate in theory-building – to ensure that feminist theories adequately incorporate the experiences of working-class and black women.

Feminist theory is also political: it sets out not just to explain society but to transform it. Feminist theories are concerned to analyse how women can transform society so that they are no longer subordinated, by understanding how patriarchal relations control and constrict them. Consequently the adequacy of feminist theory is tested by its usefulness: that is, the extent to which it provides useful and useable knowledge for women. Feminist sociology is concerned, then, to build what Dorothy Smith (1987) has called a sociology for women – a sociology that relates to women, with which women can identify, in which women recognize themselves as the subject of what is being said, and which helps us to understand our everyday lives as well as the ways in which they are structured and established within a male-dominated society.

A sociology for women empowers women because knowledge is power. Women have inhabited a cultural, political, and intellectual world from whose making they have been excluded and in which they have been recognized as of no more than marginal relevance. Malestream scientific knowledge, including sociology, has been used to justify the exclusion of women from positions of power and authority in cultural, political, and intellectual institutions of society. Feminist knowledge, including sociology, challenges the objectivity and truth of that knowledge (which is presented as neutral) and seeks to replace it with more adequate knowledge – more adequate because it arises from the position of the oppressed and seeks to understand that oppression.

Some radical feminists would argue that we should not seek to develop new, feminist theories because the theoretical approach is an essentially masculine way of working. Theorizing is seen as a task undertaken by an elite that devalues, or even ignores, the experiences of women not included in the elite. Feminist sociologists, they argue, are trying to replace one 'truth' with another 'truth' and in doing so fail to recognize the validity of the experience of all women. The feminist task, they suggest, is to use the experiences of all women in making sense of women's lives and fighting oppression.

However, we would argue that all explanation and research is an essentially theoretical activity, whether the theory is made explicit or remains implicit. 'Facts' – our experiences and our observations – do not speak for themselves; we have to explain them, that is, to theorize them. Feminist theories have enabled women to do this; to make sense of their lives and the cultural, political, and intellectual worlds that they inhabit. Experience itself is a product of our theories; we interpret and make sense of what is happening in our lives. In the past women have had to use malestream theories; we need to replace them with more adequate feminist theories.

It could be argued that attempts to develop feminist *sociology* are themselves a contradiction (in much the same way as it has been argued that a Marxist sociology is a contradiction): that the Women's Movement and feminism are themselves concerned with understanding women's lives and developing strategies that will enable women to liberate themselves from oppression. Feminists have sought to break down artificial – man-made – barriers between disciplines and to develop interdisciplinary studies that recognize that we cannot compartmentalize knowledge or women's lives into discrete areas. A Women's Studies syllabus would include, for example, women's literature, women's art, women's history, and feminist biology as well as feminist social science. The subjects would not necessarily be taught as disciplines, but on a topic basis. We agree with this. What we have sought to do in this book is to explore the criticisms and contributions that feminist ideas have brought to sociology – not to construct a feminist sociology. Likewise, feminist theories are not bound by discipline. The feminist theories that we have used in this book and which we examine in more detail in this chapter are not restricted to sociology – they are not *sociological* theories, but *feminist* theories. Nevertheless, feminists have been interested in many areas that concern sociologists, and some female sociologists would regard themselves and the work they do as feminist. Feminists have never claimed to be scientific observers of the world and would argue that no knowledge is neutral; malestream knowledge has been used to control women, and feminist knowledge is an aid to the emancipation of women.

Collecting feminist evidence

Theories are world-views that enable us to make sense of the world. They guide us in terms of what is important and relevant to question and how to interpret what is going on. However, to understand the world it is also necessary to collect evidence – to carry out research. Research methods are the means by which sociologists gather material about society. The main research methods used in sociology are usually divided into 'quantitative' methods – most notably the survey and the statistical analysis of secondary-source data, and 'ethnographic' or 'qualitative' methods, most notably participant observation, in-depth interviewing, and the qualitative analysis of secondary sources of data. One could argue that no research method is explicitly feminist or anti-feminist; it is the ways in which research is carried out and the theoretical framework within which the results are interpreted that determine if research is feminist or not. However, many feminists have rejected quantitative methods of data collection and analysis because they argue these assume a scientificity that sociology cannot and should not strive to attain, and because they treat people as objects, as natural scientists treat chemicals or rocks, rather than as human subjects.

Feminist research has been concerned to move away from the positivistic view of sociology as a science and to argue that research should involve a commitment to the emancipation of women. While some feminists have suggested that feminist research should be research by women, for women, and with women, others have argued that it should include both men and women in its 'subject-matter', explicitly recognizing and investigating the sex/gender system that exists in the society being researched.

Harding (1987b) has suggested that it is not the method of research that makes feminist research significantly different from malestream research, but:

1 the alternative origin of problems – raising problems and issues that are of concern to women rather than to men;
2 the alternative explanatory hypotheses that are developed and the evidence that is used;
3 the purpose of the inquiry – to facilitate an understanding of women's views of the world and to play a role in female emancipation;
4 the nature of the relationship between the researcher and the 'subjects' of her inquiry.

She points to the need to distinguish between methods, methodologies, and epistemologies. Methods are techniques for gathering evidence. Methodologies are theories of how research should proceed. Epistemologies define what counts as an adequate theory and how research findings can be judged: what makes the findings of one piece of research more adequate than the findings of other research in the same area. The question of epistemology raises the issue of who the knower (researcher) can be, what tests something must pass to count as legitimate knowledge, and what class of things can be known.

What is distinctive about feminist research is the methodology and epistemology that underlie it. However, feminists are not in total agreement; there are competing theories and arguments about the ways in which feminists should undertake research. There is, however, some measure of agreement about the reasons for rejecting malestream research:

1 In the name of science, malestream sociologists have helped to sustain an ideology that supports the continuing subordination of women.
2 Women, and women's concerns, have not been seen as a major aspect of the research project. When women are included in research they are seen as marginal and viewed from the perspective of men. There has also been a tendency to present man as the norm, and when women do not conform to this norm to present them as deviant.
3 Those who have been researched have been treated as objects to be worked on. Researchers have also used those studied to serve the researchers' purposes rather than to meet the needs and aspirations of the researched. Feminists have referred to this as the 'research as rape' model. Shulamit Reinharz captures this criticism well:
   ...conducted on a rape model, the researchers take, hit and run. They intrude into their subjects' privacy, disrupt their perceptions, utilise false pretences, manipulate the relationships, and give little or nothing in return. When the needs of the researchers are satisfied, they break off contact with the subjects.

                                                        (Reinharz, 1983: 80)

Feminists are concerned to develop research strategies to incorporate women and not to treat the researched as objects to be used by the researcher. There are differences among feminists as to how this is to be done and as to what exactly feminist research is and how to go about doing it. Initially much feminist scholarship and research was deconstructionalist – that is, concerned to expose the male-centred nature of existing sociological research, to point out that it was biased and ideological because it ignored the experiences and perceptions of women. The second stage was research on women by women. This research asked new questions and was concerned to provide knowledge from the perspective of women. It was recognized that it was necessary to develop theories to provide an understanding of women's experience.

Many feminists see this as the main objective of feminist research – especially radical feminists. The third stage has been the development of the argument that feminists can develop a feminist sociology only if they research men as well as women, but with the proviso that the research is from the perspective of women, providing a fuller and more adequate knowledge.

The logic of the feminist position on research seems to demand non-individual co-research, where the researcher helps the women involved to undertake their own research, so that researcher and researched decide together on the object of the research, how the research is to be conducted and how the findings are to be used. In practice, few feminists have adopted this method. This is partly because it is not possible for the researcher to share her knowledge and expertise, and to imply that she *is* sharing them conceals a power relationship rather than overcoming it. Furthermore, most researchers are middle-class women with a university education, and many of those who are researched lack this privileged background.

Most feminists have argued, however, that feminist researchers in sociology must use qualitative methods, so that the women (and men) who are the subjects of research can be 'heard', so that it becomes possible to see and understand the world from the position of the research subjects. They have also rejected the view that feminist researchers can be objective in the sense of being uninvolved, because as researchers they are part of what is being researched. Involvement is seen as necessary and inevitable: necessary because the researcher must and does identify with the women she is researching, and inevitable because she is a part of what is being researched – she *is* involved. This means that reflexivity is essential – the researcher must be constantly aware of how her values, attitudes, and perceptions are influencing the research process, from the formulation of the research questions, through the data-collecting stage, to the ways in which the data are analysed and theoretically explained.

In practice, feminist sociologists have found it difficult to carry out research that lives up to the demands of the methodology that has been set out above. This is because of the sheer difficulty of doing research at all, because the training of most female researchers has taken place within malestream assumptions, because there are inevitably power relationships involved in research, because the funders of research have certain views about what constitutes 'good' research practice, and because feminist sociologists are part of a wider academic community to which they have to justify their research practices and findings. One of the main traps into which they fall is to take on a neutral stance, so that the research is on women, asks questions of interest to women, and uses qualitative methods, but the researcher tries to stand back and remain detached from what is going on rather than being a part of the research process and making explicit her involvement as a woman. Ann Oakley (1982) suggests that she was often aware of how much of a danger this was when she was interviewing women about the events surrounding maternity and childbirth – a subject of central interest to the women being researched and to Oakley herself as a woman and mother.

Feminist sociologists also frequently use the research findings for publications that are as much for their career advancement as to help the women (and men) who were the subjects of research – although, of course, the publication of research findings can influence policy-makers and could result in changes in women's lives that meet their needs. The danger here is that the researcher does not have control over how others interpret and use the research findings.

Most feminists would argue against the view that the researcher/ scientist is not responsible for how the findings of research are used, but once research is published the researcher has lost control. Janet Finch's research finding (1983b) that working-class mothers find it difficult to organize pre-school play groups for their children could as easily be used to argue that this means that they are responsible for their children *not* having pre-school education as to argue that the state should organize and run pre-school facilities for working-class children. This does not mean that we reject feminist research or that we do not publish our findings. It means that we have to be constantly aware of the dangers of appearing to be a neutral scientist and of the ways in which research findings can be distorted by anti-feminist interpretation.

A major problem is that feminist research can be accused of being 'subjective' and therefore of no value. If it is seen as subjective then there is no way of showing how feminist conclusions are any better than those reached by anyone else and why the findings of feminist research are better than those of malestream research. There are three main responses to this – three feminist epistemological stances which have been adopted in response to this criticism: feminist empiricism, 'standpoint' feminism, and feminist relativism.

Feminist empiricism

Feminist empiricists are critical of malestream research because it has been male-centred. They suggest that feminists are more likely to produce adequate knowledge because they include women and women's experiences in their research as central and normal rather than as marginal and deviant. The logical goal of this perspective is the development of non-sexist research. Magrit Eichler (1988) has produced guide-lines for such research:

1 to avoid sexism in titles: titles should be sexplicit (for example, the Affluent Worker study should be retitled the Male Affluent Worker study);

2 sexism in language has to be eliminated: language should be used that makes it clear whether men or women or both are being addressed or referred to;

3 sexist concepts need to be eliminated (for example, defining class by reference to the occupation of the head of household);

4 sexism in research designs has to be overcome so that men and women are both included in the research where this is relevant;

5 sexism in methods has to be eliminated;

6 sexism in data-interpretation has to be eliminated – the interpretation of data from the perspective just of men or just of women;

7 sexism in policy evaluation has to be eliminated, so that policies that serve the needs of both men and women are advocated.

Most feminists would agree with Eichler but argue that what she says is insufficient. They would reject the positivistic research stance that underlies her preoccupation with non-sexist methods, arguing that given the power relations that exist in society such research practices would continue to be male-dominated and meet the needs of men rather than of women. This is because such research does not challenge the underlying assumptions inherent in malestream research, which are presented as truths.

Liz Stanley and Sue Wise (1983) argue that research carried out in the traditional sociological framework, whether 'positivistic' or 'naturalistic', draws on a pre-chosen framework – the findings are abstracted from reality and presented as if given research logics had been followed. Material is organized for the reader, and information is not given about what happened, when it happened, how it happened, and how the people involved (including the researchers) felt about it. They argue that it is essential to recognize that malestream sociological research is written up as if a formal pattern of procedures were carried out, but that in practice this is rarely what happens. We would argue that non-sexist research as advocated by Eichler would fall into the same trap. This type of research account fails to examine the relationships between experience, consciousness, and theory because it acts as if they are unimportant or do not exist. The researcher is presented as an objective, neutral, and value-free technician who is following set procedures. All that Eichler does is to replace what she and feminists would agree are sexist practices with practices which attempt to overcome *only* the sexism. Most feminists would argue that following such a set of procedures would not produce feminist knowledge because they reject the view that the researcher can be neutral and value-free.

'The feminist standpoint'

'Standpoint' feminists argue that they are concerned to produce socially relevant knowledge that is 'adequate' or 'good enough'; that is, they seek to justify their research findings as better, more adequate, than those produced by the malestream or other feminist researchers. The research findings should be both useful to and useable by women. It is a position taken mainly by academic feminists who want their work to be accepted as scholarship and to make a contribution to sociological knowledge as well as to produce research that will be of benefit to women. They are concerned that their research will advance the understanding of social life and to have a basis for claiming that those who do not share their starting position should be convinced by the conclusions. They are concerned to demonstrate why their research findings should be believed and why their research should be funded.

They recognize that the production of knowledge is a politically engaged activity. Malestream researchers have often refused to acknowledge this, but it is a problem which feminist researchers have confronted. They want to reject the view that all knowledge is equally valid (relativism) and to argue that it is essential to be able to justify some research findings and theoretical explanations as more adequate than others. If this is not possible then it is difficult to see why feminist research findings and explanations should be seen as better or more true than malestream ones. It is necessary to be able to demonstrate that some statements are better accounts of social reality than others, while recognizing their inevitable partiality.

Researchers cannot avoid some selection and interpretation of their material, and it is essential that this is acknowledged. All knowledge is based on experience, and standpoint theorists claim their research is scientifically preferable because it originates in and is tested against a more complete and less distorted kind of experience than malestream research. Human activity, it is suggested, structures and sets limits to human understanding, and what we do shapes and constrains what we can know. However, human activity is structured for and experienced differently by men and women because the latter are subordinated. Standpoint theorists argue that men's knowledge can never be complete. It is not just that the oppressed can see more, but also that their knowledge emerges through their struggle against oppression – women's knowledge emerges from a struggle against men and the attempt to replace the distorted knowledge produced by men which is used to control and subordinate women. The feminist standpoint is an achievement – it is the portrayal of social life from the viewpoint of the activity which produces women's social experience, not from the partial and perverse perspective available from the 'ruling gender' experiences of men.

Standpoint feminists argue that their accounts of the social world are less partial and less distorted than malestream ones. Feminist science is better able to reflect the world as it is and is able to replace the distorted and distorting accounts produced by malestream sociology and consequently to advance sociological knowledge. It is based on the view that there is a real world, but that our accounts of it are always and inevitably partial, and that feminist accounts are less partial and less distorted than malestream ones.

Feminist relativism

Some feminists reject the standpoint position because they argue that there cannot be a feminist science and that all that the academic feminists who advocate the standpoint position are doing is trying to set up a new truth. These feminists are deeply sceptical about claims to universal knowledge and argue that there is no world or set of social structures 'out there' waiting to be known, but only many subjective experiences. All that feminist (or indeed any) researchers can do is to uncover the many stories that different women tell and reveal the different knowledges that they have (Stanley and Wise, 1983).

These feminists are critical of malestream research because of its claims to objectivity, to reveal truth, and because of the claim that the researcher is not involved in the research process. Also, they argue that it is only possible for women, because of their shared experiences of oppression, to do research on women. Stanley and Wise (1983), for example, argue that, in presenting accounts of their research, researchers 'do not tell it as it happened' but present a reconstructed account of how the research was undertaken that accords with textbook accounts. Not only are these accounts false, but they fail to reveal the ways in which the researcher was involved in the research process. Consequently they argue that feminist research must be genuinely reflexive – that is, the accounts of the research must make available to the reader the procedures which underlie the way the knowledge which is presented was produced out of the research, and draw on the experience of 'being a researcher', and the experiences of being a feminist in any social situation. It is also essential not to deny one's experiences and feelings as a feminist, but to use them as part of the process of validating one's research, rather than vice versa – that is, we should accept the validity of our own experiences as women. The adequacy of knowledge is based on the extent to which it enables us to understand better our situation as women and gives us the resources with which to emancipate ourselves.

The major problem with this position is its relativism. While we agree that researchers must be reflexive, that women must speak for themselves, and that research findings should help the oppressed, we are sceptical of the view that all women's accounts are equally valid and that there is no way of selecting between them.

Summary

1 Research methods are not just 'tools of the trade': what gives meaning to the research is the underlying theory and epistemology used. The methods at the more quantified 'positivistic' end of the spectrum claim to be more scientific and neutral and for this reason feminists have attacked them, arguing that they in fact represent a malesteam view of the world under the guise of science.
2 Feminists have tended to espouse qualitative methods as the better means for carrying out feminist research because:
   • they imply more equality between researcher and researched;
   • they allow the viewpoint of the researched to be taken into account;
   • they do not turn the researched into fragmented objects.
3 Three feminist positions on methodology have been described – empiricist, standpoint and relativist.

Feminist theories

Feminism is not a unified intellectual movement. While all feminists are agreed that it is necessary to understand women's subordination and to emancipate women, they are not agreed on the causes of that subordination or how emancipation is to be achieved. In this book we have mostly organized our analysis around four feminist theories: liberal/reformist, radical/revolutionary, Marxist, and socialist. Not all feminism is encompassed within these four broad perspectives, nor would we argue that they represent four entirely distinct feminist theories. Furthermore, not all feminists whom we have labelled as belonging to a given perspective would agree with the way in which we have labelled them. We should stress again, as we did in Chapter one, that this is a heuristic device, a way of classifying a large body of feminist theorizing in order to make explanation and analysis possible.

Liberal/reformist feminist theory

Historically, liberal feminism has been concerned to argue for equal rights for women – for women to have the same citizenship rights as men. Equal rights feminists have fought against laws and practices that give rights to men and not to women, or which are designed to 'protect' women. Recognizing that mere formal equality is insufficient, they have also advocated the passing of laws to outlaw discrimination against women and to give women rights in the workplace such as maternity leave and pay.

Women, they argue, are human beings and have the same inalienable natural rights as men. A woman's sex is irrelevant to her rights; women are capable of full rationality and are therefore entitled to full human rights. However, in western industrial societies women are discriminated against on the basis of sex; that is, certain restrictions are placed on women as a group without regard to their own individual wishes, interests, abilities, and needs. Women are denied equal rights with men, and as a group are not allowed some freedoms that men as a group are permitted to enjoy. Furthermore, while men are judged on merit as individuals, women tend to be judged on their accomplishments as females – that is, they are denied the same right as men to pursue their own interests.

In sociology, liberal/reformist feminists have been concerned to demonstrate that the observable differences between the sexes are not innate but a result of socialization and 'sex-role conditioning'. The ways in which boys and girls are treated differently, from about the moment of birth, arguably discourage women from developing their full potential as human beings. Feminist researchers have carried out research to demonstrate that women are discriminated against and treated differently from men, and argue that this explains women's subordinate position in society. To liberate women it is necessary to demonstrate that men and women are equal in potential, that women are fully human, that the differences between men and women in western society are due to the different ways in which boys and girls are socialized and the different social expectations they face, together with discriminatory legislation.

However, sociological research from a reformist position does not explore women's experiences, nor challenge the use of concepts and tools developed to explore society from the standpoint of men. Nor does it adequately challenge malestream views of what the major issues are to be researched. It argues for the incorporation of women in research samples and for women to carry out research, but leaves intact the foundations of existing theoretical perspectives. However, research from this perspective has demonstrated the ways in which women are denied equal opportunities and are discriminated against, and has challenged the view that the sexual division of labour is adequately explained by biological sex differences.

213

Marxist feminism

Marxist feminism has developed out of the attempts by women to develop Marxist theory so that it provides an adequate explanation for the subordination and exploitation of women in capitalist societies. Marxist feminists recognize that Marxism is inadequate as it stands and needs to be developed in order to explain adequately why women are excluded from the public sphere and are the main unpaid workers in the domestic sphere. They have also had to deal with the 'fact' that women did not become subordinated under capitalism but were subordinated already, and with the strong suspicion that the overthrow of the capitalist mode of production would not result in the emancipation of women. However, while they recognize that the struggle between the sexes is not reducible to the class struggle, they give primacy to the latter. For Marxist feminists the defining feature of contemporary society is capitalism, within which women are subject to a special form of oppression which is mainly the effect of their exclusion from wage labour and of their role in the domestic sphere reproducing the relations of production. That is, women's unpaid work in caring for the labour force and raising the next generation of workers benefits capitalism and is essential to its continuation. The main beneficiary of women's unpaid labour is capitalism, although individual men also benefit to some extent.

A major problem that Marxist feminists confront is that Marx himself was not concerned with the position of women in capitalist society. Marx rejected notions of morality, justice, and equal rights as bourgeois ideas. He was concerned not with reform, but with developing a scientific account of the exploitation of the working class under capitalism with a view to overthrowing that system.

The concepts Marx uses appear to be neutral, but they are in fact sex-blind; he fails to recognize that women are subject to a special form of oppression within capitalist societies and does not analyse gender differences and gender ideologies. Although he uses abstract categories such as 'labour power', his specific analyses suggest that he assumed a *male* waged labour force. He also adopted a naturalistic approach to the family, maintaining that women should provide care in the domestic sphere. The paid labour of women and children was seen by Marx as a threat to male workers – women and children, he argued, were used by capitalists to reduce the costs of production. Cheap female labour was or could be used to replace more expensive male labour. (Marx did not challenge the practice of paying women less than men.) This analysis ignores the fact that women have always made a contribution to the economic survival of the household and does not challenge the view that men should be paid more for their labour than women – presumably because men should be paid a family wage.

Marxist feminists want to retain the Marxist analysis of capitalist societies, integrating into it an explanation for the subordination of women. A starting point for the development of an adequate Marxist feminist theory has been the work of Engels, Marx's collaborator. In Engels' analysis of the relationship between the origins of the family and the development of capitalism he argues that the bourgeois nuclear family was formed because of the needs of the capitalist system, and specifically because men wanted to pass on their property to their legitimate heirs. Engels argues that this meant that men needed to control women in marriage so that they knew who their heirs were. Women's subordinate position was/is a form of oppression that serves the interests of capitalism. All women are oppressed, whether they are married to bourgeois or proletarian men.

Marxist feminists have adapted this line to develop a theory which attempts to provide an adequate account of the subordination of women as well as forms of class exploitation, and which overcomes the theoretical marginalization of women in conventional Marxist theory. They seek to analyse and explain the relationships between the subordination of women and other aspects of the organization of the capitalist mode of production. The attempt to marry feminism with Marxism has been difficult, but Marxist feminists have argued that it is essential to recognize that the oppression of women is inextricably linked with the capitalist order. Given this and given Marxism's sex-blindness, it is necessary to reformulate it so that it provides an adequate explanation for the subordination of women, and of ethnic minorities and other exploited groups in such societies as well. Such a theory it is argued, will enable us to develop strategies that result in the emancipation of subordinated groups – something that the overthrow of the capitalist system would not automatically achieve by itself.

One of the most fully developed of Marxist feminist accounts is Michelle Barrett's in *Women's Oppression Today* (1980). She sets out to construct a Marxist analysis of the relationship between women's oppression and class exploitation in capitalist society that rejects the view that women's exploitation can be explained either by the biological differences between men and women or by reference to the 'needs' of the capitalist system, nor by dominant ideas (ideologies) which posit that women are inferior to men, that women's role is as a wife and mother, or the like. She argues against approaches such as Domestic Labour Theory which begin from the premiss that women's oppression is an integral part of the capitalist system, by maintaining that it cannot be demonstrated that privatized (family) reproduction using the unpaid domestic labour of women is the cheapest way of reproducing labour power. Also, it does not explain why it is *women* who work in the domestic sphere and not men.

The need is to understand women's social position as exploited by capital and their dependent and powerless relationship with husbands and fathers. Patriarchal relationships need to be incorporated into class analysis; that is, it is necessary to recognize that men have privileges as men and wield power over women even within the working class. She rejects the view that class and gender hierarchies are two separate systems (a point of contrast with the socialist feminists discussed below, p. 220) and argues that what is necessary is to revise and develop Marxist theory so that gender relations are placed at the centre of its analysis.

The key to women's oppression, she suggests, is the 'family/household' system, a complex which includes a social structure and a given ideology – familialism. The household is made up of a number of people, usually biologically and legally related, who live together and share domestic arrangements. Familial ideology defines the nuclear family as 'naturally' based and universal and specifies a 'natural' division of labour such that the man is seen as the provider of economic resources and the woman as the carer and provider of unpaid domestic labour. This family/household system is not an inevitable aspect of capitalist society but has come to form a historically constituted element of class relations. It was not inevitable, but emerged through a historical process in which an ideology that maintained that a woman's natural role is as a domestic labourer – that is, as a wife and mother – became incorporated into the capitalist relations of production. This ideology came in part from pre-capitalist views of a woman's place, but mainly developed because it fitted the way in which bourgeois family relations had become established with the emergence of industrial capitalism. This ideology, Barrett argues, became accepted by the organized working class in the early nineteenth century. The family/household system became established in the mid nineteenth century as a result of an alliance of craft unions and capitalists, both arguing that women should be excluded from the labour force and that men should earn a family wage. Thus, the male fight for a family wage and protective legislation passed by the state eliminated the low-waged competition from women in the labour market and forced women into the domestic sphere. (See Chapters four and six.)

While the family/household system was in the short-term interests of men, it was not in their long-term interests because it split the working class so that working-class men and women came to have different interests. It *was* in the long-term interests of capitalism because it divided the working class, and women came to provide a pool of lowly paid workers who could be used as a flexible, disposable extra workforce. Women's oppression did not have a material basis in the period in which it was formed but has now come to acquire one. It has come to form an essential element in the relations of production, in the sexual division of labour in paid work, and between wage labour and domestic labour. The oppression of women is necessary for the reproduction of the capitalist mode of production in its present form.

The major problem with Marxist feminist theory is that it fails to place sufficient emphasis on the ways in which men oppress women and the ways in which men benefit from their unpaid domestic labour. While Marxist feminists have recognized that it is necessary to allow the importance of patriarchal relationships and how these are intertwined with capitalism, they see them as unchanging and fail to recognize that there is no necessary and inevitable congruence between the interests of patriarchy and the interests of capitalism. Barrett, for example, fails to explain why it is in capitalism's interests to exclude cheap female labour, given its concern to maximise profit. Marxist feminism tends to reduce explanations to the categories of Marxist theory. It fails to take account of patriarchal relationships in societies other than capitalist ones, nor does it fully consider the specific location of black or Third World women. It also tends to be abstract and far removed from the everyday experiences of women in their relationships with men.

Radical/revolutionary feminist theory

The central tenet of radical/revolutionary feminists is that gender inequalities are the outcome of an autonomous system of patriarchy and that gender inequalities are the primary form of social inequality. They argue that there has always been a sexual division of labour under-pinning and reinforcing a system of male domination. Patriarchy is a universal system in which men dominate women. Radical feminism is primarily a revolutionary movement for the emancipation of women. Its exponents argue that no area of society is free from male definition, and consequently every aspect of women's lives currently accepted as 'natural' has to be questioned and new ways of doing things found. Theory, they argue, is not a separate area of activity, carried out by an elite, but is an integral aspect of feminist practice. Theory arises out of practice and is continually measured against experience and continually reformulated. The revolution, for radical feminists, begins here and now, by women taking positive action to change their lives and to remove oppression.

Radical and revolutionary feminism is not a unified area. There are three major issues within it:

1 the relationship between feminist politics and personal sexual conduct – a key question being whether women can continue to live with men, or whether separation is essential;

2 whether sex differences are biologically or socially constructed;
3 the political strategy that should be adopted – withdrawal or revolution.

One of the first substantial and systematic expositions of radical feminism was by Shulamith Firestone in her book *The Dialectic of Sex* (1974). The opening words of the book are: 'Sex class is so deep as to be invisible.' The aim of her work (and that of subsequent radical feminists) is to make this visible. She argues that the subordination of women occurs not only in obvious areas such as law and employment but also in personal relationships. The difference between genders structures the whole of life – women are not only differentiated from men, but subordinated to them. Man is the main enemy. The theoretical task must be to understand the sex-gender system and the political task must be to end it.

Shulamith Firestone argued that the division between men and women had a biological base; women are physically weaker than men because of their reproductive physiology and because they have to care for the helpless human infant. This, she suggests, necessitated social relationships whereby women came to depend on men for physical security. This biological imperative has subsequently been overlaid by social institutions, especially sexual and child-rearing practices, that reinforce male domination. However, she suggests that there is no necessity for male domination, as advances in reproductive technology make it possible to eliminate the biological basis of women's subordination. This has freed or will free women from having to have children (by contraception) and the child-bearing and child-rearing role can be shared by men and women.

More recent radical feminists have rejected the view that women's subordination is anything to do with women's biological inferiority. They reject the idea that the victim (woman) is to blame. Male biology, they argue, is to blame: men are naturally aggressive and use their aggression to control women (as, for example, in rape). Mary Daly, in *Gyn/Ecology* (1978), documents the horrors of the ways in which men have used aggression to control women. She cites Indian suttee, Chinese foot-binding, African genital mutilation, European witch-hunts, and American gynaecology as examples of ways in which men have abused women and used violence to control them (and continue to do so). These feminists encourage women to create a new identity for themselves founded on 'true' femaleness, based in the biological nature of women which has been distorted by patriarchy. Women are encouraged to celebrate a new female creativity, based on sisterhood and self-identification. They reject androgyny because they argue that the most valuable qualities are those that are specific to women. Also, because men dominate women even in the most intimate of relationships, women must live separately from men. The ideal, they argue, is for women to live freed from patriarchy, which divides and mutilates them.

A rather different radical feminist position, one that rejects biological explanations, has been developed by the French radical feminists, of whom the two best known are Christine Delphy and Monique Wittig. They argue that to give birth is not a biological process, a natural given, but a social/historical construction of 'forced production'. They argue that it is birth that is planned and women are socially programmed (socialized) to give birth. Women are forced to behave in ways that are seen as natural, and this has resulted in the creation of two discrete biological sexes. But this division falsifies the reality of human variation – the wide variety of sexual characteristics – because an over-gendered society has evolved. Society is structured around the belief that there are two polar opposite sexes, male and female.

Biological theories of sex differences are social constructs which, they argue, serve the interests of the socially dominant group. Women are a class in themselves because the category 'woman' (as well as the category 'man') is a political and economic one, not an eternal, biological category. What is necessary is to eliminate the sex distinction itself. Wittig (1979) argues that 'Our fight aims to suppress men as a class not through a genocidal but a political struggle. Once the class "men" disappears, women as a class will disappear as well, for there are no slaves without masters' (Wittig, 1979: 72).

For radical feminists the subordination of women is the central concern, and their theories seek to uncover and eliminate the subordination of women by men. Men, it is argued, systematically dominate women in every sphere of life, and all relationships between men and women are institutionalized relationships of power and therefore an appropriate subject for political analysis. Thus, radical feminists are concerned to reveal how male power is exercised and reinforced in all spheres of life, including 'personal' relationships such as child-rearing, housework, and marriage and in all kinds of sexual practices including rape, prostitution, sexual harassment, and sexual intercourse.

Women's subordination is seen to be universal and primary, as not having changed significantly over time or place. Men, it is maintained, benefit as a class (and as individuals) from women's subordination. The relationship between the sexes is thus political, and any permanent and far-reaching change will necessitate the transformation of sexual relationships – the elimination of male domination of women.

Radical feminists argue that women's culture, women's knowledge, and women's subjective understanding have all been denied by men. What is taken as truth and is seen to be valued has been defined by men. Male science has been used to legitimate the ideologies that define women as inferior, and women's role to be that of domestic labourers. Sociology is seen as part of this male-defined, distorting male culture. Radical feminists, then, do not want to participate in sociology – to bring women in – but to transform the way knowledge is produced so that women's subjective understandings are revalued. Much radical feminist research has been concerned with analysing male violence towards women and the ways in which this is hidden, marginalized or blamed on the women by malestream social science and patriarchal values. Radical feminists have also been concerned to uncover 'herstory', to recover for women their history and their cultural heritage and to reveal the ways in which women's knowledge has been devalued both historically and in other societies.

Radical feminism has uncovered the ways in which even the most intimate and personal relationships are political – that is, are power relationships. Also they have documented the universality of patriarchal relationships. However, they have failed to explain adequately the ways in which women are subordinated and exploited by men. They fail to take sufficient account of the different forms that patriarchal relationships have taken in different societies. They also tend to discount the differences that exist in the experiences of women from different social classes. Radical feminist biological explanations, while very different from those developed by malestream theorists, are equally reductionist and fail to take account of ideology and culture. Also, they give the opportunity for sociobiological theories to be developed as a counter to the feminist ones – ones that argue that women's role as presently constituted is naturally determined. However, not all radical feminists accept biological theories, arguing that they are developed to justify the subordination of women and that it is necessary to challenge the argument that there are two biologically determined sexes.

Socialist feminism

This position, often referred to as 'dualism', attempts to develop an analysis that recognizes two systems: the economic, and the sex-gender. Patriarchy is seen as trans-historical – that is, men exercise power over women in all societies. However, an adequate feminist theory, socialist feminists argue, has to recognize that patriarchy takes a specific form in capitalist societies. Capitalism and patriarchy are seen as two separate systems. The aim is to develop a theory of capitalist patriarchy that makes possible an understanding of the ways in which the capitalist system is structured by male domination.

In contemporary societies all human beings belong to a social class and a specific gender. Socialist feminists argue that gender, class, race, age, and nationality all shape women's oppression, but they are not committed to any one of these oppressions as being any more fundamental than any other. The specific forms of women's subordination in capitalist society are seen as specific to that particular socio-economic system. Women's lack of freedom is a result of the ways in which women are controlled in the public and domestic spheres, and women's emancipation will come about only when the sexual division of labour is broken down in all spheres: the abolition of social relationships that construct people as workers and capitalists, and as women and men.

Marxist theory presents the world from the position of the proletariat (working class); what is necessary, socialist feminists argue, is to develop a world view from the position of women. Traditional Marxist theory ignores women's labour outside the market (domestic labour) and the gender-defined character of women's work within the market, and therefore obscures the systematic domination of women by men. Women, however, are controlled both by the ruling class and by men; male capitalists determine the conditions under which women sell their labour, and male workers receive monetary and other advantages from the fact that women's waged labour is remunerated at a lower rate than men's, and that women perform unpaid domestic labour. Also, men's sexual desires are taken as primary in the definition of women as sexual objects.

To understand women's oppression fully it is necessary to examine the sexual division of labour in the domestic sphere as well as in the labour market, and the relationship between the two. Women's reproductive labour limits their access to wage labour, but the limited range of wage labour available to women is what drives many of them into marriage. The ideology of marriage and motherhood as women's primary role serves to conceal this. The public/private distinction not only benefits capitalism but also men. The exclusion of women from the public sphere benefits men as well as capitalists, while women's unpaid domestic labour also benefits both men and capitalists.

Sylvia Walby (1988b), emphasizing the need for a dual analysis, argues that patriarchy is never the only mode of production but is always articulated with another mode. She also points out the need to analyse variations in the forms of patriarchy. She argues that in capitalist society the key sets of patriarchal relations are to be found in domestic work, paid work, the state, and in male violence and sexuality. Social relations in domestic work constitute the patriarchal mode of production, and this, she argues, is of particular significance in the determination of gender relations. However, when patriarchy is articulated with the capitalist mode of production, patriarchal relations in paid work are of central importance to the maintenance of the system. The form that patriarchy takes under capitalism is different from the form that it takes in other socio-economic systems. Patriarchy pre-dates capitalism, but takes new forms with capitalist development. There was a well developed sexual division of labour in feudal and proto-industrial England. In agricultural work in pre-industrial England men had to leave the home to work, and poor women worked in the fields. With industrialization men went out to work and poor women continued to work for others than their families, though gradually women were excluded from much paid work. The confining of women to the home is not unique to capitalist society; in most Islamic societies – industrial and pre-industrial – women are confined to the home, and upper-class women did not work in pre-industrial or industrial Britain.

However, the development of industrial capitalism did lead to changes. Women were excluded from certain types of paid work, especially skilled work, and lost certain legal rights they had previously held over property. Men also made gains: men had control over credit, and some men, but no women, had access to political arenas including Parliament. Men developed many new bases of power in the public sphere from which women were barred, and domestic ideologies became more dominant. The form that women's subordination takes in capitalist society is not an outcome of the logic of capitalism or patriarchy, but the result of a shift in the resources of male power consequent upon the development of capitalism. Men were in a position to develop new power bases as the domestic economy contracted and was replaced by capitalist production.

Walby also argues that the form of patriarchy changes. Since the rise of capitalism there has been a move from private patriarchy to public patriarchy both because of the capitalist demand for labour and because of feminist political activity. However, the interests of patriarchy and of capitalism are not necessarily the same; the main basis of tension between the two lies in the exploitation of women's labour. It is in capital's interests, she argues, to recruit and exploit cheap female labour, labour which is cheaper than men's because of patriarchal structures. This is resisted by patriarchy, which seeks to maintain the exploitation of women in the household. In the nineteenth century, when men struggled to exclude women from from competition for jobs, there was a strong cross-class patriarchal alliance. However, this cross-class alliance is weakened when it is in the interest of employers (capitalists) to recruit women, and then there is conflict between capitalism and patriarchy, as during the First World War. An alternative strategy is for capital to recruit women to jobs defined as women's jobs – that is, jobs which pay less than men's and have a lower status. When this happens patriarchy fights to ensure that women are recruited only for women's work. Walby argues that the power of capital prevents the exclusionary strategy working in the long term and that segregation as an alternative develops at least in part because of the feminist movement – women demanding the right to have paid employment. Consequently, in Britain there has been a move from private patriarchy where women were kept in the house to a public form where women are controlled by men in all spheres.

The adequacy of feminist theories

Feminist theory and research has contributed to our understanding of the subordination of women. All feminists are concerned to develop theories that enable women to understand their situation and to enable them to work towards liberating themselves. We have seen in this book that feminists are not united and have developed a number of theories that seek to uncover the causes of women's subordination and develop strategies for emancipating women.

The key questions become: what are the criteria of adequacy for a feminist theory, and which (if any) of the existing theories satisfy these criteria? All theory, including feminist theory, is simultaneously political and scientific. Feminist scholars have a common political interest in ending women's oppression and see their work as contributing to a comprehensive understanding of women's subordination. Feminist theory has to be politically adequate as well as scientifically adequate. A political theory puts forward values that are seen as morally desirable and acts as a guide to conduct. A scientific theory should be self-consistent, well supported by the available evidence, comprehensive in accounting for all the data, and have explanatory power. However, the competing feminist theories disagree as to what is to count as evidence, what needs explaining and which explanations are illuminating.

Liberal/reformist feminists tend to take a positivistic position, arguing for unbiased and impartial research. Theories and research developed within this perspective are seen as more adequate because they overcome the biases of malestream positivistic research by incorporating women so that gender-fair knowledge is produced.

Radical feminists are critical of malestream or patriarchal forms of knowledge. They argue that men, as the dominant group or class, impose their own distorted view of reality. Women's subjective understandings must be researched if they are to free themselves from the constraints of the distorting patriarchal knowledge. The ways in which women's knowledge can be revealed is by 'consciousness-raising', by small groups of women getting together and sharing their experiences. They argue that when women discuss their lives they will become aware of the ways in which they are oppressed by men. Shared experiences will make possible the constant development of the understanding of women's situation and ways to change it. The collective knowledge that is developed is guided by the special interests and values of women. The aim is to produce practical knowledge, and theory development is guided by practical interests and informed by the experiences of all women. It is argued that all women should be included in the production of knowledge, and that it is impossible to separate the observer from the observed and the knower from the known.

Marxist and socialist feminists have developed a Marxist epistemology to justify the way that their knowledge is produced. For traditional Marxists knowledge is seen as socially constructed: knowledge production is one aspect of human productivity and consequently the basic categories of knowledge are always shaped by the human purposes and values on which they are based. Empirical knowledge is never value-free because the conceptual frameworks which are used to make sense of our lives and our place in them are shaped and limited by the interests and values of the society in which we live. In capitalist society the interests and values of the most powerful class – the bourgeoisie – shape and limit knowledge production, and the knowledge (ideologies) produced as truth tends to obscure or to justify the oppression of the proletariat. It is only in a classless society that it will be possible to produce undistorted knowledge.

However, in capitalist society it is evident that despite the dominance of ruling-class ideology, reality is perceived very differently by different groups. The different understandings of reality depend on group positions within society. A different view of reality is produced from the standpoint of the bourgeoisie rather than from the standpoint of the proletariat. The Marxists argue that the view of the proletariat is more adequate because as the subordinate class it has a wider vision, because it includes the perspective of the subordinate class which is ignored in middle-class knowledge. Marxist theory, it is argued, is the most adequate, because it has the most comprehensive picture of the world – it reflects the interests and values of the working class, which it is argued are those of the totality of humans.

Marxist and socialist feminists have developed this Marxist epistemology to argue for women's standpoint as the basis for adequate knowledge. The special position of women gives them a special epistemological standpoint and therefore enables them to produce a less distorted view of the world than those available to capitalist or proletarian men. The adequacy of a feminist theory is tested by the extent to which it presents the world from the standpoint of women. The class position of the bourgeoisie prevents them from understanding the suffering of the oppressed; the position of men in the sex-gender system prevents them understanding the position of women. Women's standpoint is able to produce a less biased and more comprehensive view of reality than is provided by bourgeois science or male-dominated-left alternatives.

To reveal the standpoint of women it is necessary to go beyond appearances to the essence of things: to go beyond the appearance of the naturalness of women's place and women's work to reveal the relations of subordination and domination of the sex-gender system. Feminist knowledge and feminist consciousness are not abstract or divorced from experience, but come from practice, from working on and changing the world – from revealing that women's subordination is not natural and inevitable, but socially constructed, and ideologically justified. This involves struggle because the ruling class and men want to preserve the *status quo* and prevent the development of women's knowledge and the emancipation of women. Women's knowledge transcends masculinist knowledge in the same way as proletarian knowledge transcends ruling-class knowledge. Hilary Rose (1976) illustrates this by reference to time. Time, she points out, has been a major issue between workers and the ruling class, but women's time has been ignored; the time that women spend on domestic labour has been naturalized – women are said to do it for love. However, women are aware of the hard, long hours that they work performing domestic labour, and this led women to search for explanations for the unequal sexual division of labour, for why women do the unpaid domestic labour and for ways of transforming the situation. Marxist feminists have argued that this can be explained by capitalist class relations – the relationship between women and the capitalist system. Socialist feminists, however, argue that this is inadequate because it does not take account of patriarchal relationships and that it is necessary to understand how the two systems – patriarchy and capitalism – work together; that man as well as capitalism benefits from women's unpaid domestic labour.

Conclusions

We are not suggesting that one feminist theory is correct and the others are wrong. We have tried to point out some of the inadequacies of theoretical positions. This we see as constructive rather than destructive; it is by recognizing what a theory cannot explain that we can develop more adequate theory. Our major contention in this book has been that mainstream sociology is inadequate because it ignores, or distorts, or marginalizes women. It is inadequate not only because it does not fully incorporate women, but because the knowledge it produces is, at best, partial because it does not take account of over half the population – women. Women have found the knowledge provided by conventional sociology does not relate to their lives or their concerns.

Feminism does seek to speak to the experiences of women, to understand reality from the viewpoint of women, to ask questions that relate to women's lives, and to uncover the systematic biases and distortions in malestream knowledge. In this book we have tried to show the ways in which feminist scholarship has made a contribution to sociology. We have argued that this does not mean that we can just add one more perspective to the list of sociological topics. What is necessary is a total rethinking of sociological knowledge and the ways in which that knowledge is produced. This is because it is not accidental or the result of an oversight that women have been ignored, marginalized, or distorted in sociology, but the outcome of the theoretical underpinning of the discipline. Malestream sociology failed to confront the view that women are naturally determined and women's role the outcome of biological imperatives. Consequently, the concepts developed to carry out sociological research, and the issues seen as there to be researched, ignored women. To produce adequate sociological knowledge it is necessary to reformulate these concepts and questions so that women become central to the concerns of the discipline.

Summary

1 In this chapter it is argued that the production of knowledge from a woman's point of view leads to a less distorted view of society than has hitherto been the case in malestream sociology.
2 This production of an alternative knowledge is a key part of the feminist struggle – although in feminism it is part of the process of being a feminist, not just an elite activity.
3 We have examined liberal, Marxist, radical, and socialist feminisms as distinct perspectives.

Further reading

Mitchell, J. and Oakley, A. (eds, 1986) *What is Feminism?*, Oxford: Blackwell.
Spender, D. (ed., 1981) *Men's Studies Modified: the impact of feminism on the academic disciplines*, Oxford: Pergamon.
Stanley, L. and Wise, S. (1983) *Breaking Out*, London: Routledge & Kegan Paul.

References and further reading

Abbott, P. A. (1982) *Towards a Social Theory of Mental Handicap*, PhD. Thesis; Thames Polytechnic.

Abbott, P. A. (ed., 1988) *Deprivation and Health Status in the Plymouth Health District*, Plymouth: Plymouth Polytechnic, Department of Social and Political Studies.

Abbott, P. A. and Sapsford, R. J. (1987a) *Women and Social Class*, London: Tavistock.

Abbott, P. A. and Sapsford, R. J. (1987b) *'Community care' for Mentally Handicapped Children: The Origins and Consequences of a Social Policy*, Milton Keynes: Open University Press.

Abbott, P. A. and Sapsford, R. J. (1988) 'The body politic: health, family and society', unit 11 of Open University Course D211 *Social Problems and Social Welfare*, Milton Keynes: The Open University.

Abbott, P. A. and Wallace, C. (1989) 'The family' in P: Brown and R. Sparks (eds) *After Thatcher: social policy, politics and society*, Milton Keynes: Open University Press.

Abel-Smith, B. (1960) *A History of the Nursing Profession*, London: Heinemann.

Acker, J. R. (1973) 'Women and social stratification' *American Journal of Sociology*, 78: 2–48.

Allen, H. (1987) *Justice Unbalanced*, Milton Keynes: Open University Press.

Allen, I. (1988) *Any Room at the Top? A Study of Doctors and their Careers*, London: Policy Studies Institute.

Allen, S. (1982) 'Gender inequality and class formation' in A. Giddens and G. Mackenzie (eds) *Social Class and the Division of Labour*, Cambridge: Cambridge University Press.

Allen, S. and Walkowitz, A. (1987) *Homeworking: myths and realities*, London: Macmillan.

Amir, M. (1971) *Patterns in Forcible Rape*, Chicago: University of Chicago Press.

Amos, V. and Parmar, P. (1981) 'Resistance and responses: the experiences of black girls in Britain', in A. McRobbie and T. McCabe (eds) *Feminism for Girls: An Adventure Story*, London: Routledge & Kegan Paul.

Anderson, M. (1980) *Approaches to the History of the Western Family*, London: Macmillan.

Arber, S., Dale, A., and Gilbert, N. (1986) 'The limitations of existing social class classifications of women ', in A. Jacoby (ed.) *The Measurement of Social Class: proceedings of a conference*, Guildford: Social Research Association.

Arber, S., Gilbert, N., and Dale, A. (1985) 'Paid employment and women's health: a benefit or a source of role strain?' *Sociology of Health and Illness*, 7: 375–400.

Aries, P. (1962) *Centuries of Childhood*, London: Vintage Books.

Arnot, M. (1984) 'A feminist perspective on the relationship between family life and school life', *Journal of Education*, 166: 15–24.

Ashton, D. N. and Field, D. (1976) *Young Wales*, London: Hutchinson.

Ashton, D. N. and Maguire, M. (1980) 'Young women in the labour market: stability and change', in R. Deem (ed.) *Schooling for Women's Work*, London: Routledge & Kegan Paul.

Banks, O. (1981) *Faces of Feminism*, Oxford: Martin Robertson.

Barrett, M. (1980) *Women's Oppression Today*, London: Verso.

Barrett, M. and McIntosh, M. (1980a) *The Antisocial Family*, London: Verso.

Barrett, M. and McIntosh, M. (1980b) 'The family wage – some problems for socialists and feminists', *Capital and Class*, 11: 51–72.

Barron, R. D. and Norris, E. M. (1976) 'Sexual divisions and the dual labour market', in D. Barker and S. Allen (eds) *Dependence and Exploitation in Work and Marriage*, London: Longman.

Bayley, M. (1973) *Mental Handicap and Community Care*, London: Routledge & Kegan Paul.

Beechey, V. (1976) 'Women and production: a critical analysis of women's work', in A. Kuhn and A. Wolpe (eds) *Feminism and Materialism*, London: Routledge & Kegan Paul.

Beechey, V. (1977) 'Some problems in the analysis of female wage labour in the capitalist mode of production', *Capital and Class*, 3: 45–66.

Beechey, V. (1986a) 'Familial ideology', in V. Beechey and J. Donald (eds) *Subjectivity and Social Relations*, Milton Keynes: Open University Press.

Beechey, V. (1986b) 'Studies of women's employment', in Feminist Review (eds) *Waged Work: a Reader*, London: Virago.

Beechey, V. and Perkins, T. (1982) *Women's Part-Time Employment in Coventry: a study in the sexual division of labour*, report submitted to the EOC–SSRC. Joint Panel, May.

Beechey, V. and Perkins, T. (1986) *A Matter of Hours: an investigation of women's part-time employment*, Cambridge: Polity.

Bell, C. and Roberts, H. (eds, 1984) *Social Researching: politics, problems, practice*, London: Routledge & Kegan Paul.

Bernard, J. (1973) *The Future of Marriage*, London: Souvenir Press.

Beveridge, W. (1942) *Social Insurance and Allied Services*, London: HMSO, Cmd 6404.

Beyres, T. J, Crow, B., and Wan Ho, M. (1983) 'The green revolution in India', in Open University course U204 *Third World Studies*, Milton Keynes: The Open University.

Black Report (1978) *A Report of a Royal Commission on Health Inequalities*, London: HMSO.

Blaxter, M. (1985) 'Self-definition of health status and consulting notes in primary care', *Quarterly Journal of Social Affairs*, 1: 131–171.

Blondel, J. (1965) *Voters, Politics and Leaders*, Harmondsworth: Penguin.

Blumberg, R. L. (1981) 'Rural women in development', in N. Black and A. B. Cottrell (eds) *Women and World Change*, Beverley Hills: Sage.

Boserup, E. (1970) *Women's Role in Economic Development*, New York: St Martin's Press.

Boulton, M. (1983) *On Being a Mother*, London: Tavistock.

Bourque, S. and Grosshaltz, J. (1974) 'Politics and unnatural practice: political science looks at female participation', *Politics and Society*, 4: 225–66.

Bowlby, J. (1963) *Child Care and the Growth of Love*, Harmondsworth: Penguin.

Bowles, S. and Gintis, H. (1976) *Schooling in Capitalist America: education reform and contradictions of economic life*, London: Routledge & Kegan Paul.

Box, S. (1971) *Deviance, Reality and Society*, London: Holt, Rinehart and Winston.

Box, S. and Hale, C. (1983) 'Liberation and female criminality in England and Wales', *British Journal of Criminology*, 23: 35–49.

Brah, A. (1986) 'Unemployment and racism: Asian youth on the dole', in S. Allen, K. Purcell, A. Waton, and S. Woods (eds) *The Experience of Unemployment*, London: Macmillan.

Braverman, H. (1974) *Labour and Monopoly Capitalism*, New York: Monthly Review Press.

Britten, N. and Heath, A. (1983) 'Women, men and social class', in E. Gamarnikow, D. Morgan, J. Purvis, and D. Taylorson (eds) *Gender, Class and Work*, London: Heinemann.

Brown, C. (1985) *Black and White Britain*, Aldershot: Gower.

Brown, G. W. and Harris, T. C. (1978) *Social Origins of Depression: a study of psychiatric disorder in women*, London: Tavistock.

Brownmiller, S. (1976) *Against Our Will: men, women and rape*, Harmondsworth, Penguin.

Bruegel, I. (1979) 'Women as a reserve army of labour: a note on recent British experience', *Feminist Review*, 3: 12–23.

Bryan, B, Dadzie, S., and Scafe, S. (1985) *The Heart of the Race: black women's lives in Britain*, London: Virago.

Burgess, A. and Holmstrom, L. (1979) *Rape, Crisis and Recovery*, Bowie: Robert J. Brady.

Buswell, C. (1987) 'Training for low pay', in C. Glendinning and J. Millar (eds) op. cit.

Butler, D. E. and King, A. (1965) *The British General Election of 1964*, London: Macmillan.

Byrne, E. M. (1978) *Women and Education*, London: Tavistock.

Cain, M. (1973) *Society and the Policeman's Role*, London: Routledge & Kegan Paul.

References and further reading

Cain, M. (1987) *Realist Philosophy, Social Policy and Feminism: on the reclamation of value-full knowledge*, paper presented to the annual conference of the British Sociological Association in Leeds.

Campbell, A. (1984) *The Girls in the Gang*, Oxford: Blackwell.

Campbell, D. T. (1969) 'Reforms as experiments', *American Psychologist*, 24: 409–29.

Carby, H. V. (1982) 'White women listen! Black feminism and the boundaries of sisterhood', in Centre for Contemporary Cultural Studies, op. cit.

Carlen, P. (1983) *Women's Imprisonment*, London: Routledge & Kegan Paul.

Carlen, P. and Worrall, A. (eds, 1987) *Gender, Crime and Justice*, Milton Keynes: Open University Press.

Carlen, P., Hicks, J., O'Dwyer, J., Christina, P., and Tchaikovsky, C. (1985) *Criminal Women*, Cambridge: Polity Press.

Cashmore, E. E. and Troyna, B. (1983) *Introduction to Race Relations*, London: Routledge & Kegan Paul.

Cavendish, R. (1982) *Women on the Line*, London: Routledge & Kegan Paul.

Centre for Contemporary Cultural Studies (1982) *The Empire Strikes Back: race and racism in '70s Britain*, London: Heinemann.

Central Statistical Office (1988) *Social Trends*, 18, London: HMSO.

Chaney, J. (1981) *Social Networks and Job Information: the situation of women who return to work*, report presented to the EOC–SSRC Joint Panel.

Chapman, A. D. (1984) *Patterns of mobility among men and women in Scotland, 1930-1970*, PhD. Thesis, Plymouth Polytechnic.

Chapman, D. (1968) *Sociology and the Stereotype of the Criminal*, London: Tavistock.

Clark, A. (1919) *Working Life of Women in the Seventeenth Century*, London: Routledge & Kegan Paul (reprinted 1982).

Clark, L. and Lewis, D. (1977) *Rape: the price of coercive sexuality*, Toronto: The Women's Press.

Clarricoates, K. (1978) 'Dinosaurs in the classroom: a re-examination of some aspects of the 'hidden curriculum' in primary schools', *Women's Studies International Quarterly*, 1: 353–64.

Clarricoates, K. (1980) 'The Importance of Being Ernest – Emma...ture: reperception and categorization of gender conformity and gender deviation in schools', in R. Deem (ed.) *Schooling for Women's Work*, London: Routledge & Kegan Paul.

Cloward, R. and Ohlin, L. (1961) *Delinquency and Opportunity: a theory of delinquent gangs*, London: Routledge & Kegan Paul.

Cockburn, C. (1983) *Brothers: male dominance and technological change*, London: Pluto Press.

Cockburn, C. (1987) *Two-Track Training: sex inequalities and the YTS*, London: Macmillan.

Coleman, J. C. (1980) *The Nature of Adolescence*, London: Methuen.

Comer, L. (1974) *Wedlocked Women*, New York: Feminist Books.

Cook, D. (1987) 'Women on welfare', in Carlen, P. and Worrall, A. (eds) op. cit.

Cooper, C. L. and Davidson, M. J. (1982) *High Pressure: working lives of women managers*, Glasgow: Fontana.

230

Cooper, D. (1972) *The Death of the Family*, Harmondsworth: Penguin.

Corea, G. (1985) 'The reproductive brothel', in G. Corea and R. Duelli Klein (eds) *Man-Made Women: how new reproductive technologies affect women*, London: Hutchinson.

Cornwell, J. (1984) *Hard-Earned Lives*, London: Tavistock.

Coser, R. A. and Rokoff, G. (1971) 'Women in the occupational world: social description and conflict', *Social Problems*, 18: 535–54.

Cowie, J., Cowie, V., and Slater, E. (1968) *Delinquency in Girls*, London: Heinemann.

Coyle, A. (1984) *Redundant Women*, London: The Women's Press.

Crewe, I. *et al.* (1979) 'Who swung Tory?', *The Economist*, 12 May, 25–6.

Crompton, R. and Jones, G. (1984) *White-Collar Proletariat: deskilling and gender in manual work*, London: Macmillan.

Crompton, R. and Mann, M. (1986) *Gender and Stratification*, Cambridge: Polity Press.

Crompton, R. and Sanderson, G. (1986) 'Credentials and careers: some implications of the increase in professional qualifications amongst women', *Sociology*, 20: 24–42.

Dalton, K. (1961) 'Menstruation and crime', *British Medical Journal*, 2: 1792.

Daly, M. (1978) *Gyn/Ecology: the metaethics of radical feminism*, Boston: Beacon Press.

Datesman, S., Scarpitti, F., and Stephenson, R. (1975) 'Female delinquency: an application of self and opportunity theories', *Journal of Research in Crime and Delinquency*, 12: 107.

David, M. (1985) 'Motherhood and social policy – a matter of education?', *Critical Social Policy*, 12: 28–43.

Davidoff, L., L'Esperance, J., and Newby, H. (1976) 'Landscape with figures: home and community in English society', in J. Mitchell and A. Oakley (eds) *The Rights and Wrongs of Women*, Harmondsworth: Penguin.

Davies, L. (1984) *Pupil Power: deviance and gender in schools*, Brighton: Famer Press.

Davies, M. L. (1915) *Maternity: letters of working women*, London: Bell.

Davin, A. (1978) 'Imperialism and motherhood', *History Workshop Journal*, 5: 9–65.

Davin, A. (1979) 'Mind that you do as you are told: reading books for board school girls 1870-1902', *Feminist Review*, 3: 89–98.

Delphy, C. (1977) *The Main Enemy*, London: Women's Research and Resource Centre.

Delphy, C. (1981) 'Women in stratification studies', in H. Roberts (ed.) *Doing Feminist Research*, London: Routledge.

Delphy, C. (1984) *Close to Home: a materialist analysis of women's oppression*, London: Hutchinson.

Department of Employment (1976) 'Teachers' pay – how and why men's and women's earnings differ', *Employment Gazette*, 84: 963–8.

Dex, S. (1985) *The Sexual Division of Work*, Brighton: Wheatsheaf.

Dex, S. (1987) *Women's Occupational Mobility*, London: Macmillan.

Dobash, P. R. and Dobash, R. E. (1980) *Violence against Wives: a case against the patriarchy*, Shepton Mallet: Open Books.

Dobash, P. R., Dobash, R. E., and Gutteridge, S. (1986) *The Imprisonment of Women*, Oxford: Blackwell.

Donnison, J. (1977) *Midwives and Medical Men*, London: Heinemann.

Downing, H. (1981) 'They call me a life-size Mechano set: super-secretary or super-slave?', in A. McRobbie and T. McCabe (eds) *Feminism for Girls: An adventure story*, London: Routledge & Kegan Paul.

Dowse, R. and Hughes, J. (1971) 'Girls, boys and politics', *British Journal of Sociology*, 22: 53–67.

Doyal, L. (1987) 'Women and the National Health Service: the careers and the careless', in E. Lewin and V. Olsen (eds) op. cit.

Doyal, L. and Elston, M. (1983) *Medicine and Health*, unit 14 of Open University course U221 *The Changing Experience of Women*, Milton Keynes: The Open University.

Doyal, L, Hunt, G., and Mellor, J. (1981) 'Your life in their hands: immigrant workers in the National Health Service', *Critical Social Policy*, 1: 54–71.

Durant, H. (1966) 'Voting behaviour in Britain', in R. Rose (ed.) *Studies in British Politics*, London: Macmillan.

Durkheim, E. (1897) *Suicide: a study in sociology*, London: Routledge & Kegan Paul, 1952.

Dyhouse, C. (1981) *Girls Growing Up in Late Victorian and Edwardian England*, London: Routledge & Kegan Paul.

Eaton, M. (1986) *Justice for Women*, Milton Keynes: Open University Press.

Edgell, S. (1980) *Middle-Class Couples*, London: Allen & Unwin.

Edwards, S. (1984) *Women on Trial*, Manchester: Manchester University Press.

Edwards, S. (1985) 'Male violence against women: excusatory and explanatory ideologies in law and society', in S. Edwards (ed.) *Gender, Sex and the Law*, London: Croom Helm.

Edwards, S. (1987) 'Prostitutes: victims of law, social policy and organised crime', in J. Carlen and A. Worrell (eds) op. cit.

Ehrenreich, B. and English, D. (1973) *Witches, Midwives and Medical Men*, New York: The Feminist Press.

Ehrenreich, B. and English, D. (1978) 'The 'sick' women of the upper classes', in J. Ehrenreich (ed.) *The Cultural Crisis of Modern Medicine*, New York: Monthly Review Press.

Ehrenreich, B. and English, D. (1979) *For Her Own Good: 100 years of the experts' advice to women*, London: Pluto Press.

Eichler, M. (1988) *Non-Sexist Research Methods*, London: Allen & Unwin.

Eisenstein, Z. R. (1979) 'Developing a theory of capitalist patriarchy and socialist feminism', in Z. R. Eisenstein (ed.) *Capitalist Patriarchy*, New York: Monthly Review Press.

Eisner, M. W. C. (1986) 'A feminist approach to general practice', in C. Webb (ed.) *Women's Health Care*, Chichester: Wiley.

Ellis, H. H. (1910–28) *Studies in the Psychology of Sex*, (Seven vols), Philadelphia: F. A. Davis.

Elston, M. A. (1980) 'Medicine', in R. Silverstone and A. Ward (eds) *Careers of Professional Women*, London: Croom Helm.

Elston, M. A. and Doyal, L. (1983) 'Health and Medicine', unit 14 of Open University course U225 *The Changing Experience of Women*, Milton Keynes: The Open University.

Equal Opportunities Commission (1982a) *Sixth Annual Report, 1981*, Manchester: EOC.

Equal Opportunities Commission (1982b) *Caring for the Elderly Handicapped*, Manchester: EOC.

Equal Opportunities Commission (1984) *Eighth Annual Report, 1983*, Manchester: EOC.

Equal Opportunities Commission (1983) *Occupational Segregation by Sex*, Manchester, EOC Research Bulletin 9.

Erikson, R. (1984) 'The social class of men, women and families', *Sociology*, 18: 500–14.

Eysenck, H. J. (1970) *Crime and Personality*, London: Paladin.

Eysenck, H. J. (1971) *The IQ Argument: race, intelligence and education*, New York: Library Press.

Family Policy Studies Centre (1988) *Fact Sheet 1*, London: FPSC.

Figueira-McDonough, T. (1980) 'A reformation of the "equal opportunity" explanation of female delinquincy', *Crime and Delinquency*, 333.

Finch, J. (1983a) *Married to the Job: wives' incorporation in men's work*, London: , Allen & Unwin.

Finch, J. (1983b) 'Dividing the rough and the respectable: working-class women and pre-school play-groups', in E. Gamarnikow, D. Morgan, J. Purvis, and D. Taylorson (eds) *The Public and the Private*, London: Heinemann.

Finch, J. and Groves, D. (1980) 'Community Care and the Family: a case for equal opportunities?', *Journal of Social Policy*, 9: 437–51.

Finch, J. and Groves, D. (1983) *A Labour of Love: women, work and caring*, London: Routledge & Kegan Paul.

Firestone, S. (1974) *The Dialectic of Sex: the case for feminist revolution*, New York: Morrow.

Ford, J. (1969) *Social Class and the Comprehensive School*, London: Routledge & Kegan Paul.

Forster, M. (1984) *Significant Sisters*, Harmondsworth: Penguin.

Friedan, B. (1963) *The Feminine Mystique*, New York: Norton.

Fuller, M. (1980) 'Black girls in a London comprehensive school', in R. Deem (ed.) *Schooling for Women's Work*, London: Routledge & Kegan Paul.

Gamarnikow, E. (1978) 'Sexual division of labour: the case of nursing', in A. Kuhn and A. Wolpe *Feminism and Materialism*, London: Routledge & Kegan Paul.

Garnsey, E. (1978) 'Women's work and theories of class stratification', *Sociology*, 12: 223–43.

Gittins, D. (1985) *The Family in Question: changing households and familial ideologies*, London: Macmillan.

Glass, D. V. (ed., 1954) *Social Mobility in Britain*, London: Routledge &

References and further reading

Kegan Paul.

Glendinning, C. and Miller, J. (eds, 1987) *Women and Poverty in Britain*, Brighton: Wheatsheaf.

Goffee, R. and Scase, R. (1985) *Women in charge: the experiences of female entrepreneurs*, London: Allen & Unwin.

Goldthorpe, J. H. (1983) 'Women and class analysis: in defence of the conventional view', *Sociology*, 17: 465-488.

Goldthorpe, J. H., Llewlyn, C., and Payne, C. (1980) *Social Mobility and Class Structure in Modern Britain*, Oxford: Oxford University Press.

Goldthorpe, J. H., Lockwood, D., Bechhofer, F., and Platt, J. (1969) *The Affluent Worker in the Class Structure*, Oxford: Oxford University Press.

Goldthorpe, J. H. and Payne, C. (1986) 'On the class mobility of women: results from different approaches to the analysis of recent British data', *Sociology*, 20: 531–55.

Goot, M. and Reid, E. (1975) *Women and voting studies: mindless matrons or sexistscientism?*, London: Sage.

Graham, H. (1984) *Women, Health and the Family*, Brighton: Wheatsheaf.

Graham, H. (1985) 'Providers, negotiators and mediators: women as hidden carers', in E. Lewin and V. Olsen (eds) op. cit.

Graham, H. (1987) 'Women's poverty and caring', in C. Glendinning and J. Miller (eds) op. cit.

Graham, H. and Oakley, A. (1981) 'Competing ideologies of reproduction: medical and maternal perspectives on pregnancy', in H. Roberts (ed.) op. cit.

Greenhalgh, C. and Stewart, M. B. (1982) *Occupational Status and Mobility of Men and Women*, University of Warwick: Warwick Economic Papers No. 211.

Greenstein, F. (1965) *Children and Politics*, Yale University Press.

Gregory, J. (1986) 'Sex, class and crime: towards a non-sexist criminology', in R. Matthews and J. Young (eds) *Confronting Crime*, Beverley Hills: Sage.

Griffin, C. (1985) *Typical Girls?*, London: Routledge & Kegan Paul.

Hakim, C. (1979) *Occupational Segregation: a comparative study of the degree and patterns of differentiation between men's and women's work in Britain, the United States and other countries*, London: Department of Employment, Research Paper No. 9.

Hall, R. (1985) *Ask Any Woman*, Bristol: Falling Wall Press.

Hall, S. and Jefferson, T. (1977) *Resistance through Ritual*, London: Hutchinson.

Halson, J. (1989) 'The sexual harassment of young women', in L. Holly (ed.) *Sex in Schools*, Milton Keynes: Open University Press.

Hammersley, M. and Turner, G. (1980) 'Conformist pupils?', in P. Woods (ed.) *Pupil Strategies*, London: Croom Helm.

Hanmer, J. and Leonard, D. (1984) 'Negotiating the problem: the DHSS and research on violence in marriage', in C. Bell and H. Roberts (eds) *Social Researching: politics, problems, practice*, London: Routledge & Kegan Paul.

Hanmer, J. and Maynard, M. (eds, 1987) *Women, Violence and Social Control*, London: Macmillan.

Hanmer, J. and Saunders, S. (1984) *Well-Founded Fear*, London: Hutchinson.

Harding, J. (1980) 'Sex differences in performance in science examinations', in R. Deem (ed.) *Schooling for Women's Work*, London: Routledge & Kegan Paul.

Harding, S. (ed., 1987a) *Feminism and Methodology*, Milton Keynes: Open University Press.

Harding, S. (1987b) 'Introduction: is there a feminist method?', in S. Harding (ed.) *Feminism and Methodology*, Milton Keynes: Open University Press.

Hargreaves, D. (1967) *Social Relations in a Secondary School*, London: Routledge & Kegan Paul.

Harris, A. (1977) 'Sex and theories of deviance', *American Sociological Review*, 42: 3–16.

Harris, A. I. and Clausen, R. (1967) *Labour Mobility in Great Britain 1953–1963*, London: HMSO.

Hartmann, H. (1978) 'The unhappy marriage of Marxism and feminism: towards a more progressive union', *Capital and Class*, 8: 1–33.

Hartsock, N. C. M. (1987) 'The feminist standpoint', in S. Harding (ed.) *Feminism and Methodology*, Milton Keynes: Open University Press.

Haugh, M. R. (1973) 'Class measurement and women's occupational roles', *Social Forces*, 52: 85–97.

Hearn, J. (1982) 'Notes on patriarchy, professionalisation and the semi-professions', *Sociology*, 16: 184–202.

Heath, A. (1980) *Social Mobility*, Edinburgh: Fontana.

Heath, A. and Britten, N. (1984) 'Women's jobs do make a difference', *Sociology*, 18: 475–90.

Heath, A, Jowell, R., and Curtice, J. (1985) *How Britain Votes*, Oxford: Pergamon.

Heidensohn, F. (1986) *Women and Crime*, London: Macmillan.

Himmelweit, S. (1988) 'In the Beginning', Unit 1 of Open University course D211 *Social Problems and Social Welfare*, Milton Keynes: The Open University.

Home Office (1986) *The Ethnic Origins of Prisoners*, London: HMSO.

Home Office (1987) *Criminal Statistics, England and Wales 1986*, London: HMSO.

Homer, M, Leonard, A., and Taylor, P. (1984) *Private Violence and Public Shame*, Middlesbrough: Cleveland Refuge and Aid for Women and Children.

Humphries, J. (1977) 'Class struggle and the persistence of the working class family', *Cambridge Journal of Economics*, 1: 241–58.

Humphries, S. (1981) *Hooligans or Rebels?: an oral history of working-class childhood and youth 1889–1939*, Oxford: Blackwell.

Hunt, A. (1975) *Management Attitudes and Practices towards Women at Work*, London: OPCS.

Hunt, P. (1980) *Gender and Class Consciousness*, London: Macmillan.

Jennings, M. K. and Niemi, R. G. (1974) *The Political Character of*

Adolescence: the influence of families and schools, Princeton: Harvard University Press.

Jensen, A. R. (1973) *Educability and Group Differences*, New York: Harper & Row.

Johnson, N. (ed., 1985) *Marital Violence*, London: Routledge & Kegan Paul.

Johnson, T. (1972) *Professions and Power*, London: Macmillan.

Jones, G. (1986) *Stratification in youth*, Paper presented to the annual conference of the British Sociological Association at Loughborough.

Joshi, H. (1987) 'The cost of caring', in C. Glendinning and J. Miller (eds) *Women and Poverty in Britain*, Brighton: Wheatsheaf.

Kelly, A. (ed., 1981) *The Missing Half: girls and science education*, Manchester: Manchester University Press.

Kelly, A. (1985) 'The construction of masculine science', *British Journal of Sociology of Education*, 6: 133–54.

Kelly, A. (1982) 'Gender roles at home and school', *British Journal of Sociology of Education*, 3: 281–96.

Kelly, E. (1988) *Surviving Sexual Violence*, Cambridge: Polity.

Kelsall, R. K. (1980) 'Teaching', in R. Silverstone and A. Ward (eds) *Careers of Professional Women*, London: Croom Helm.

Kiel, T. and Newton, P. (1980) 'Into work: continuity and change', in R. Deem (ed.) *Schooling for Women's Work*, London: Routledge & Kegan Paul.

Land, H. (1978) 'Who cares for the family?', *Journal of Social Policy* 7(3): 257–84.

Land, H. (1982) 'The family wage', in M. Evans (ed.) *The Woman Question*, London: Fontana.

Land, H. (1987) 'Social policies and women in the labour market', in F. Ashton and G. Whitting (eds) *Feminist Theory and Practical Policies*, Bristol: School of Advanced Urban Studies.

Lansing, M. (1977) *Comparison of the Voting Turnout and Party Choice of British and American Women*, paper presented to the European Joint Sessions, Berlin.

Larkin, G. (1983) *Occupational Monopoly and Modern Medicine*, London: Tavistock.

Laslett, P. (1972) *The World We Have Lost*, Harmondsworth: Penguin.

Lawrence, B. (1987) 'The fifth dimension: gender and general practice', in A. Spencer and D. Podmore (eds) *In a Man's World*, London: Tavistock.

Lazarsfeld, P. F, Berelson, B., and Gaudet, H. (1968) *The People's Choice*, (2nd Edition), Chicago: University of Chicago Press.

Leach, E. (1967) *A Runaway World?*, London: BBC Publications.

Lees, S. (1986) *Losing Out: sexuality and adolescent girls*, London: Hutchinson.

Lees, S. (1989) *Naggers, Whores and Libbers: provoking men to violence*, paper presented to the annual conference of the British Sociological Association, Plymouth.

Leeson, J. and Gray, J. (1978) *Women and Health*, London: Tavistock.

LeGrande, J. (1982) *The Strategy of Equality*, London: Allen & Unwin.

Leonard, E. B. (1978) *Women, Crime and Society*, London: Longman.

Lewin, E. and Olsen, V. (eds, 1985) *Women, Health and Healing: towards a new perspective*, London: Tavistock.

Lewis, J. (1980) *The Politics of Motherhood: child and maternal welfare in England 1900-1939*, London: Croom Helm.

Lewis, J. and Piachaud, D. (1987) 'Women and poverty in the Twentieth Century', in C. Glendinning and J. Miller (eds) *Women and Poverty in Britain*, Brighton: Wheatsheaf.

Llewelyn Davies, M. (1915) *Letters from Working Women Collected by the Women's Cooperative Guild*, Republished London: Virago.

Lobban, G. (1975) 'Sex roles in reading schemes', *Forum*, 16: 57-60.

Lobban, G. (1978) 'The influence of the school on sex-role stereotyping', in J. Chetwynd and O. Hartnell (eds) *The Sex Role System*, London: Routledge & Kegan Paul.

Locker, D. (1981) *Symptoms and Illness*, London: Tavistock.

Lockwood, D. (1958) *The Black-Coated Worker*, London: Allen & Unwin.

Lomax, P. (1980) 'The school careers of West Indian immigrant girls', *Journal of Applied Educational Studies* 9: 29–36.

Maccoby, E., Matthews, R., and Morbin, A. S. (1954) 'Youth and political change', *Public Opinion Quarterly*, 18: 23–9.

MacGuire, J. (1980) 'Nursing', in R. Silverstone and A. Ward (eds) *Careers of Professional Women*, London: Croom Helm.

Mackie, l and Pattullo, P. (1977) *Women at Work*, London: Tavistock.

MacIntyre, S. (1977) *Single and Pregnant*, London: Croom Helm.

McRobbie, A. (1978) 'Working-class girls and the culture of femininity', in Centre for Contemporary Cultural Studies (ed.) *Women Take Issue: aspects of women's subordination*, London: Hutchinson.

McRobbie, A. and Garber, P. (1977) 'Girls and Subcultures: an exploration', in S. Hall and T. Jefferson (eds) *Resistance through Ritual*, London: Hutchinson.

McRobbie, A. and McCabe, T. (eds, 1981) *Feminism for Girls: an adventure story*, London: Routledge & Kegan Paul.

Mandaraka-Sheppard, K. (1986) *The Dynamics of Aggression in Women's Prisons in England*, London: Gower.

Marsland, D. (1988) *The Seeds of Bankruptcy*, London and Lexington: Claridge Press.

Martin, J. and Roberts, C. (1984) *Women and Employment: a lifetime perspective*, London: HMSO.

Massey, D. (1983) 'The shape of things to come', *Marxism Today*, April, 18–27.

Matthews, R. and Young, J. (eds, 1986) *Confronting Crime*, Beverley Hills: Sage.

Mawby, R. (1980) 'Sex and crime: the results of a self-report study', *British Journal of Sociology*, 31: 525.

Mead, M. (1943) *Coming of Age in Samoa: a study of adolescence and sex in primitive societies*, Harmondsworth: Penguin.

Measor, L. (1983) 'Gender and the sciences: pupils' gender-based conceptions of school subjects', in M. Hammersley and A. Hargreaves (eds) *Curriculum Practice: some sociological case studies*, Brighton:

Falmer Press.

Meyers, B. (1980) 'The development of girl's sex-role attitudes', *Child Development* 51: 508–14.

Milkman, R. (1976) 'Women's work and economic crises', *Review of Radical Political Economy* 9: 29–36.

Mill, J. S. and Mill, H. T. (1869) *The Subjection of Women*, reprinted in A. S. Rossi (ed.) (1970) *Essays on sex Equality by John Stuart Mill and Harriet Taylor Mill*, Chicago: University of Chicago Press.

Miller, J. and Glendinning, C. (1987) 'Invisible women, invisible poverty', in C. Glendinning and J. Miller (eds) *Women and Poverty in Britain*, Brighton: Wheatsheaf.

Millett, K. (1977) *Sexual Politics*, London: Virago.

Mills, C. W. (1954) *The Sociological Imagination*, Harmondsworth: Penguin.

Mitchell, J. (1986) 'Women and equality', in J. Donald and S. Hall (eds) *Politics and Ideology*, Milton Keynes: Open University Press.

Mitchell, J. and Oakley, A. (eds, 1976) *The Rights and Wrongs of Women*, Harmondsworth: Penguin.

Mitchell, J. and Oakley, A. (eds, 1986) *What is Feminism?*, Oxford: Blackwell.

Morris, A. (1987) *Women, Crime and Criminal Justice*, Oxford: Blackwell.

Muncie, J. (1984) *The Trouble with Kids Today: youth culture and post-war Britain*, London: Hutchinson.

Murphy, R. (1984) 'The structure of closure: a critique and development of the theories of Weber, Collins and Parkin', *British Journal of Sociology*, 35: 574–602.

Myrdal, A. and Klein, V. (1956) *Women's Two Roles: home and work*, London: Routledge & Kegan Paul.

National Union of Teachers (1980) *Promotion and the Woman Teacher*, London and Manchester: NUT/EOC.

Newsom Report (1963) *Half Our Futures*, London: HMSO.

Nissell, M. and Bonnerjea, L. (1982) *Family Care of the Handicapped Elderly: who pays?*, London: Policy Studies Institute.

Nuttall, P. (1983) 'Male takeover or female giveaway?', *Nursing Times*, 12 January, 10–11.

Oakley, A. (1972) *Sex, Gender and Society*, London: Temple Smith.

Oakley, A. (1974a) *Housewife*, London: Allen Lane.

Oakley, A. (1974b) *The Sociology of Housework*, London: Martin Robertson.

Oakley, A. (1980) *Women Confined: towards a sociology of childbirth*, Oxford: Martin Robertson.

Oakley, A. (1982) *Subject Women*, London: Fontana.

Oakley, A. (1984a) *The Captured Womb*, Oxford, Blackwell.

Oakley, A. (1984b) 'The importance of being a nurse', *Nursing Times*, 12 December, 24–7.

Oakley, A. (1987) 'From walking wombs to test-tube babies', in M. Stanworth (ed.) *Reproductive Technologies: gender, motherhood and medicine*, Cambridge: Polity.

Oakley, A. and Oakley, R. (1979) 'Sexism in official statistics', in J. Irvine (ed.) *Demystifying Social Statistics*, London: Pluto Press.

Obbso, C. (1980) *African Women: their struggle for economic independence*, London: Zed Press.

Office of Population Censuses and Surveys (1982) *Labour Force Survey 1981*, London: HMSO.

Office of Population Censuses and Surveys (1986) *Occupational Mortality: December Supplement, England and Wales, 1979-1980*, London: HMSO.

Olsen, V. and Lewin, E. (1985) 'Women, health and healing: a theoretical introduction', in E. Lewin and V. Olsen (eds) *Women, Health and Healing: towards a new perspective*, London: Tavistock.

Orr, J. (1987) 'In conclusion', in J. Orr (ed.) *Women's Health in the Community*, Chichester: Wiley.

Osborne, A. F. and Morris, T. C. (1979) 'The rationale for a composite index of social class and its evaluation', *British Journal of Sociology*, 30: 39–60.

Pagelow, M. (1985) 'Violent husbands and abused wives: a longtitudinal study', in J. Pahl (ed.) *Private Violence and Public Policy*, London: Routledge & Kegan Paul.

Pahl, J. (1980) 'Patterns of money management within marriage', *Journal of Social Policy*, 19: 313–35.

Pahl, J. (1983) 'The allocation of money and the structuring of inequality within marriage', *Sociological Review*, 31: 237–62.

Pahl, J. (ed., 1985) *Private Violence and Public Policy*, London: Routledge & Kegan Paul.

Pahl, J. and Pahl, R. (1971) *Managers and their Wives*, Harmondsworth: Penguin.

Pahl, R. and Wallace, C. (1985) 'Household work strategies in economic recession', in E. Mingione and N. Redclift (eds) *Beyond Employment*, Oxford: Blackwell.

Parkin, F. (1979) *Marxism and Class Theory: a bourgeois critique*, London: Tavistock.

Parsons, T. and Bales, R. F. (1955) *Family, Socialisation and Interaction Process*, New York: Free Press.

Payne, G. (1987a) *Employment and Opportunity*, London: Macmillan.

Payne, G. (1987b) *Mobility and Change in Modern Britain*, London: Macmillan.

Penfold, P. S. and Walker, G. A. (1984) *Women and the Psychiatric Paradox*, Milton Keynes: Open University Press.

Petchesky, R. P. (1987) 'Foetal images: the power of visual culture in the politics of reproduction', in M. Stanworth (ed.) *Reproductive Technologies: gender, motherhood and medicine*, Cambridge: Polity.

Pfeffer, N. (1987) 'Artificial insemination, in-vitro fertilisation and the stigma of infertility', in M. Stanworth (ed.) *Reproductive Technologies: gender, motherhood and medicine*, Cambridge: Polity.

Phillips, A. (1987) *Divided Loyalties: dilemmas of sex and class*, London: Virago.

Phillips, A. and Taylor, B. (1980) 'Sex and skill: notes towards a feminist economics', *Feminist Review*, 6: 79–88.

Phizacklea, A. (ed., 1983a) *One-Way Ticket: migration and female labour*,

London: Routledge & Kegan Paul.

Phizacklea, A. (1983b) 'In the front line', in Phizacklea, A. (ed.) *One-Way Ticket: migration and female labour*, London: Routledge & Kegan Paul.

Pill, D. and Stott, N. (1986) 'Concepts of illness causation and responsibility: some preliminary data from a sample of working-class mothers', in C. Currer and M. Stacey (eds) *Concepts of Health, Illness and Disease: a comparative perspective*, Leamington Spa: Berg.

Pinchbeck, I. (1977) *Women Workers and the Industrial Revolution 1750–1850*, London: Cass.

Pollack, O. (1950) *The Criminality of Women*, Philadelphia: University of Pennsylvania Press.

Pollert, A. (1981) *Girls, Wives, Factory Lives*, London: Macmillan.

Prandy, K. (1986) 'Similarities of life-style and occupations of women', in R. Crompton and M. Mann (eds) *Gender and Stratification*, Cambridge: Polity Press.

Pratt, J. *et al.* (1984) *Option Choice: a question of equal opportunity*, Windsor: NFER/Nelson.

Radford, J. (1987) 'Policing male violence – policing women', in J. Halmer and M. Maynard (eds) *Women, Violence and Social Control*, London: Macmillan.

Ramazanoglu, C. (1987) 'Sex and violence in academic life, or you can keep a good woman down', in J. Hanmer and M. Maynard (eds) *Women, Violence and Social Control*, London: Macmillan.

Rapaport, R. and Rapaport, R. N. (1969) 'The Dual-Career Family: a variant pattern and social change', *Human Relations*, 22: 3–30.

Reid, I. and Wormald, N. (1982) *Gender Differences in Britain*, London: Grant McIntyre.

Reinharz, S. (1983) 'Experiential analysis: a contribution to feminist research', in G. Bowles and R. D. Klein (eds) *Theories of Women's Studies*, London: Routledge & Kegan Paul.

Roberts, E. (1982) 'Working wives and their families', in T. Barker and M. Drake (eds) *Population and Society in Britain 1850–1980*, London: Batsford.

Roberts, H. (ed., 1981) *Women, Health and Reproduction*, London: Routledge & Kegan Paul.

Roberts, H. (1985a) *The Patient Patients: women and their doctors*, London: Pandora.

Roberts, H. (1985b) 'Women and social class', *Survey Methods Newsletter*, Spring: 3–4.

Roberts, H. (1986) *The social classification of women: a life-cycle approach*, paper presented to the annual conference of the British Sociological Association at Loughborough.

Roberts, H. (1987) *Women and Social Classification*, Brighton: Wheatsheaf.

Rose, H. (1976) 'Women's work: women's knowledge', in J. Mitchell and A. Oakley (eds) *The Rights and Wrongs of Women*, Harmondsworth: Penguin.

Rose, N. (1985) *The Psychological Complex*, London: Routledge & Kegan Paul.

Rose, R. (1976) 'Social structure and party differences', in R. Rose (ed.)

Studies in British Politics, London: Macmillan.

Rosser, J. and Davies, C. (1987) 'What would we do without her? Invisible women in the National Health Service administration', in A. Spencer and D. Podmore (eds) *In a Man's World*, London: Tavistock.

Royal College of General Practitioners (1974) *Oral Contraception and Health*, London: Pitman Medical.

Rutter, M., Graham, P., Chadwick, O., and Yule, W. (1970) 'Adolescent turmoil: fact or fiction?', *Journal of Child Psychology and Psychiatry*, 17: 35–56.

Sarsby, J. (1983) *Romantic Love and Society*, Harmondsworth: Penguin.

Savage, W. (1986) *A Savage Enquiry*, London: Virago.

Scambler, G. and Scambler, A. (1984) 'The illness iceberg and aspects of consulting behaviour', in R. Fitzpatrick, T. Hinton, S. Newman, G. Scambler, and T. Thompson (eds) *The Experience of Illness*, London: Tavistock.

Scott, H. (1984) *Working Your Way to the Bottom: the feminisation of poverty*, London: Pandora Press.

Scully, D. and Bart, P. (1978) 'A funny thing happened on the way to the orifice: women in gynaecology textbooks', in J. Ehrenreich (ed.) *Cultural Crisis of Modern Medicine*, New York: Monthly Review Press.

Seager, J. and Olsen, A. (1986) *Women in the World: an international atlas*, London: Pluto Press.

Secombe, W. (1974) 'The housewife and her labour under capitalism', *New Left Review*, 83: 3–26.

Shaklady Smith, L. (1978) 'Sexist assumptions and female delinquency', in C. Smart and B. Smart (eds) *Women, Sexuality and Social Control*, London: Routledge & Kegan Paul.

Sharpe, S. (1976) *Just Like a Girl*, Harmondsworth, Penguin.

Sharpe, S. (1984) *Double Identity: the lives of working mothers*, Harmondsworth, Penguin.

Shaw, J. (1976) 'Finishing school: some implications of sex-segregated education', in D. Barker and S. Allen (eds) *Sexual Divisions and Society: process and change*, London: Tavistock.

Shaw, J. (1983) *Romantic Love and Society*, Harmondsworth: Penguin.

Siltanen, J. and Stanworth, M. (1984) *Women and the Public Sphere: a critique of sociology and politics*, London: Hutchinson.

Silverstone, R. (1980) 'Accounting', in R. Silverstone and A. Ward (eds) *Careers of Professional Women*, London: Croom Helm.

Smart, C. (1976) *Women, Crime and Criminology*, London: Routledge & Kegan Paul.

Smart, C. and Smart, B. (eds, 1978) *Women, Sexuality and Social Control*, London: Routledge & Kegan Paul.

Smith, D. E. (1979) 'A peculiar eclipse: women's exclusion from men's culture', *Women's Studies International Quarterly*, 1: 281–95.

Smith, D. E. (1987) *The Everyday World as Problematic: a feminist sociology*, Milton Keynes: Open University Press.

Snell, M. W., Glucklich, P., and Povall, M. (1981) *Equal Pay and Opportunity: a study of the implementation and effect of the Equal Pay and Sex Discrimination Act in 26 organisations*, London: HMSO, Department of Employment Research Paper No. 20.

Spencer, A. and Podmore, D. (eds, 1987) *In a Man's World*, London: Tavistock.

Spender, D. (1980) *Man-made Language*, London: Routledge & Kegan Paul.

Spender, D. (ed., 1981) *Men's Studies Modified: the impact of feminism on the academic disciplines*, Oxford: Pergamon.

Spender, D. (1982) *Invisible Women: the schooling scandal*, London: Writers' and Readers' Publishing Co-operative.

Spender, D. and Sarah, E. (1980) *Learning to Lose: sexism and education*, London: Women's Press.

Springhall, J. (1983) 'The origins of adolescence', *Youth and Policy*, 2.

Sping-Rice, M. (1939) *Working-class Wives: their health and conditions*, London: Virago, 1981.

Stacey, M. (1981) 'The division of labour revisited, or overcoming the two Adams', in P. Abrams, R. Deem, J. Finch, and P. Rock (eds) *Practice and Progress: British Sociology 1950–1980*, London: Allen & Unwin.

Stacey, M. and Price, M. (1981) *Women, Power and Politics*, London: Tavistock.

Stanley, L. (1984) 'Why men oppress women, or how experiences of sexism can tell us interesting and useful things about women's oppression and women's liberation', in S. Webb and C. Pearson (eds) *Looking Back: some papers from the BSA Gender and Society conference*, Manchester: Manchester University Department of Sociology, Studies in Sexual Politics.

Stanley, L. and Wise, S. (1983) *Breaking Out*, London: Routledge & Kegan Paul.

Stanworth, M. (1983) *Gender and Schooling: a study of sexual divisions in the classroom*, London: Hutchinson.

Stanworth, M. (1984) 'Women and social class analysis: a reply to Goldthorpe', *Sociology*, 18: 159-170.

Stanworth, M. (ed., 1987a) *Reproductive Technologies: gender, motherhood and medicine*, Cambridge: Polity.

Stanworth, M. (1987b) 'Reproductive technologies and the reconstruction of motherhood', in M. Stanworth (ed.) *Reproductive Technologies: gender, motherhood and medicine*, Cambridge: Polity.

Stone, K. (1983) 'Motherhood and Waged Work: West Indian, Asian and white mothers compared', in A. Phizacklea (ed.) *One-Way Ticket: migration and female labour*, London: Routledge & Kegan Paul.

Sutherland, E. and Cressey, D. (1966) *Principles of Criminology*, Philadelphia: J. P. Lippincott.

Sydie, R. A. (1987) *Natural woman, cultured man*, Milton Keynes: Open University Press.

Taylor, I., Walton, P., and Young, J. (1973) *The New Criminology: for a social theory of deviance*, London: Routledge & Kegan Paul.

Taylor, P. J. and Johnstone, R. J. (1979) *The Geography of Elections*, Harmondsworth: Penguin.

Thorne, B. (1982) *Feminist Rethinking of the Family: an overview*, New

York: Longman.

Thorne, B. and Yalom, M. (1982) *Rethinking the Family*, London: Longman.

Tiano, S. (1987) 'Gender, work and world capitalism: Third World women's role in development', in B. B. Hess and M. M. Ferree (eds) *Analysing Gender: a handbook of social science research*, Beverley Hills: Sage.

Toner, B. (1977) *The Facts of Rape*, London: Hutchinson.

Townsend, P., Phillimore, A., and Beattie, A. (1987) *Health and Deprivation: inequality and the North*, London: Croom Helm.

Verslusyen, M. C. (1980) 'Old wives' tales? Women healers in English history', in C. Davies (ed.) *Rewriting Nursing History*, London: Croom Helm.

Verslusyen, M. C. (1981) 'Midwives, medical men and 'poor women labouring of child': lying-in hospitals in eighteenth-century London', in H. Roberts (ed.) *Women, Health and Reproduction*, London: Routledge & Kegan Paul.

Wacjman, J. (1983) *Women in Control*, Milton Keynes: Open University Press.

Walby, S. (1986) *Patriarchy at Work*, Cambridge: Polity.

Walby, S. (1988a) 'Gender, politics and social theory', *Sociology*, 22: 215–32.

Walby, S. (1988b) *The historical periodization of patriarchy*, paper presented to the annual conference of the British Sociological Association, at Edinburgh.

Walkerdine, V. (1981) 'Sex, power and pedagogy', *Screen Education*, 38: 14–23.

Wallace, C. (1986) 'From girls and boys to women and men: the social reproduction of gender', in S. Walker and L. Barton (eds) *Youth, Unemployment and Schooling*, Milton Keynes: Open University Press.

Wallace, C. (1987) *For Richer for Poorer: growing up in and out of work*, London: Tavistock.

Wallace, C. (1989) 'Youth', in R. Burgess (ed.) *Investigating Society*, London: Longmans.

Webb, C. (ed., 1986) *Feminist Practice in Women's Health Care*, Chichester: Wiley.

Weber, M. (1920) *The Protestant Ethic and the Spirit of Capitalism*, London: Allen & Unwin, 1952.

Weiner, G. (1986) 'Feminist education and equal opportunities: unity or discord?', *British Journal of Sociology of Education*, 7: 265–74.

Weiner, T. S. (1978) 'Homogeneity of political party preferences between spouses', *Journal of Politics*, 40: 208–11.

West, D. J. (1967) *The Young Delinquent*, Harmondsworth: Penguin.

West, J. (1978) 'Women, sex and class', in A. Kuhn and A. Wolpe (eds) *Feminism and Materialism*, London: Routledge & Kegan Paul.

West, J. (ed., 1982) *Work, Women and the Labour Market*, London: Routledge & Kegan Paul.

West, W. M. (1974) *Occupational Choice*, London: Allen & Unwin.

Westwood, S. (1984) *All Day Every Day: factory and family in the making of women's lives*, London: Pluto Press.

Westwood, S. and Bhachu, P. (1988a) 'Images and realities', *New Society*, 6

May: 20–2.

Westwood, S. and Bhachu, P. (1988b) *Enterprising Women: ethnicity, economy and gender relations*, London: Routledge.

Whitehead, M. (1987) *The Health Divide*, London: Health Education Council.

Williams, A. (1987) ' Making sense of feminist contributions to women's health', in J. Orr (ed.) *Women's Health in the Community*, Chichester: Wiley.

Williams, R. G. (1983) 'Concepts of health: an analysis of lay logic', *Sociology* 17: 185–205.

Williams, W. M. (ed., 1974) *Occupational Choice*, London: Allen & Unwin.

Willmott, P. and Young, M. (1957) *Family and Kinship in East London*, Harmondsworth: Penguin.

Willis, P. (1977) *Learning to Labour*, Farnborough: Saxon House.

Wilson, D. (1978) 'Sexual codes and conduct: a study of teenage girls', in B. Smart and C. Smart (eds) *Women, Sexuality and Social Control*, London: Routledge & Kegan Paul.

Wilson, E. (1977) *Women and the Welfare State*, London: Tavistock.

Wittig, M. (1979) 'One is not born a woman', in *Proceedings of the Second Sex Conference*, New York: Institute for the Humanities.

Witz, A. (1985) 'Patriarchy and the labour market: occupational control strategies and the medical division of labour', in D. Knights and M. Willmott (eds) *The Gendered Labour Process*, Brighton: Gower.

Wollstonecraft, M. (1792) *A Vindication of the Rights of Women*, republished 1929, London: Dent.

Wolpe, A-M. (1977) 'Some processes in education', Women's Research and Resource Centre, *Explorations in Feminism* 1.

Yeandle, S. (1984) *Women's Working Lives: patterns and strategies*, London: Tavistock.

Young, M. (1952) 'Distribution of income within the family', *British Journal of Sociology* 3: 305–21.

Young, M. and Willmott, P. (1973) *The Symmetrical Family*, London: Routledge & Kegan Paul.

Young, S. (1981) 'A woman in medicine: reflections from the inside', in H. Roberts (ed.) *Women, Health and Reproduction*, London: Routledge & Kegan Paul.

Youthaid (1981) *A Study of the Transition from School to Working Life*, vols 1–3, London: Youthaid.

Yudkin, S. S. and Holme, A. (1963) *Working Mothers and their Children: a study of the Council for Children's Welfare*, London: Michael Joseph.

Author index

Subject index